PRES

God has provided His evaluation of who is truly saved, and who is merely presumptuous!

A Book on Assurance

God in His sovereignty placed 1 John in the New Testament to provide clarity for the genuineness of Christian profession.

PRESUMED FAITH

A Study of 1 John Verse-by-Verse

Jim Bryant

Presumed Faith: A Study of 1 John Verse-by-Verse

Copyright © 2014 Jim Bryant

All rights reserved. Except for brief quotations in printed reviews, no part of this publication may be reproduced, stored in a retrieval system, or transmitted in any form or by any means (printed, written, photocopied, visual electronic, audio, or otherwise) without the prior written permission of the copyright holder.

Unless otherwise noted, Scripture taken from the NEW AMERICAN STANDARD BIBLE, © Copyright 1960, 1962, 1963, 1968, 1971, 1972, 1973, 1975, 1977, 1995 by the Lockman Foundation
Used by permission — www.Lockman.org

Library of Congress Cataloging-in-Publication Data

ISBN–13: 978-1500699765
ISBN–10: 978-1500699764

Dedication

To my parents, Aubrey & Pansy Bryant, who brought me up in the Scriptures, always holding them in the highest regard, and teaching me to search them diligently.

Acknowledgments

I am very grateful to Dr. J. D. "Doc" Watson, not only for providing the foreword, but also for his expertise in preparing this book for publication; to Trudie Elmer for editing this work, and to Jan Bryant for her proofreading.

Contents

	Foreword	9
	Introduction	11
	Outline of Book	19
1	The Certainty and Communication of Christ	25
2	The Conditions for Fellowship	35
3	The Challenge for Fellowship	70
4	The Characteristics of Fellowship	111
5	The Cautions for Fellowship	150
6	The Consequences of Fellowship	178
7	The Confidence from Fellowship	192
8	The Conclusion from the Writing	199
	Closing Thoughts	215
	About the Author	218

Foreword

WE live in a day unlike any other in history. It is a day of unprecedented materialism, secularism, relativism, and many other "isms" that are like a creeping plague infecting our world, our culture, our families, and indeed, even our churches. The latter is most dramatically evident by what is perhaps the broadest definition of salvation that has ever existed in Church History. It has digressed so far, in fact, that each individual person has the inherent right to define salvation in whatever nebulous terms so as not to offend his or her sensitivities, and will fulfill one's "felt needs."

In stark contrast, the Bible is unambiguous, unapologetic, and unwavering in defining salvation in extremely narrow terms. One passage, in fact, uses those very words: "Enter through the narrow gate; for the gate is wide and the way is broad that leads to destruction, and there are many who enter through it. For the gate is small and the way is narrow that leads to life, and there are few who find it" (Matt. 7:13–14).

A few verses later, we read some of the most sobering and terrifying words in all of Scripture:

> "Not everyone who says to Me, Lord, Lord," will enter the kingdom of heaven, but he who does the will of My Father who is in heaven will enter. Many will say to Me on that day, "Lord, Lord, did we not prophesy in Your name, and in Your name cast out demons, and in Your name perform many miracles?" And then I will declare to them, "I never knew you; DEPART FROM ME, YOU WHO PRACTICE LAWLESSNESS" (vv. 21–23).

Further, Jesus was so "narrow" is His thinking that He declared, "I am the way, and the truth, and the life; no one comes to the Father, but through Me" (John 14:6), using the definite article "the" three times to indicate limitation, and that He alone is each of those things.

Therefore, just *saying* one is a Christian does not make it so. That is why the apostle Paul wrote that we must "test [ourselves] to see if [we] are in the faith [and] examine [our]selves" (2 Cor. 13:5), and why Peter echoed that we should "be all the more give diligence to make certain about His calling" (2 Pet. 1:10). It is not enough to *call* yourself a Christian or even to *say* Jesus is Lord. What *proves* that one is a Christian? Doing "the will of My Father in heaven." As the old expression goes, "Words are cheap," and they seem to get cheaper every day as the Gospel is redefined in increasingly broader terms. But our Lord could not have been more clear: the two greatest evidences of true conversion are obedience to God's Word (Jn. 14:15, 23; 1 Jn. 2:1–5), and holiness of life (Eph. 4:24; 1 Thess. 4:17; etc.). It was because of that certain clarity that the apostle John, by the inspiration of the Holy Spirit, expounded on that theme in his First Epistle. This epistle could be subtitled "God's Salvation Exam," for it contains God's standards by which those who *profess* salvation can test themselves, and prove whether or not they really *possess* salvation. The present volume, which is expositional, devotional, and practical, flows from the heart and through the pen of a concerned pastor, one who I am blessed to know and honored to call a friend. It expresses the author's deep burden concerning today's church and its *Presumed Faith*, a faith that is alleged but far from proven. While certainly a commentary, this book is more than that. It is a reflection on, a reminder of, and a rallying to the standards by which God tests true conversion to Christ. Pastor Jim Bryant is to be commended for standing on and proclaiming truths that are not popular in our day. He is also to be thanked for his outline of an epistle that admittedly resists systematizing. I pray that God will use this discerning work to His glory and the church's good.

Dr. J. D. Watson
Pastor, Grace Bible Church; Meeker, CO
Director, Sola Scriptura Ministries
Author, *A Hebrew Word for the Day*
and *Truth on Tough Texts*

Introduction

PAUL'S statement to Timothy that "in the latter days there will be *difficult* times" (2 Tim. 3:1-4:4), applies directly to our day in the twenty-first century. Among the prominent descriptions prophesied in the perilous "last days" are the decline of true spirituality, and marks of advanced apostasy in the professing church. This church apostasy has had a direct affect on the godless, degenerating condition of society. This is evident not only in America, but throughout the world. The churches "salt" has lost its savor (Mat 5:13), its influence, and this has resulted in a generation "who does not know God" (Judges 2:10). This is sadly seen by the philosophy and acceleration of evil activity. How should a concerned person respond to these morally declining, and troublesome times? This question becomes very personal, and is associated with individual awareness and accountability. What must be recognized is that God's warning of this age through Paul, is directly associated with the spiritual condition of churches. There is a correlation between the faithfulness of professing Christianity, and what is occurring today. Prophecy has come to pass. The truth of Christianity, in the majority of places claiming to worship God, has been exchanged for another gospel. The fruit of this "other gospel" is described in 2 Tim. 3:1-4:4. It does not produce saving faith, nor is it beneficial in pointing people to Christ. The idea of "difficult" or "perilous" relates to exposure to spiritual danger at every turn. Many professing Christians are, with good intentions, attending churches where the truth is not being presented. This false teaching is under the guise of being beneficial, but it is just the opposite. This complexity of spiritual deception in our day is influencing many people.

The impression that the general populous reasons as Christianity, and what or who is a Christian, is distorted. Many sum up Christianity as philosophies of morality, conservative politics, and old fashioned patriotism. For example, the more conservative television news is found on the "FOX" network. They have as their primary religious spokesperson, representing Christianity, a Roman Catholic priest. When they want to bring in the Christian viewpoint, they turn to him for his ideas and perspective. As this network represents the more conservative thinking in America, the general conclusion is that Christianity, and therefore a Christian by definition, can be defined under a broad philosophical umbrella. The impression is that Christianity is something that can be shaped by the person calling himself a

Christian. According to the Bible this is not true. The Bible emphatically defines true Christianity, and provides detailed instruction that warns of the many avenues of deception. To recognize the truth from distortion and deception matters significantly. First, as these are the latter days, Christ is coming soon, and many will not be prepared to meet Him. Second, because the truth is not preeminent in the present time, many are unknowingly following falsehood. The truth must be wisely evaluated, and sought with considerable effort. For even in places claiming awareness and objection to the decline of spirituality, there is often more affiliation with those deceived, than those with the clarity of the truth. The tendency of many churches is to compromise with the trends of society leading away from Christ. Compromising is rationalized, with good intentions, in order to maintain relevance and popularity. Many places of worship have embraced, by varying degrees, the "New Age" belief which teaches that truth is relative or overvalued. This philosophy is seen either directly in what is taught, or indirectly by what is not taught. There is too much concern for maintaining entertainment and a comfortable message ("ears tickled" 2 Tim. 4:3), than for upholding the only saving Gospel. The Gospel, on the other hand, is the true essential. It is specific to the Person of Christ, and it is the singular means that God uses for salvation. It cannot be improved upon, and must not be diminished.

Paul writes that anyone proclaiming a gospel that is not the Gospel of Christ is accursed (Gal. 1:8). Therefore, the new theology, and message of today is neither innocent nor without consequence–it is apostasy! It is the result of years of neglect of the Word of God, and the consequence is generations of biblical ignorance. This has allowed the proliferation not only of false teaching, but an inability to deal effectively with false belief systems. The new thinking is bad enough in itself, but it is actually claiming to be the Gospel. Further, because it claims to represent God's relevant message and plan for man, Christianity has by many been redefined. The new message has no power (2 Tim. 3:5). This is because the unchangeable, real focus; Christ, has been exchanged for a focus on man (Rom. 1:23). In the churches of the "new gospel," when measured against the Word of God, worship has also been changed "away" from a God-fearing, high regard for and determination to know the God of the Scriptures, to man's carnal immediate desires. The character of God's love has been incorrectly construed, and then this faulty concept emphasized, without regard for a more complete biblical picture of God's total character. Love, in such places, has become God's blind affection, and perverted acceptance of evil, sin, and rebellion. People living for self, and in sin, receive a false sense of comfort. Instead of man being proclaimed as a hopeless sinner under the wrath of God (John 3:36), and in need of a Savior; he needs only to improve his attitude and find fulfillment. After all, he is told that God *already loves him*, and God *wants him to be happy*. The matter of man's separation from God as a sinner is considered too negative to be discussed. So the new branding of Christianity is focused on attitude improvement, not on the necessary transforming work of God in the heart (John 3:3).

Some of the most popular churches that now serve as what is considered the Christian "standard" proudly advertise and practice only the so-called *positive aspects* of the Bible. Those attending these churches are led to believe that God's highest priority is their immediate gratification. The chief goal is to make people feel good. People are placing their eternal well-being in ministries that are void of biblical substance. In reality, there is no basis for such confidence because the basis for confidence, the Scripture, is either directly rejected or deliberately twisted. But nonetheless, the confidence of the audience foolishly builds as they see others finding, what appears to be energy for God. They are in a well-attended place, with nice, enthusiastic, and sincere people. The masses of church attendance in such places are being manipulated into a false sense of well-being. Those attending are exposed to *music* that is more like the world's entertainment, followed by *man-centered* talks. Although God *terms* are used, the substance is humanistic. This has replaced true repentance and faith in the Lord Jesus Christ. Often in services, the Bible is *not opened*, or if it is opened, it serves as a launching point for non-biblical subjects, or for philosophies actually contrary to the true Gospel. Those attending never seem to question whether the motive behind the gathering is really for God's glory.

Many people have happily and embraced this new standard, and the audiences have naively assumed it pleases God. The actual top priority in such places is not God, or knowing God, but self promotion. What is really being developed is a supposed happier version of the people in the sinful world that are loyal to these ministries. These churches have found a way to be popular by getting along with society's antagonism to historic Christianity, by neglecting truth, tolerating sin, and thereby being less controversial. The teaching may contain elements of truth, but it veers from the Bible because it is presented in narratives with the primary objective being not to offend. It does not honor the Lord, and is not representative of the worship required from Scripture.

But, be clear on this, this "new gospel" has no life changing ability. It does not conform to the message of the Bible or what man needs. It fails to address the essence of the Bible; man's alienation from God because of sin, and therefore, man's need for and total dependence on God for reconciliation. It is perilous because it is given in the *name* of Christ, but does not reflect the *nature* of Christ. It is a diversion because it is not honestly attempting to communicate the truth of the Bible. Many of these assemblies produce Christians in name only. As such, they are incapable of fighting the good fight of faith or of being a true light, and they are not "overcoming" as required by Scripture. They are most often superficial and indistinguishable in lifestyle from those with no profession.

Never addressed, in the churches described, is the authenticity of their faith. True salvation, as a work of God in the heart, is unknown and considered unnecessary. The subject is completely neglected, even though it is most important, and the reason for the death of the Son of God at Calvary. If the truth is known in these ministries, it is buried behind many activities and other focus. The attitude of many churches is that to speak biblical is old fashioned, too judgmental, unloving, divisive, and considered neither socially nor politically correct. The deception within these churches can be summed up in Proverbs 14:12; "There is a way that seems right unto man, but the end thereof is the way of death." Such is the evil of ministries that are substitutes for the true Gospel. A biblical evaluation shows them unworthy of any association with the name of Christ. As Christ warned in His letters to the seven churches (Revelation 2-3), these churches have lost their "lamp stand," or their ability to be a light. They should not be attended or supported, but should be exposed for their apostasy. "Love rejoices in the truth" (1 Cor. 13:6). Love is not accepting that which God reveals as detrimental. It is instead love to warn others of the peril of being religious, but without Christ (Matt. 7:13-14). It is heartbreaking because these ministries often draw large crowds of people who are not hearing the life changing words of Christ. These are people who are sincere, and yet deceived. They are not under the true message of Christ, and are missing the narrow way that leads to life (Matt. 7:13–14).

Then, there are others in these perilous times who find their sense of spiritual well-being in established historic denominations. These claim their church history as the basis for their confidence. Their denomination has been around for a long time, and they take comfort in what they believe are time-tested traditions. Ultimately, their confidence is placed in the church's longevity and religious practice. The problem is that most of these institutions have long abandoned the faith of the Bible, replacing it with evolving traditions developed by men. The individuals attending have fallen into the trap of assuming that their church pastor or priest, is feeding the flock with a right understanding of acceptability to God. These have trusted their eternity on the institution. For many, the assumptions, whether stated or not, are, "My church has been around a long time, and the people running the church, and promoting what is presented, have the foundation of time-tested tradition. Therefore, it must be right."

Interestingly, similar thinking prevailed during the time of Christ. Those confident in religious traditions never seem to realize that Satan is not opposed to religion; he is instead opposed to Christ, and to His truth. This kind of unchecked religious apostasy led, in the providence of God, to the execution of the Lord Jesus Christ (Acts 2:23). That execution was pressed by the religious leaders of that time who were blind to the truth of God, so much so, that they would hate and condemn the Lord of life, whom they claimed to represent. Although their unbelief was, in the sovereignty of God, used to accomplish the work of the Savior on the cross, they were fully accountable for their unbelief. People create institutions, and the Bible warns us about placing confidence in anything but the Scripture (Ps. 118:8, 146:3; Jer. 17:5). We must put confidence exclusively in the Word of God. Placing confidence in traditions, a church, a denomination, or an institution formed upon traditions, is a foundation built on sand (Matt. 7:24–28). Paul stated after his conversion from the highest testimony of religion; "put no confidence in the flesh" (Phil. 3:3).

Other people place their confidence for eternity on general assumptions. There are many non-church goers that simply believe they are better than most other people, and if there is a God, their good outweighs their bad. In their mind they are acceptable. They disregard that the revealed God is holy, and that all sinners outside of Christ are unacceptable in His sight. Others have confidence that what a person believes, in relation to God, is unimportant, as long as the person is sincere. Sincerity can easily be misplaced, and it should never run contrary to, or replace the teaching of Scripture. Sincerity, when it is not supported by truth, is foolish.

Some other persons take comfort in the large numbers of people who are not associated with any kind of faith, morality, or accountability. They think: *How can that many people be wrong?* Again, Christ Himself gave this clear warning, "Broad is the way the leads to destruction and narrow the way that leads to life and few there be that find it" (Matt. 7:13). God is not a democracy. His standard of acceptance is not based on popularity. In fact, the Bible consistently demonstrates that God is not impressed with big numbers of people. The narrow way to life is not indicated as a way naturally taken by the masses, but a way that must be sought, and prayerfully found (Matt. 7:14). Even though Christianity is by grace, it is still the way that God has made theologically impossible without His help. The broad road of religion, leading to destruction, and the broad road of non-religion are false. Both are deceived ways leading to destruction.

Then there are those who reason, *Religious thinking has come a long way for many years, and modern Christianity is much smarter today.* Are we? Christianity does not advance in the fallen world like technology. There are two things to recognize that have not, and cannot change. The first is truth. The truth of God "abides forever" (1 Pet. 1:25), and in conjunction with the truth (the Word), Christ (who is the Word), is "the same yesterday, today, and forever" (Heb. 13:8). The discerning need is to recognize that this *new*, and supposedly *improved*, redefining of salvation is false. Second, man's sinful nature has not changed. Jeremiah stated, "The heart is deceitful above all else and desperately sick, who can know it?" (Jer. 17:9). He unambiguously declared that we cannot trust ourselves, that is, our own thinking and reasoning.

In regard to most issues, wrong assumptions might matter little, but not so with regard to the eternal soul. The consequences of being wrong cannot be overstated. Neither can they be reversed beyond this life. This issue far surpasses any other matter. Simple reasoning screams out that our eternal destination is not a matter to be considered based on anything but absolute surety. The never changing standard, and only sure foundation as the source for confidence, must be placed exclusively in God, as He is revealed in His Word. There is no deception or falsehood in the Bible. The Word of God is "the truth" (John 17:17)! It is to be cherished above denominations, religions, churches, people, or self-thinking. It is to be read and studied, because it is the source of truth that brings eternal life.

My intention in writing this commentary is to warn and awaken individuals concerning their most valuable possession, their soul. Thankfully, the truth can still be found as honored and taught from some church pulpits, although it must be carefully and wisely sought. Christianity is not defined by the world, society, or the modern church. It is defined by God in His Word. The definition of a Christian is also defined exclusively in the Bible. The Bible alone must be the source for all understanding, and through it comes a right relationship with God. I praise God for those ministries that continue to proclaim the message of Christ. I love the true church of God, and desire with all my heart for the truth to go forth reaching as many as God is pleased to save.

I am soberly convinced that many people today, calling themselves Christians, have no basis for assurance. In the closing remarks of His Sermon on the Mount, Christ gave serious warning about people being religiously deceived. In Matthew 7:24–27, Christ spoke of making a commitment for building a person's house. The decision was either to build it on sand, or to build it on the rock. We know that He was not literally talking about houses, sand, and rocks. He was instead describing whether a person establishes his spiritual life and eternal future on something as insecure as sand (an unsubstantiated belief), or on "the Rock." The Rock is Christ, and the only true hope is found in believing His Gospel. Christ was addressing the most important question of all time for every person; where am I really placing my confidence for eternity? Is it on "the Rock," or is it merely something built on sand?

If the reader is not sure of his salvation, there is a means of finding the true answer. The answer lies with God. God Himself has revealed this in His Word. The Bible is the message of God for salvation. God uses the Scriptures exclusively to bring men to Himself (1 Pet. 1:23; Jas. 1:18). The Scriptures are exclusively reliable in communicating to us the validity of our personal salvation.

The most important, fundamental matter of all time, for every person, is where he will spend eternity? This issue should be addressed with the highest priority of care and consideration. It is not something to be overlooked, or something anyone else can do for the individual. It is too intimate, too personal, and too serious. It is between the person and God. It is the same question for every soul who has ever lived. The refinement of the matter is this; how do I know that I am on that narrow way spoken of by Christ (Matt. 7:14)? How do I know that I am truly saved? Could I be fooled like the masses described by Christ, and really be on the broad road (Matt.7:13)? Every individual's eternal destiny is based on what Christ says, not on what one wishes or what someone else says. Is the reader looking exclusively to Christ in His Word for reasoning and faith? Should one believe assumptions, without reasoning through the Word, to discover what God says? Should not one reflect on his beliefs to see if they agree with the teaching of the Bible? God has spoken to us in His Word. The only place for real confidence for the truth, and nothing but the truth, is the Bible. What can we trust? God's Word!

The Epistle of 1 John was written, and purposefully placed within the Canon of Scripture for soul assurance (1 John 5:13). It defines true Christianity, and thereby the true Christian. This epistle is God's provision to understand a right relationship with God. Only in the careful assessment of John's arguments can personal confidence, devoid of foolish assumption, be settled. Since every book of the Bible has a distinct revelatory assignment, John thus stated his; **These things I have written ... that you may know you have eternal life** (1 John 5:13). To study 1 John is to encounter God's evaluation or His exam. An honest study of 1 John is the most necessary and valuable experience anyone can undertake. John's writing serves as the measure of real spiritual life, and addresses clearly the most significant question; am I right with God; am I really saved?

Theme:

The writing of 1 John is about reality—how can people know that they have eternal life? Many people from a variety of backgrounds, knowledge, experiences, and life practices, profess to be Christians. Are mere professions from the lips of individuals, when asked if they are Christian, the seal of God's approval? Obviously not, for the Bible abundantly addresses the difference between profession and possession. This same writer (John), wrote of one of the most profound teaching encounters with Christ in the Gospel of John, chapter 3. A religious leader named Nicodemus came to Christ by night, and Jesus explained true salvation. He stated that all truly saved "must be born again." The person must undergo a supernatural work of God in order to be in a right relationship with God.

The spiritually discerning person will be reminded of the theology of Romans 8:28–30. This is what I call the unbroken chain of God's true salvation. There are three main essential components of salvation spoken of in Scripture: justification, sanctification, and glorification. All three of these are seen in this passage. The point is that no person can be justified without also "being conformed to the image of His Son" (sanctified). 1 John is about the marks of sanctification, the evidence that the person is somewhere in God's defined sanctification process. In other words, 1 John shows us who is "born again" and who is not. For the reader, it is as though they are taking a self-evaluation. But, unlike any other evaluation, this one has eternal consequences. It is God's perfect exam. Its purpose is to bring about assurance of salvation for the saved, and for those who do not find assurance, to seek the Savior, who alone can save. Those in the latter category may then also find assurance, and the joy of true salvation.

Author
John the Apostle (abundance of internal evidence and early church)

Date
85–90 AD (according to early church father, Irenaeus)

Place
Ephesus (according to Irenaeus)

Recipients
Those professing faith in Christ - believers (1 John 2:12-14)

Purpose
Assurance of possession of eternal life (1 John 5:13)

Outline
Our exposition will proceed according to the following outline.

I. The Reality of the Person of Christ (1:1–4)
    A. The Certainty of Christ (1:1)
        1. The Parallel
        2. The Proof
        3. The Person
    B. The Communication of Christ (1:2–4)
        1. The Power of the Proclamation (1:2–3)
        2. The Blessing of the Proclamation (1:4)

II. The Requirement of Fellowship with Christ (1:5—5:12)
    A. The Conditions for Fellowship (1:5—2:11)
        1. Walking in the light (1:5–7)
            a. The Position of God (1:5)
            b. The Practice of Christians (1:6–7)
        2. Walking by Confession (1:8—2:2)
            a. Our Sin (1:8–10)
                (1) Comprehension (1:8)
                (2) Confession (1:9)

    (3) Contempt (1:10)
   b. Our Advocate (2:1–2)
    (1) Essential (2:1)
    (2) Exclusive (2:2)
  3. Walking In Obedience (2:3–6)
   a. Our Assurance (2:3–4)
    (1) Condition (2:3)
    (2) Commandments (2:3)
   b. Our Assertion (2:4)
   c. Our Affirmation (2:5–6)
    (1) Conduct (2:5, 6b)
    (2) Credential (2:5b)
    (3) Cause (2:6)
  4. Walking In Love (2:7–11)
   a. The Authority (2:7–8)
    (1) Expressed (2:7)
    (2) Exhibited (2:8)
   b. The Antithesis (2:9)
    (1) Claimed (2:9a)
    (2) Contradicted (2:9b)
   c. The Associations (2:10–11)
    (1) Love with Light (2:10)
    (2) Lost showing Darkness (2:11)
 B. The Challenge for Fellowship (2:12–29)
  1. Absolute Foundation in Reality (2:12–14)
   a. True for All (2:12a)
    (1) Forgiveness (2:12b)
    (2) Freedom from Doubt (2:12c)
   b. True for Fathers (2:13)
    (1) Firsthand Knowledge (2:13b)
    (2) Fellowship (2:13a)
   c. True for Young Men (2:14)
    (1) Fight (2:14b)
    (2) Faith (2:14c)
    (3) Favorable Outcome (14d)
   d. True for Children (13b)
  2. Appeal Against Loving the World (2:15–17)
   a. The Command (2:15a)
   b. The Consequence (2:15b)

      c. The Considerations (2:16–17a)
        (1) The Singular Elements (2:16a)
        (2) The Source (2:16b)
        (3) The Short Span (2:17a)
      d. The Contrasting Promise (2:17b)
    3. Assurance from Abiding in the Truth (2:18–25)
      a. Nurturing your Perception (2:18–19)
      b. Nurturing your Position (2:20–25)
        (1) Manifested by Anointing You (2:20-21)
        (2) Manifested by the One Lying (2:22-23)
        (3) Manifested by You Abiding (2:24-25)
    4. Admonition to Avoid Deceivers (2:26–29)
      a. Necessity of Being Vigilant (2:26)
      b. Necessity of Being Selective (2:27)
      c. Necessity of Being Focused (2:28)
      d. Necessity of Bearing His Image (2:29)
C. The Characteristics for Fellowship (3:1—3:24)
    1. Practicing Moral Excellence (3:1–10a)
      a. Our Prospect (3:1–2)
        (1) Actual Standing (3:1a)
        (2) Ambiguous Identity (3:1b)
        (3) Assured Revealing (3:2)
        (4) Attention on Him (3:3a)
        (5) Actions Affected (3:3b)
      b. Our Propriety (3:4–6)
        (1) Association to Sin (3:4)
        (2) Antithesis of Sin (3:5)
        (3) Antagonistic to God (3:6)
      c. Our Production (3:7–8)
        (1) Association with God (3:7)
        (2) Association with Satan (3:8)
      d. Our Proof (3:9–10)
        (1) Affiliation in God (3:9)
        (2) Activity of God (3:10)
    2. Practicing Love (3:10b–24)
      a. The Distinction Exemplified (3:10b–16)
        (1) Critical from Beginning (3:11)
        (2) Contrasted (3:12)
        (3) Corrupted Expectation (3:13)

        (4) Contrasts Providing Proof (3:14–15)
        (5) Christ's Right Example (3:16)
     b. The Distinction Examined (3:17–24)
        (1) Challenge to Our Heart (3:17–18)
        (2) Confidence within Our Heart (3:19–20)
        (3) Confident Action (3:21)
        (4) Complementary Association (3:22)
        (5) Commanded Expectation (3:23)
        (6) Conclusive Evidence (3:24)
D. The Cautions for Fellowship (4:1–21)
  1. Practicing Cautions (4:1–6)
     a. The Caution concerning False Prophets (4:1–4)
        (1) Command to Test (4:1a)
        (2) Composition of the World (4:1b)
        (3) Confession as a Means of Examination (4:2–3)
        (4) Capability to Overcome (4:4)
     b. The Caution regarding listening (4:5–6)
        (1) Communication (4:5)
        (2) Communion (4:6)
  2. Production of Love (4:7–21)
     a. The Caution of an Unloving Spirit (4:7–14)
        (1) Call for Indispensable Love (4:7–8)
        (2) Commencement of Love (4:9)
        (3) Conveyance of Love (4:10)
        (4) Conclusive Call for Love (4:11)
        (5) Chosen Portrayal of Love (4:12)
        (6) Confirmation from Love (4:13)
        (7) Convicting Testimony of Love (4:14)
     b. The Caution against False Presumption (4:15–21)
        (1) Causes Genuine Peace (4:15–18)
        (2) Causes Us to Love as He Loves (4:19–21)
E. The Consequences of Fellowship (5:1–12)
  1. Victory over the World (5:1–4)
     a. Observable Earmarks of New Birth (5:1–3)
        (1) Its Belief (5:1a)
        (2) Its Love (5:1b–3a)
        (3) Its Obedience (5:2b–3a)
     b. Overcoming Nature of New Birth (5:4)
        (1) Its Power (5:4a)

       (2) Its Passion (5:4b)
    2. Validity through Christ's Authentication (5:5–12)
      a. The Centrality of Christ (5:5)
        (1) Identification of the Recipient (5:5a)
        (2) Identification of the Means (5:5b)
      b. The Certainty of His Credentials (5:6–11)
        (1) Authentication by Unique Agreement (5:6–8)
        (2) Authentication by the Father's Testimony (5:9)
        (3) Authentication by Changed Lives (5:10–11)
        (4) Authentication of His Ownership (5:12)

III. The Reassurance of Eternal Fellowship with Christ (5:13–21)
  A. The Confidence from Fellowship (5:13–15)
    1. Assurance from the Writing (5:13)
      a. Evident Purpose (5:13b)
      b. Exclusive Recipients (5:13a)
      c. Eternal Life (5:13c)
    2. Assurance from Confident Prayer (5:14–15)
      a. Expectation He Hears (5:14)
      b. Expectation He Answers (5:15)
  B. The Conclusions from the Writing (5:16–21)
    1. Prayer Guidance (5:16–17)
      a. Possible Interpretations (5:16a)
      b. Position of Responsibility (5:16b)
      c. Personal Discernment (5:17)
    2. Proper Perspective (5:18–20)
      a. Protection (5:18)
      b. Position (5:19)
      c. Partnership (5:20)
    3. Practical Command (5:21)

I encourage the reader to go with me on a journey through the epistle of 1 John, and prayerfully allow the verses to provide an honest self-assessment leading to personal application. In doing so, I recognize that God the Holy Spirit must be actively involved. My purpose and prayer is that this study will be used of God to edify the reader by producing either, concern for, or confidence in personal salvation. Ultimately, my desire for every reader is for him to know, and to possess true salvation. Real peace comes from the assurance of embracing the faith "that was once for all delivered unto the saints" (Jude 3). God has given John's first epistle as a means of knowing God's assessment. Having such information to study is a treasure. Nothing is more important because it addresses our most valuable possession–our personal relationship and standing before God!

Soli Deo Gloria!

1

The Certainty and Communication of Christ

1:1–4

I. The Reality of the Person of Christ

Several years ago one of my sons, who at that time was around 20 years of age, was taken to the emergency room with a swollen stomach, and he was in significant pain. After receiving morphine, he was relieved of the severity of the pain, but yet he was obviously quite stressed about his immediate circumstances. He began dialogue with an unfamiliar emergency room doctor dealing with his case. He immediately inquired about the doctor's credentials. The usual kind of pleasantries, and more mannerly discussion was cast aside. The doctor had stated that surgery would be required, and my son, who was very concerned, even alarmed, was bold enough to ask;"Do you know what you're talking about? Do you have experience? Are you sure you have the ability to successfully deal with my situation?"

By the grace of God, this doctor was, indeed, a wise physician and surgeon who handled my son's situation with precision, and undoubtedly, saved his life. This situation serves as a good example to lead off our study into the epistle of 1 John. My son was correct in wanting to make sure he was in the best hands possible; the hands of a reliable and competent surgeon. He was in a helpless and very difficult situation, one that is analogous to our desperate situation as citizens of earth who have a certain future of death, and the facing of eternity beyond. Knowing that, we need to be sure that whoever or whatever is directing our steps toward an eternal cure is capable, reliable, and true so that we might have confidence as we face eternity.

Where shall we find such a Great Physician who will heal our soul and fit us for all eternity? The answer, of course, is found exclusively in Christ Jesus. He is the **Word of Life**, as declared here in these first four verses. This epistle relates to John's Gospel, which also specifically begins with Christ: "In the beginning was the Word." John begins this epistle, which is about reliable assurance, on Christ's credentials and reliability. Simply put, John's epistle is built on the foundation of the worthiness of Christ, not only as the authority to examine our *condition* and provide a truthful and absolutely relevant and impeccable diagnosis, but also as the exclusive *cure*. He gained that right by His death for sinners on the cross.

John correctly begins by reminding us about Christ. His credentials are so complete, so absolute, and so exclusive that He is the only source suited for examination of the soul. All other sources, unless they are following His book, as He is the Word, are unqualified frauds. Those not following Christ therefore cannot be trusted. It is upon the reliability of Christ and His Word that John is staking the validity of his arguments for examining the authenticity of each reader's claim to eternal life.

A. The Certainty of Christ (1:1)

What was from the beginning, what we have heard, what we have seen with our eyes, what we have looked at and touched with our hands, concerning the Word of Life.

The opening phrase, What was from the beginning (beginning is the Greek, *archē*) means that Christ (**the Word of Life**) was chief or paramount at the beginning. Christ's chief credential is that He is God. Only God can be stated as **from the beginning**. As John writes this epistle to define who is saved (has assurance), and who is not, the epistle is built on the foundation of the Person of Christ and His authority. He was present in eternity past with God the Father, and the infinite value of His credentials serves as the foundation for the reader's confidence in what has been written. Without His reality as the Savior, and without His presence as God eternal, and the ultimate author of this message through John, this book would have no validity. This book is a very dogmatic and defining epistle. Its statements would be mere opinions with no basis for acceptance of the message, except for the superintending of Christ. He is the foundation on which salvation has reality. Therefore, John places Christ's credentials at the beginning of his writing. This introduction corresponds to his Gospel. In both cases, he is establishing Christ as God, and as inseparable from His **Word**. As Christ has supreme authority, so His **Word** has the same authority. This writing of John was written under divine inspiration, and therefore, is sealed by the authority of Christ. It is the same as the Word of Christ.

John's next statement, **what we have heard, what we have seen with our eyes, what we have looked at and touched with our hands**, introduces a personal validation. He wants the readers to understand that Jesus Christ is real. He is the "God-man." How does John know that? All of his senses were fully engaged with Christ. This is the apostle so close to Christ that he often rested his head physically against Him (John 13:23). He was intimately acquainted with Him personally and physically for a period of approximately three years. John is stating this not only as a personal witness to validate the reality of Christ, but also as evidence so that the reader can know that John was a personal, present recipient of the teaching of Christ (**what we have heard**), and that John's writing was not merely his writing, but more importantly, the message of Christ. John has written majestically of Him so the reader will know He is no ordinary religious man. He is reminding the reader of Christ's glory in the most concise yet profound manner. By doing so, he brings the same sense of inseparable authority to this epistle, and says in effect: this is the Word of God; hear Him (Christ).

1. The Parallel

The parallel with John's Gospel is striking. Just as the Gospel of John states "We beheld His glory" (John 1:14), so this epistle has the same sense. In both this epistle and his Gospel, John makes it dogmatically and profoundly evident that Christ is God, and that He is the central figure and foundation for his writing. There are at least four major similarities between John's Gospel and his epistle of 1 John.

First, Christ is presented as eternal and as God. John's reference to the eternal nature of Christ, in both writings, emphatically proclaims His deity and His equality with God the Father.

Second, Christ is described as **the Word**. This presents Christ as inseparable from the message of Scripture, and provides His absolute endorsement of the Word of God. John further shows Christ's authority as the author of Scripture in conjunction with the purpose of the Father, and the essential work of the Spirit. As **the Word**, He is also the object of Scripture, and as such, has the final say on all things.

Third, Christ (**the Word of life**) is the Creator of all things. This is again not only a statement of His deity, but also of His role in the Godhead. He is spoken of here as the Creator of life both physical and spiritual, who has the right over all creation (see also Col. 1:16). With regard to this epistle, He (Christ) will be defining the spiritual life He created.

Fourth, Christ is the source of all truth, knowledge, and the only hope for man. As the Word, He is the revealed knowledge about God, and He is the provider of the means God uses (the Word), to set men free. As John also describes Him as the proclamation of **the eternal life (1:2)**, which is the message of salvation; He is the only hope for man.

> **Pause and Reflect**
>
> Christ is the foundation of everything about Christianity. John begins with Christ in the most majestic description and terms because he wants the reader to understand the deity, authority, and solid foundation of which he writes. That foundation is Christ. As his message is built upon Christ, it is totally reliable, and the reader can have absolute confidence in the arguments presented. John is further saying that if anyone loses sight of Christ, or bases ideas on anything other than a foundation on Christ, they are perilously off course. Those veering from Christ are placing their confidence on something worthless that will ultimately lead to ruin. Therefore, John makes it clear that the foundation of his writing is the Person of Jesus Christ.

2. The Proof

John makes the argument of his personal and unique witness. His witness, that would be affective in any honest courtroom, is powerful and unique because it involved all of his senses over a period of three years. John was one of the "inner circle" of apostles (Peter, James, and John) who were with Christ at the most significant occasions of His ministry, such as the transfiguration, and at key opportunities throughout Christ's ministry. John called himself the disciple Jesus loved (John 13:23). The words he uses to describe his witness demonstrate its thoroughness and accuracy.

First, there is **heard**, which is *akouō*, a primary verb meaning "to hear" (in various senses).

Second, **seen** is *horaō*, to *stare* at, gaze at, that is, (by implication) "to discern clearly."

Third, **touched** is *psēlaphaō*, to manipulate, that is, verify by contact. Combined with **looked at** (*theaomai)*, the full sense is "to look at closely, examine with a combination of hands and eyes."

This witness takes on a progressive tone. John says, in effect, "We didn't just hear, we also saw; and we didn't just see, we also felt Him." He alludes to the fact that he spent long periods of examination with Christ.

These words provide, to any reasonable person, the personal, comprehensive proof of the genuineness of Jesus Christ. The reader should compare this claim to Peter's statement (2 Pet. 1:16–18), and the accounts given in John 13:25, 20:27, and Luke 24:39. This togetherness was obviously more than any normal relationship would be today because of the demands of work, family, and other obligations. These men moved together, almost in continuous and constant interaction daily for three years, and through many different circumstances.

The ministry of Christ was providentially controlled, dynamically rich, and so well-defined that John would state at the end of his Gospel: "there are also many other things Jesus did, which if they were written in detail, I suppose the world itself would not contain the books that would be written" (John 21:25). The other disciples were each severely persecuted, following Christ's resurrection and ascension, and yet maintained a steadfast testimony, and all but one finally were martyred.

> **Pause and Reflect**
>
> Christ is real, and John has an obligation to speak about Him because of his personal, intimate witness and first-hand knowledge. Because Christ is real, there is a real salvation. The basis of the real salvation is the reality of the Savior of whom John bears absolute substantiated witness. Implied here is that, as a result, the reader should be wary of any claims that are not founded on Christ and His Word. These include religion in general, even religion in the name of Christ. There are many ministries claiming Christianity, but when carefully examined, many are not built on the Word. They are built on precepts of their own making, or wishful concepts. Such things must not be confused with John's writing or even considered to be on the same level as John's writing. This writing is the inspired testimony and Words of Christ. He is writing under divine providence and guidance, and that is why his writing is included in the canon of Scripture. The Word of God is the only true source whereby the reader can have absolute confidence, as Christ is the only genuine Savior.

3. The Person

John uses very particular terms to describe Christ, and this is purposefully by design. For as John is writing this epistle to define true Christianity, and to provide a guide for who has salvation and who does not, he must bring Christ into an inseparable relationship with what is written. The validity of salvation is founded on the author and means of salvation. Christ holds that unique position, and therefore, He alone has the final word when it comes to defining the characteristics of His great salvation.

John makes the connection with Christ using the term **Word of life (1:1)**. **Word** is *logos*, something said (thought, spoken, written). **Life** is *zōe,* the phenomena or condition that is distinguished from things inorganic, such as objects or dead organisms. The qualities of life include: growth, reproduction, and certain powers of adaptation to environment. Interestingly, no person can define life. Man can only observe it and know that life exists. Christ is the author and creator of all life, both physical and spiritual. He is the life giver (John 5:26; 5:40; 6:48, 53; 1 John 5:11–12; John 14:6). In Hebrews 4:12, Christ is again shown to be inseparable from the Word (where Christ and the Word are intermingled in the context), and He is shown to be as **the Word**, a possessor of living power and supernatural ability. In John 10:27–28, as **the Word**, He is shown to have a drawing power upon His elect (sheep), which cannot be taken away.

> **Pause and Reflect**
>
> Christ is brought into the writing as the author and means of salvation, and as having a mysterious, inseparable dynamic with His Word. In so doing, John has brought fundamental validity to everything he writes under inspiration. It can be trusted. As his writing is defining salvation and thereby providing assurance to those who meet the definitions in this epistle, it is appropriate that the focus and provider of so great a salvation is appropriately shown linked to the writing of John, even as Christ was intimately acquainted with John during His earthly ministry. The validity of the writing lies not in John, but in Christ.

B. The Communication of Christ (1:2–4)

And the life was manifested, and we have seen and testify and proclaim to you the eternal life, which was with the Father and was manifested to us—what we have seen and heard we proclaim to you also, so that you too may have fellowship with us; and indeed our fellowship is with the Father, and with His Son Jesus Christ. These things we write, so that our joy may be made complete.

1. The Power of the Proclamation (1:2–3)

John tells us **the life was manifested**. The word **manifested** (*phaneroō*) means "to make apparent." When John described Christ in his Gospel, he declared: "We beheld His glory" (John 1:14). The same concept is here. This was no ordinary man—this was the man described in Isaiah 7:14 as "Immanuel," God with us. This **life . . . manifested** has in it the truth of the incarnation. Just as the incarnation is supernatural because it is of God, so is the message supernatural because that which is proclaimed is of God. It also carries the power and authority of **eternal life**. The concept of **eternal life** has to do not only with the *quantity* of life, but it also includes the *quality* of life, because the life is in the presence of God. The context of the **eternal life** defines it as life with the Father and with the Son, for a co-equal description is given of the Savior being from the beginning in eternity past with the Father. Here, then, John describes eternity future, a life of living eternally in the very presence of God the Father and the Lord Jesus Christ, and thereby, also describes the glorious salvation emanating from the Gospel that is stated in the simple but dynamic term: **eternal life**.

Fellowship (*koinonia*) is defined as "the experience of sharing something significant in common with others." This fellowship is of the highest order, not only because it is of God, but also because true fellowship has with it the pleasure of being in a group where everyone sees eye-to-eye on every matter. It is complete harmony because everyone has the same values and desires, and each responds with the same affection. This view is the opposite of the current fallen world, where there is a mixture of people who are continually out of step with one another on almost every subject. This full agreement (in a state of total harmony and joy) is what provides a glorious tone to every Christian relationship. There is no true fellowship among people who do not share the same view of Christ, the same faith, the same doctrine, and the same desires. Without the intervention of God, such fellowship is impossible.

So, **fellowship (1:3)** with God describes fellowship with all members of the Godhead, but with specific reference to **Jesus Christ**. Having this fellowship means that those sharing fellowship with the Godhead have the righteousness of Christ (for God cannot associate with wickedness), and the same holy desires. Those in fellowship love what He loves. Having this fellowship with God, practically means that God is not a stranger. The person in this fellowship wants to be in God's presence because his nature has been remade in order to be like God's nature. This person is somewhere along the path of sanctification (Rom. 6:22; 2 Thess. 2:13; Hebrews 12:14), where growth takes place and the person becomes more and more like Christ. The saving work of God is not justification only, but the active, on-going process (sanctification) that places the person in fellowship with God. In this life (the fallen world), this fellowship is never *broken*, but it can be *hindered* (1 Pet. 3:7) by sinful behavior. This fellowship with God will be fully realized when the person is glorified (removed from the cursed environment and made into the perfect likeness of Christ), and the transformation is completed. It is therefore impossible for someone who does not love what God loves, and does not share the same mindset of desires, to have true fellowship with Him. Unless a person is "born from above," he remains under the separation that exists between the lost persons (outside of Christ) of the world, and God (Isa. 59:2). Only in Christ can there be reconciliation, and thus fellowship. This epistle is about the fellowship that exists in the sanctification process; this fellowship is for those whom He has chosen for salvation. They will bear the marks of God's work of sanctification in their lives.

The reader should be aware that fellowship with God was destroyed in the Garden of Eden at the fall. This was seen initially when Adam and Eve hid from the Lord (Gen. 3:8), with whom they had formerly enjoyed fellowship with no reservations (Gen. 2:25). It is the glorious plan of God, of which the Bible progressively unfolds through history, to restore fellowship with men. The restoration is by faith in and through Christ Jesus alone (Rom. 5:1). The underlying purpose of justification, sanctification, and glorification is the goal of restoring the fellowship that was broken in the fall (Gen. 3). Just prior to the cross, Christ prayed specifically for those chosen for salvation to complete their restoration of fellowship with God. This desire is the predominate issue in His high priestly prayer (John 17:22–24). As we progress through the epistle of 1 John, we should be aware that fellowship with God is the underlying factor. The ultimate defining matter is whether a person is in Christ Jesus, and therefore restored in fellowship through Him and with Him. All of the personal evaluation for determining eternal life found within 1 John is in the context of the significance of restoration of fellowship. More specifically, this restoration of fellowship is not perfected in this life, but is in the process in what theologians call "sanctification" (being set apart unto God). This process is exclusive to all persons who are the objects of God's saving faith; those who have experienced repentance, and are committed to following Christ by faith.

> **Pause and Reflect**
>
> John is building his case for defining those who have assurance of eternal life. He immediately interconnects this with the nature of the persons addressed. He describes himself as a person having fellowship with God. He tells his readers that they can have fellowship with him, and one another, by their fellowship with God. Therefore, the reader, who passes the fellowship provision described, will of necessity have to be of the same nature as those with whom they are fellowshipping, and the same nature as God the Father and the Lord Jesus Christ. To have this fellowship is to be truly joined with others in a relationship of like-mindedness, desire, and affection. This fellowship includes a supernatural change of nature that has purposely taken place in the person's life. The understanding of fellowship serves as a lead-off for the "black and white lines" of demarcation that John uses throughout his writing as he describes who is saved and who is not. It will be described according to who they are, what they love, and what they do. All of the factors that will be presented in this epistle, indicating whether a person is truly saved or not, fall within the boundaries of the fruit of fellowship. This fruit must be viewed as part of the sanctification process taking place within every true believer (Heb. 12:14). Within the beauty of the restored fellowship with God, is the glory and joy of a true relationship with Him. Nothing is more wonderful or more joyful than having fellowship with God. Indeed, that is what John says when he provides insight into the blessing of this writing. Salvation is the restoration of fellowship with God, and the marks of that fellowship are real and are the basis for John's epistle. He will fully explore and expose these earmarks and their significance in relation to assurance.

2. The Blessing of the Proclamation (1:4)

These things we write, so that our joy may be made complete.

The word used here to describe the **joy** of being eternally in fellowship with God is *chara*. This term is exclusive to a biblical understanding of "true joy." This is a kind of joy or sense of well being that goes beyond the bounds of circumstances. In Scripture we find that Christians can have joy in the worst of physical conditions (Acts 16:25). This is a supernatural joy that comes with having peace and fellowship with God. John 15:11 provides focus on the source of real happiness, and this same happiness is defined here as being **complete**. This is the word *pleroō*, which means "to cram it to level up or fill it to the top." The idea is that nothing can compare with this measure of **joy**.

John states this as one of the goals of his writing. He desires individuals to know for sure whether they are acceptable to God (truly saved), or not. He wants those who are acceptable to find an immediate joy of the highest measure in the anticipation and assurance of eternal life. In making this proclamation of truth—for that is what this defining epistle is—John delivers a blessing of assurance, and with it, brings immediate joy to God's elect. While not stated explicitly, John's words certainly allude to a sobering word of rebuke (and possible conviction) to those who have no assurance of acceptance by God. Instead of assurance, many can be better defined as in a state of personal deception. This sobering word from John may well be, and I am quite sure it has many times, been used to bring those with false assurance to real salvation and true assurance.

Pause and Reflect

John has laid the foundation for his epistle. It is a work that is built on the authority of Christ, and it points to the joy of true, eternal fellowship with other saints, and with the Father and Son. John is already experiencing that joy because of the privilege of being used by God to write this epistle. The importance of this letter is sobering. This is not a work to be taken lightly, but to be studied and believed. The study and correct understanding of this epistle has the greatest imaginable value, because that value is the highest form of joy for those truly saved. For those who are not saved, however, it brings a sobering rebuke and warning that may be used of God to bring about a true salvation.

2

The Conditions for Fellowship

1:5—2:11

Outline context:

I. The Reality of the Person of Christ

II. The Requirement of Fellowship with Christ (1:5—5:12)

A. The Conditions for Fellowship (1:5—2:11)

Over the years there have been many professing Christians, often in highly visible positions, who were caught in open sin and paraded in the news. In the late twentieth century and moving into the twenty-first century there has been a flurry of such scandals finding their way into the public eye. The world in general shows great interest in these scandals, and delights at those who profess Christianity being caught in sin. Those caught become the object of ridicule, jokes, and much conversation.

What is not understood by the world is that there is a significant difference between *profession* and actual *possession*. One of the reasons there are scandals is because the person claiming one thing and doing another is obviously living in hypocrisy. Even those dead in sins realize the hypocrisy. In some cases the person might truly be a Christian who will repent, and seek to move on in the Christian life. However, many are not Christians at all, but are Christian in name only. It is relatively easy to be religious, but it is impossible to counterfeit the true work of God that transforms the heart (Jer. 13:23). God is about the business of doing the impossible. He transforms His elect into new creations (2 Cor. 5:17). God is not about *profession* only, rather, He is about *possession*. Part of any reality of possession is a new relationship with God that results in true fellowship. Fellowship is not theoretical; it is real and comes by the power of God. It is a real state of being whereby persons are remade to have the same interest, likes, and dislikes as God. There is a harmony of mindset and a binding of hearts, because of a relationship dominated by unified desires. It is not perfect in this life, but it does have an obvious testimony. True fellowship among the saved can only exist by spiritual birth (1 Cor. 1:9).

> ### Pause and Reflect
> God sets the conditions that identify His own, and one of those conditions is fellowship. Fellowship with God is a key desire and definer of true Christianity. God also determines the definition of fellowship, and only His definition is acceptable. In a real sense, all other marks of true salvation in this epistle are related to the defining of true fellowship with God. Fellowship is essential. The derivative of fellowship is joy, because to know God, and to be in His presence is the fullness of joy (Ps. 16:11). Therefore, every Christian desires and has the kind of fellowship with God that is described in this epistle.

1. Walking in the Light (1:5–7)

a. The Position of God (1:5)

Now this is the gospel message we have heard from Him and announce to you: God is light, and in Him there is no darkness at all.

The word **this** is simply a connector to the prologue "so that our joy may be made complete" (v. 3). That joy comes by being associated with Him, what the Psalmist calls being in His "presence" (Ps. 16:11), which is the pinnacle of fellowship. The **message** (*aggelia*) has its root in the word "angel," which is often translated messenger. John is communicating or giving "the message." It is not just any message but the **Gospel message**. In other words, it is fundamentally related to salvation. This phrase is used again in 3:11, reflecting back on the source of the message. It has with it the authority of a message that **we heard from Him**, the **Him** being a reference to Christ, and therefore, it carries with it full authority, or full reality. This is not something that John dreamed up, so he wants us to know that the message has its roots in his personal attention to the words of Christ, and therefore it is a true message deserving close attention. It is this message that is being announced to the readers. **Announce** means "to declare in detail." John will give us the message from Christ in thoughtful detail so that nothing relevant is left out. It is a divine message that he declares is sure, important, and informative.

What is the message? Interestingly, John again begins with Christ and His position in majesty. Christ is always the fixed foundation of any discussion. He is the beginning, the end, and the standard. The position that John wants to address is given in specific terms, **God is light (1:5).** The word for **light** is *phos*, which means "to shine or make manifest." John is addressing what God is like. God is Himself all light in the sense of His essential quality, attribute, and character. Christ made this claim of Himself in John 8:12. Light in Scripture is always associated with His righteous nature, a nature that is all truth! In Psalm 27:1 and 36:9, the light has reference to appreciating all that is relevant and important related to God's essential nature. By contrast, men in sin are described by Christ in John 3:19 as those who "love darkness because their deeds were evil." This verse tells us two important truths about light. First, light, which is the opposite of darkness, is associated with God's righteousness, and second, men in their natural state of sin hate light. Men, because of sin, are comfortable only when hiding from God, just as Adam and Eve hid from God in the garden (Gen. 3:10) after their sin.

Why does John, in a context where fellowship is an indicator of man's relationship with God, bring up that **God is light and in Him is no darkness at all (1:5)?** John is letting the readers know that each person's affinity for **light** or **darkness** serves to reveal the nature of the person. God's nature or Christ's nature is pure light. He has no darkness whatsoever. In fact, the idea is that for Him to have anything but light is impossible. Therefore, if any person is to have fellowship (similar tastes, harmony, the same likes and dislikes) with Christ, then that person must love the light, because Christ is Light and has no darkness at all. There is no neutrality here. There is either a love of light or a love of darkness. If there is no love of light, then John is indicating that there can be no true fellowship with Christ. It would be impossible to fellowship with Christ, who is the Light, while at the same time love darkness. Christ is so related to light that not loving the light is the same as not loving Christ.

Pause and Reflect

John is showing us the position of Christ. That position is a position that is immovable, and uncompromising. It is a position of absolute light, and if one is to be associated with Christ in essential fellowship, he must have a nature that prefers light to darkness. To love light is to love Christ, and therefore the reverse is true. To hate the light, is to hate Christ. That does not mean that the person loving the light is in a state of perfection without any darkness. It does mean, however, those truly saved have a *desire* for the light, as compared to those who hate the light. It points to Christ as the

> Light, and therefore to those who have an attraction to light as those who desire Christ's fellowship.

b. The Practice of Christians (1:6–7)

If we say that we have fellowship with Him and *yet* walk in the darkness, we lie and do not practice the truth; but if we walk in the Light as He Himself is in the Light, we have fellowship with one another, and the blood of Jesus His Son cleanses us from all sin.

The phrase **if we say** demonstrates the difference between saying and doing. This phrase will be repeated again in 1 John 1:8, and 10. Its inclusion addresses the theme of this epistle; the separation of false Christianity from real Christianity. It is only the genuine that brings assurance. Real Christianity must be based, not on mere words, but actions. The idea is that saying is much easier than doing. Speech can just as easily be a lie, but living it out is where the real accountability is demonstrated. John is showing the inconsistency of saying that we have fellowship with Christ, while at the same time walking (the idea of living out the actions and decisions of life) in darkness. The Greek word for **fellowship** (*koinonia*) means "partnership, participation, or communion" (see verse 3 discussion). The idea that someone could declare that their fellowship with God is intact, while living a life practicing disobedience (**walk in darkness**), is as impossible as it would have been for Adam & Eve to deny a breach in fellowship after their sin in the garden.

That is why John uses such direct words as **we lie and do not practice the truth (1:6)**. The idea of darkness is that which is contrary to the nature of Christ, who is the Light. Darkness is unrighteous behavior in thought and action. John calls such inconsistency an emphatic lie. He goes on to say that this is a particular sin, because it means the one who is living this deception is not practicing the truth. Now, if the person is not practicing the truth, how can they have fellowship with Him who is **the Truth?** This is impossible, and that is the point. The one who says that they have fellowship with Christ, and yet continues to practice a lifestyle of showing their love for darkness, cannot possibly have a true relationship with Christ. It is clear from the beginning that John insists that a vast difference exists between those saved and those lost. The difference for the one saved exists around the concept of restoration of fellowship with God. The whole issue of fellowship becomes a sphere of attitude and action that surrounds the life of the true child of God. The life and maintenance of fellowship with Christ takes top priority in the life of the Christian, and is seen in the various ways John discusses in this letter.

The **"but"** of verse 7 is one of those many contrasting connectors used in the Greek New Testament to indicate the black and white differences essential in understanding of contrasting conditions. This one is special because it provides the very opposite condition from those who are living a lie, and have no true fellowship even when they say that they do. The opposite of walking in darkness is to **walk in the light.** To walk in the light is true fellowship because Christ is the Light. Further, this is the means whereby we (as true Christians) can have fellowship with one another. Any other basis for Christian fellowship is false. The correct connection for Christian fellowship is that we **walk in the light.** We associate and love one another because of our love for Christ and for what Christ loves.

Notice also in verse 7 that the passage does not speak of perfection. The phrase **the blood of Jesus cleanses us from all sin (1:7)** is a statement of the on-going power of Christ to forgive all sin in the life of any true Christian. He is not saying that there is no sin in the life of the Christian, but instead, that the Christian has the benefit of the cleansing power and promise of God's on-going forgiveness. One of the keys is the word **practice** in verse 6. **Practice** (*poieō*) carries the idea of the end result or effort. Practice is therefore a lifestyle, not an exception. To practice something is the norm or standard for the person practicing. In Matthew 7:17, Christ speaks of it in terms of fruit and that "every good tree bears good fruit, but the bad tree bears bad fruit." Interestingly, the word "bear" in Matthew 7:17 is the same word (*poieō*) translated **practice**. A tree is known by the practice of bearing its fruit, and so is a person known by the practice of bearing their fruit (walking in light with works pleasing to God).

Pause and Reflect

As with the tree, Christ is speaking of the general trend. If a tree is good it produces good fruit, but that does not mean that every piece of fruit on the tree is good, but it means good fruit characterizes the tree. The Christian is characterized by walking in the light, and because this is his trend, he proves or shows his relationship with Christ, and with that relationship is continuing forgiveness for yet remaining sins. This is also covered in the next verse. The bottom line is this: the Christian is known by his walk in the light, not just by what he says, but by what he does in the trend of his life. On the other hand, the false professor is also known, not by what he

> says, but by what he does in the trend of his life: he walks in the darkness, and therefore, it is impossible for him to have fellowship with God.

Finally, verse 7 specifies two marvelous rewards for those who walk in the light. First, John mentions **fellowship with one another**. This is likened unto Psalm 133:1, where David describes the wonderful nature of unity, like-mindedness, and peace among brethren. It provides a little heaven on earth, for indeed in glory there will be perfect harmony, peace with God, and with the saints.

The second reward is the on-going forgiveness that Christ gives. If we are walking in the light, Christ does not disown us when we sin. This cleansing is not addressing initial salvation or justification. It is addressing the process of sanctification. This encompasses the whole issue of the struggle of faith, elsewhere described by Paul in Philippians 2:12: "work out your own salvation with fear and trembling." It is a process of growth toward Christ-likeness, another aspect of walking in the light.

Those who have no love for the light will not be concerned about "working out their salvation." They will sin with impunity because they love the darkness. The true Christian, however, is grieved about remaining sin, and struggles to overcome it by the power of Christ, and has the promise that God will faithfully cleanse all sin. Therefore, while this walking in the light and fellowship with God is not perfect in this life, it does have some consistent characteristics shown in its practice. Part of that practice is genuine concern for the remaining sin in one's life, and this is directly linked to a consistent concern and priority for fellowship with God.

2. Walking by Confession (1:8—2:2)

a. Our Sin (1:8–10)

The doctrine of total depravity is among the most neglected and misunderstood doctrines in the Christian church. An understanding of this doctrine is the only answer for man's behavior now, and throughout history. Depravity is a theological term for the non-meritorious and sinful condition of man. The "total" description of depravity qualifies the extent of it to every aspect of man's nature. Man is inherently evil, not good, and there is nothing he can do to commend himself to God. This is the reason that sin saturates man's environment and activity from birth, and is at the source of all of mankind's problems. It is that which separates man from God, and ultimately takes every person's life ("the wages of sin is death," Rom.

6:23). Society, and even much of what is called Christianity, has lowered the bar of sin, because it is not fashionable to talk about it. Sin has also been redefined to lessen the offense for those who do not want to consider it. Sin is, whether recognized or not, the enormous issue in every person's life. The fact that mankind is immersed in it, and is so conformed to it that it is not recognized as the relentless destroyer, does not distract from the fact of its terrible reality.

The battle over personal sin is therefore huge. As Christians live in a sinful world, with sinful bodies, it continues to be a factor of stress and battle. It is a lifelong battle (Gal. 5:17): "the flesh sets its desire against the Spirit and the Spirit against the flesh." It is a battle that everyone is engaged in whether they want to be or not. It is also a fight that no person, no matter how strong or how determined, can win without God's help. As a result of this great enemy, there are different approaches to the battle in Christendom. There are those who claim Christianity but are legalistic. They make Christianity into a set of man-made rules to rigidly keep. Others of the opposite persuasion, say it is all a matter of grace, and therefore sin is of little concern. The legalist find their rules impossible, and the latter may indulge in sinful activities using what they believe is freedom under grace as an excuse for sinful behavior.

How, then, does a true Christian deal with sin in his life? That is the subject of this section. Remember, John is defining the difference between those who have a mere profession, with those who have genuine salvation. Those with true salvation are somewhere along the path of God's sanctification (Rom. 6:22). They are in a battle with sin. Sin still enters the life, but does not captivate the life as it once did.

(1) Comprehension (1:8)

If we say that we have no sin, we are deceiving ourselves and the truth is not in us.

The phrase **If we say** is used a second time, again emphasizing the difference between just talk and/or wishful thinking and actuality. John deals with a major area of controversy, and one that is often misunderstood about sin in living the Christian life. This is an essential passage dealing with the reality of sin and coming to grips with the sin battle. The word for **sin** is *harmatia*, which means "to miss the mark, do wrong, commit an offense against God, or fail God". John says that if we say we have no sin (as Christians) then **we are deceiving ourselves and the truth is not in us**.

The word **deceiving** (*planaō*) means "to roam from the truth, to wander off or go astray from the truth." It is one thing to recognize that all have sinned (Rom. 3:23), as this is addressing the fact of sin in all natural people (the unsaved), but here John is addressing whether there continues to be sin in the life of those truly born again. In dealing with sin in a believer, it should be apparent from the wording that **if we say we have no sin**, he is not only dealing with the reality of continued sin, and the battle that the Christian is engaged in, but also the attitude of the Christian in the battle. The Christian must not fall into the trap of the natural man's inclination of diluting the magnitude of sin or redefining it. John Wesley, who believed in perfectionism (that a true Christian is sinless after the new birth), did this when he stated, "If we did not intend to sin then it was not sin." This does exactly what John is saying we cannot do, that is, deny that Christians are sinless when they are not. Nor can we do as the natural man does and blame sin on something outside of ourselves. There was a phrase that became popular a few years ago that said this: *the devil made me do it*. Man blamed something or someone else for his sin. Man has made similar excuses from the very beginning. Adam, when caught in his sin of eating from the forbidden tree, blamed his sin on God who gave him his wife—"the woman you gave to be with me she gave me to eat" (Gen. 3:12). Therefore, if we skirt the personal responsibility of recognizing our sin, we are further sinning because we do not see ourselves as God sees us. We are living in the unreality stated in the phrase **deceiving ourselves**.

The phrase **truth is not in us (1:8)** is not a mere hand slap. John is saying that if we have a self-righteous attitude, we have the attitude of the Pharisees, the attitude of a man that has not truly met God. In John 8:32, we are told it is the truth that sets us free. Therefore, if the truth is not in us, we are guilty of suppressing it (Rom. 1:18). John is saying that we cannot possibly be in a state where we have been set free, nor can we be one of Christ's own as He is "the Truth" (John 14:6). Christianity is always synonymous with truth. Mere political correctness, wishful thinking, delusion with sincerity, good intentions, or positive thinking, are excuses and unreality. Deception will not be possible if the person is functioning in the light of truth. Deception and truth are of opposite spheres.

As already stated, one of the major factors included in the sin battle is our attitude. Keep in mind the first step in coming to Christ for forgiveness is the recognition of our vile condition and offenses against Him. These offenses necessitated His awful death on the cross. Repentance is a necessity for every Christian, and the attitude of initial repentance does not end with first steps in justification. In gratitude and growing understanding, the Christian continues to see more and more the depth of his natural alienation and differences from the Holy God. In short, the Christian increasingly sees himself as God sees him. Peter saw this clearly in Luke 5:8 after the miracle of Christ filling his nets with fish. He said, "Go away from me Lord, for I am a sinful man." The attitude of walking with the Lord is never one of personal worthiness or merit. It is an attitude of wonder at the grace of God (1 Pet. 5:5). As already discussed, the Christian's life is different because he walks in the light. This would indicate there is a vital difference between the character and volume of sin in the old life of darkness, and the new life in the light. In reference to the new life and sin, there is an obvious balance here. On the one hand there is the reality for every Christian to **walk in the light** (John 1:7), and on the other hand a recognition, with humble admittance, that personal sin does continue in the present body. The Christian is then a person ever finding his ambition and joy in Christ, as well as his dependence on Him for daily cleansing.

Pause and Reflect

Those who have been truly born again reflect significant changes in their life. They walk in the light. They are on the road of sanctification (Rom. 6:22). That is, they are concerned about the things of God: truth, holiness, and obedience. These things are reflected in real life circumstances and day to day living, not in a cavalier manner, but in thankful humility. Perfection in this walk, however, is not possible. Some sin continues in the life of every Christian. But the attitude of the Christian about sin is so different that sin no longer is that which characterizes or dominates his life. When sin does take place, the Christian finds his remedy, as with all his hope, in his confession, repentance, and forgiveness in Christ. By grace, the Christian's fellowship with Christ cleanses ongoing and remaining sins, and therefore the attitude is one of humble and continual dependence on Christ.

(2) Confession (1:9)

If we confess our sins, He is faithful and righteous to forgive us our sins and to cleanse us from all unrighteousness.

The Christian not only looks at sin differently, but he handles sin differently than the natural person. He recognizes his earthly remedy is confession through the priestly intervention of Christ Jesus. The word **confes-**

sion is the Greek *homologeō*. *Homo* means "one," and *logeō* has to do with "the Word" or *mind of God*. Therefore, the root meaning is *one mind* or being of the same mind. Confession is agreeing with God about our sin so that we have exactly the same mind or attitude about our sin that God does.

Regarding confession–one of the great privileges of being a Christian is to have an audience with God (Rom. 8:15). The statement **if we confess our sins** is a matter of ongoing constancy. It is a need that will continue as long as the Christian is in this body and living in a fallen world. It will only be fully remedied in glorification. Christ gave us an example of prayer in Matthew 6 where He stated "forgive us our sins." This prayer was not for initial entry into faith, but an ongoing, daily example of prayer, given for His disciples. This statement recognized the daily need and importance of confession. Our fellowship with God requires the constant renewing of the mind, and making things right. This is the blessed need of dependence on Him for continual cleansing. Again, this is associated with attitude. The Pharisee in Luke 18 was praying "to himself" in the Temple. He was not confessing his sin because he thought he had no sin. He was instead bragging that he was not like other men. On the contrary, the tax collector was seeking God's mercy, by confessing to the Lord that he was a sinner. Confession is associated directly with humility (Luke 18:14), and if there is no humility in recognizing the need for confession, then there can be no true confession or relationship of being set right.

He is faithful (1:9) is a promise of God, and statement of the surety of forgiveness upon a true confession. The idea of **faithful** is that *God is absolutely trustworthy to do what He says*. The same concept is seen in 1 Thessalonians 5:23–24. It is a characteristic of God, and therefore, it is impossible for Him to be anything but trustworthy. This statement is of great encouragement and comfort to every Christian. Not only are my sins forgiven and remembered no more by God (Heb. 10:17) at initial new birth, but so are those remaining sins since the new birth—**to cleanse us from all unrighteousness**. This is a familial forgiveness, that is, it is for family only. It is only for those who have experienced the new birth and who are walking in the light. It is not part of the initiation of the new birth, rather, a family act of restoration of fellowship and communion. The picture of the importance and necessity of this family cleansing is seen in John 13:5–11. Here, Christ washes the feet of the disciples, and uses the occasion not only to demonstrate an example of humility, but also the need for cleansing. Christ's statement in John 13:10—"He who has bathed needs only to wash his feet but is completely clean; and you are clean, but not all of you"—has an obvious reference beyond physical cleaning. Christ was saying that they had been redeemed, but still had a need for foot washing; a picture of the contamination of sin as members of Christ's family as they travel in the fallen world. The reference to "not all of you" was a reference to Judas. The absolute necessity of this on-going cleansing is seen in the statement by Christ to Peter in John 13:8: "If I do not wash you (a reference to his feet), you have no part with Me." In this statement we see the necessity of confession and forgiveness as a part of the Christian experience of restoration, communion, and vitality.

And just is a statement that is also necessary for the forgiveness to actually occur. God is a holy God, and cannot do anything that is not in perfect justice. The promise of forgiveness, because of confession, is not based on God looking the other way. It is based on the fact that Jesus paid the full penalty on the cross for all the sins of His people. As this forgiveness is appropriated for restoration of fellowship by the confession, God could do nothing else but restore fellowship based on the payment made in full by Christ and His perfect character of justice.

Pause and Reflect

Recognition of continuing sin, and confession of that sin, is an essential part of the Christian experience. It is based on the new relationship with a Holy God. It restores fellowship because God, through Christ, is both faithful to forgive, but also, just to forgive based on the work of Jesus Christ. If this kind of ongoing attitude and actual confession is not taking place, then the reader should take no comfort in the assurance of his relationship to God. If there is no concern over personal sin, and no concern for communion with God, then there can be no understanding or association with the life of a Christian as shown in this context. The true Christian is one who is first and foremost concerned about His consistent relationship in the family of God. He, therefore, seeks restoration of fellowship because of the breaches of sin, and finds that restoration in the faithful forgiveness and restoration that is freely given by Christ.

---

(3) Contempt (1:10)

If we say that we have not sinned, we make Him a liar and His Word is not in us.

This passage is very similar in construction to 1 John 1:8. However, there is a radical difference in the focus. Whereas in 1 John 1:8, the focus was on our own personal deception, here the focus is on a contempt for God Himself, because He has declared our condition and need for on-going repentance, and if we are arguing our purity when we are not pure, **we make Him a liar**.

Arrogance is a form of *pride,* and God hates pride (Prov. 8:13). In the argument of 1 John 1:8, a denial of Christian sin says the that one denying is a **liar**, but here, a denial of Christian sin goes further and says we accuse God of lying. Accusing God is the most arrogant form of error conceivable. As a Christian, I have a new standard with new marching orders. I have a different way of looking at life. Life is now viewed through the **Word** of God. If the ones claiming Christ are not viewing their life through the **Word** of God, then the phrase **His Word is not in us** means that there can be no reality of Christianity. Christianity is constructed believing the **Word**: "Your Word I have treasured in my heart, that I may not sin against You" (Ps. 119:11). If this **Word** is not an essential in the life, it means the person is still dead in sins and lost, because the **Word** has no place in them. The lost care nothing for the **Word**. Paul says it is "foolishness to them" (1 Cor. 2:14). This is the opposite of the saved. Prior to conversion, the manner of living was directed through the person's own thinking, but as a Christian it is viewed through, and directed by God's **Word**. When the **Word** is read and studied, the life is confronted with a fresh understanding of self. The **Word** pulls no punches. It does not rationalize or excuse. The **Word** addresses sin in the most egregious terms. The more the person understands the Word, the more their own condition is seen in weaknesses, failures, and the many wayward errors by contrast to the holy God. Christ said that it wasn't just the actual act of doing sin that was sin, but also the thinking of it in the heart, a reference to the mind (Matthew 5:28). John is saying that we fall short of the glory of God and His holy standard, even after the new birth. A denial of this is a denial of the reality of the **Word**. Denying what and who I am is accusing God of being a **liar (1:10),** and therefore, having contempt for God. For either I must be in absolute alignment (perfection) with the holiness of God and His **Word**, which is not possible, or I have contempt for Him by claiming that I am.

Furthermore, if I say I have no sin, I am further accusing the **Word** of error, for the **Word** speaks of the need for a Savior, not only for my initial justification, but also as my intercessor (Rom. 8:34). If I am perfect, then there is no need for Christ to stand daily on my behalf (Heb. 4:15–16) as a high priest before the Father. This advocacy will be addressed in the next verses. The point is that the person who foolishly thinks he is living a life of perfection is saying, "I don't need an advocate!" Such thinking is arrogant and not according to the truth. It is the same as stating that Christ is not needed. It is only the true Christian who really understands his remaining sins, and his understanding of himself is only because his gauge is the **Word** of God, and he is being directed by the Spirit of God. He knows that he not only needs a Savior to redeem him from past sins, but also, a Savior who will stand with him until the "day of Christ" (Phil. 1:6). Therefore, the Christian life is a life of communion that must include continuous cleansing. This reflects a life of trusting, asking for forgiveness, and being totally honest and transparent before the all-knowing God who has designed us to be dependent upon Him.

> **Pause and Reflect**
>
> John says that anyone claiming to be a Christian, but who says that they have no sin in their life, is accusing God of lying. Why? God's Word addresses remaining sin in Christians, and dependence on the ongoing advocacy of Christ for cleansing. A denial of personal sin is a denial of the truthfulness of God's Word. The issue is not that a Christian's life is given over to sin, but it is a life where sin, regretfully, still remains. As a result, there is the need for, and continual desire for, restoration of communion with God. This is viewed in the Christian life as a continual state of humility and fellowship dependence on Christ's advocacy. The Christian life is not a life of perfection, but a life of change. The change is in affections, desires, and dependency.

b. Our Advocate (2:1–2)

We now encounter our first **little children** phrase. This phrase is repeated seven times by John (2:1; 2:12; 2:28; 3:7; 3:18; 4:4; 5:21). Each time John uses it, he does so to highlight something important or unique. This is a term literally meaning "infant, diminutive in stature." It is expressive of endearment in the same manner as a parent engages his child with love in communicating something of special importance. Here, John is dealing with a harsh and difficult subject. It is a subject related to critical **sin**, and thereby, evaluates the truthfulness of one's honest relationship or lack of relationship to God. He does not do so mechanically. Instead, he does so lovingly. He is speaking to his children in the faith. And just as there is a growth process of development physically in children, there is also a growth process in spiritual children. Paul uses this same concept in dealing with the Corinthian church, and its many needs of correction (1 Cor. 4:14). The point for the reader is the sincere interest and concern by the writer, and the emphasis upon the highly sensitive subject. John is reasoning that just because God is forgiving, and there is true restoration from **sin, sin** must never be taken lightly. The Christian does not have a license to **sin**.

> ### Pause and Reflect
>
> The issue of continued sin after regeneration is a matter of some practical discussion in the Word. Since salvation is by grace, there are always those who either in false reasoning, or by desire, view "grace" as a license to sin. This is the natural thinking of the unconverted looking for an excuse to sin (Rom. 6:1). John will present the balance between perfection (being sinless), which is impossible, and the other extreme, a life of servitude to sin, which is true of the unconverted. The line between the believer and unbeliever is clearly drawn. There is a marked and significant difference between a true believer's lifestyle of reluctant sin, and the lifestyle of the sin-practicing unbeliever. John is writing this to his "newborn" spiritual children, so they will understand that sinning is no longer the rule of life, as with the old self, but is the exception.

(1) Essential (2:1)

My little children, I am writing these things to you so that you may not sin. And if anyone sins, we have an Advocate with the Father, Jesus Christ the righteous;

The term **Advocate (2:1),** speaking of Christ Himself, is the Greek word *paraklēto*. It is used five times in the New Testament. Only here is it used to refer to Christ. It is used of the Holy Spirit (John 14:16; 14:26; 15:26; 16:7–8) in the four other passages. It means "one who comes alongside another to help." There are two very important concepts regarding this glorious advocacy of Jesus Christ as a Christian's *paraklētos*.

The first pertains to His *defense of us*. In a legal sense, we are guilty. In fact, we are so guilty that there is no hope for us other than Christ Himself being our **Advocate.** If He did not intercede for us, we would be justly condemned. But because He is our perfect **Advocate,** we cannot possibly be condemned (Rom. 8:34). Therefore, He is essential, because only He is fully qualified. Without His being present and actively working as our **Advocate** between us and the justice of God, there would be no hope, no argument, and nothing to present in our defense. If we committed only one **sin**—but of course, we have all committed many—we would still be guilty and sentenced to eternal death by His justice, if it were not for the advocacy of Christ. He alone is fully qualified to be the Christian's advocate, because He is **Jesus Christ the righteous.** No other person could do what He is able to do, and must do.

Secondly, not only is He fully qualified, but He is *also patient* (Rom. 2:4). Although this quality is not stated here, it is implied. Self-restraint is His character toward those for whom He died. He is infinitely patient toward His own. Christ's patience is an amazing aspect of His glorious character. He never loses His restraint or gives up on His advocacy, throwing up, as such, His hands in disgust. He is a firm, never moving advocate of complete reliance. He always faithfully continues His role of advocacy, despite our unworthiness, because it is not based on us, but on Him.

> ### Pause and Reflect
> John must begin any discussion about the Christian life with a quick view of Christ's continuing role. The Christian exists and is sustained continually by Christ. The basis for any Christian to continue living is Christ. He is the sure foundation. It is not the Christian's strength, knowledge, wisdom, cunning, or righteousness. If it were not for Christ, the Christian's reliable and patient advocate, there would be no hope for the Christian's life. In all things, the Christian is dependent upon Christ for everything. He is the "author and perfecter of faith" (Heb. 12:2). Therefore the Christian is continually looking to Him, and certainly so in the area of greatest concern, namely, the sin that continues to beset us. Christ is our all. With Him we cannot possibly fail.

(2) Exclusive (2:2)

and He Himself is the propitiation for our sins; and not for ours only, but also for *those of* the whole world.

John must make it clear that as Jesus is serving as our advocate, He is doing so, not as a slick lawyer using loopholes, or His favored status as the Son. He is doing so in perfect justice. He is more than our advocate. He is the reason for interceding, as **He Himself** is the very **propitiation** (appeasing God's justice), or payment to curb God the Father's divine wrath, which is justifiably and righteously against us. God hates sin, is angry against sin, and because of His righteous justice must deal justly with sin. He is holy and therefore cannot simply look the other way. God, as such, has been injured, and therefore sin must be dealt with. Of course, sin is remedied completely and righteously in His Son, who is not only our advocate, but also our **propitiation**. As with advocacy, so with **propitiation**, He alone was qualified and essential to take on the horrendous role of our sin-bearer. The statement by Paul that Christ "is all in all" or "who is our life" (Col. 3:4) takes on new meaning. Christ is the exclusive basis of how any Christian can go on living as a Christian. He is exclusively our essential advocate, who alone is qualified, and enduring with us, and He is the very **propitiation for our sins.**

The phrase **not for ours only, but also for those of the whole world** is one of encouragement. He is stating that if a person is in Christ, then he can be assured that these remaining sins will not be held against him. Christ has already paid the penalty on the cross. The phrase is literally **for the whole world**. The words **those of** in the NASB were added by the translators. **World** is *kosmos*, which is used in several ways in the Scriptures, and the context must always give us the indication of what is meant. Sometimes it means "the literal physical globe" (John 1:10), sometimes it refers "to the world system of evil" (1 John 2:15), and *sometimes* "as a connotation of people," as it is in this passage. Does that mean it is referring to *every person* in the world or to a *specific* group?

John's first epistle is to read and thereby understand who is of God and who is not of God. Obviously then, the whole argument is built on identifying limited groups of people, those who are saved as compared to those who are unsaved. In this portion, John is writing to comfort little children (those new or still young in Christ) with the understanding that Christ is a true **propitiation** for sins. This means they that will be accepted by God, even though they are not yet perfect. Now, what kind of comfort would it be, then, to these weak in faith to be told that Christ also died for those in hell (every person who ever lived)? The modern idea prevalent in Christianity is that Christ's atonement was universal; that is, He died for all mankind (every person), but His payment is only applied as one accepts Christ as his Savior. The point here is emphatically the opposite. The clarification is that because Christ died for people throughout the whole world, those for whom He died have their sin propitiated. Therefore, if they are in Christ, among those for whom He died, they are blessed with eternal life.

This is a word of great comfort. It does not depend on the person's weak profession, nor is it ruined by occasional stumbling, but it is sure in Christ, if the person belongs to Him. When applied to people, the word *kosmos* was understood to have limits. For example, John 12:19 declares: "the world has gone after Him." Obviously not every person in the world had gone after Him (Christ), rather a large, yet limited number. This same sense of limitation is seen in 1 John 5:19: "the whole world lies in the power of the evil one." That contextual reference would not apply to God's own, but to all the remaining unsaved. John was a Jew writing to Jews. Gentiles were often also referred to as "the world" (Rom. 11:12–15), as they were outsiders. The most common rendering is to explain that Christ died not only for Jews, but also for Gentiles, with the understanding of a given limited number that are of the elect. This kind of use was common among the Jews. Christ is "all in all" for the Christian, but not for every man. John states, as well, that this propitiation is not just for Jews, but also, for the "whole world," meaning for persons throughout the entire world who would, in sovereign election, belong to Christ.

Pause and Reflect

Christ is essential and exclusive as both our advocate and our propitiation. Were He not so, then no person could possibly be saved. He alone fills the role perfectly, judiciously, and righteously. He also fills the role patiently and consistently. He does so for all of His own from every kindred and tongue and race from all over the world (Rev. 5:9). There is comfort in knowing that the person in Christ is acceptable to God, and even the remaining sins that remind him that he is not yet what he will be, as sinless, in the glorified state, are none-the-less also forgiven. For Christ's own, redeemed people, who, although not practicing sin as slaves to sin in the manner of the unsaved, still do sin. God has graciously provided cleansing, restoration of fellowship, and great privilege through His Son, the only advocate and propitiation. God has in His omniscience considered everything. Because of this advocacy and propitiation, those in Him are able to have real fellowship with God the Son and God the Father.

3. Walking In Obedience (2:3–6)

Politicians running for office promise many things, but rarely live up to the promises. They market themselves by presenting a picture of who they are through speeches, sound bites, advertising, etc., – all to produce an image. For many of these individuals, they present a false picture of themselves in order to secure votes. They know if they presented their true opinions to the public, they would lose the election. This deception is considered a way of life, or acceptable behavior in our society, at least by many, if not most. It is also a picture of how man is so very easily deceived. Many people are so conditioned by this kind of behavior that they apply the same thinking into the area of relationship with God. This influence has spread into church doctrines, regarding life with God. The manner of life that presents the image of a Christian as a person unchanged, except by the name Christian, is stated by John to be false. This way of life that says **we have come to know Him**, but is not seen by change in the life is rebuked in the harshest terms – the person **is a liar, and the truth is not in him**. God is not running a club whereby people merely make lip-service to Him. God is all about genuineness, truth, and reality. There are no games with God, and fellowship with Him must be based on non-compromising realities. Here, John lays out the practical assurances of real fellowship. The first is "**keep His commandments**."

a. Our Assurance (2:3–4)

(1) Condition (2:3)

By this we know that we have come to know Him, if we keep His commandments.

The phrase **By this** refers to what he will say next. He presents a new thought, but still within the broader scope of the reality of fellowship with Christ. He is showing that there are different components that will be displayed as necessary within this reality of fellowship. He has already shown us that there must be a "walking in the light" in 1 John 1:5–6, and "walking by confession" in 1:7–10, with instruction on how the Christian deals with remaining sin in 2:1–2. **By this** places a condition upon his statement: **we have come to know Him**. The word "**know**" is *ginoskō*, which has a root meaning "to know absolutely or intimately in a most special manner." It is a knowledge based on familiarity, relationship, and reality. It means more than information; it regards the "**know**" as something binding. This idea is seen clearly in the sobering words of Christ in Matthew 7:23: "Depart from Me; I never knew you." The word "knew" is the same word used as **know** in this passage. Christ is saying in Matthew, "I never really had a relationship with you." What these people thought they had, and others thought they had, was not real. But, when John says **we have come to know Him**, he means they have come to know Him experientially, personally, and as Savior and Lord. They have come to know Him in the manner God requires for true salvation.

> ### Pause and Reflect
>
> The term **by this** is stating "that by the means of this," the real test of a right relationship with God can be determined. This is the most important test anyone can take. This is the eternal test of reality. This is a test from God. He is the examiner, and He cannot be deceived. The issue is passing the test of "knowing" Christ in the manner required, and knowing Him in a personal relationship as Savior and as Lord. If anyone does know Him in this manner, then there are certain realities that will be true of his life.

(2) Commandments (2:3)

By this we know that we have come to know Him, if we keep His commandments.

The first of these conditions listed by John is **if we keep His commandments**. The **if we** implies "only if we," which is stating choices, direction, and conditions. The word **keep** (*téréō*) means "close watch or holding fast." The word carries the idea of the keeping of His commandments as being a consistent high priority. The word **"commandments"** (*entolē*) means "injunctions and precepts." There is no indication from John that these commandments are referring directly or exclusively to the Old Testament laws given by Moses to Israel. Instead, taking in the context of the epistle, the word focuses on the entirety of the revealed will of Christ and God. The closest we can come to a right understanding is shown in verse 5: **keeps His word**, not just certain specified commandments, rather the entirety of all that God reveals. The weight of the revealed will of God is not merely attempting to keep the letter of laws, but to cherish the essence of all that God reveals, and especially those things internal (from the heart), so that we might please Him.

To what commandments, then, is John specifically referring? There is no indication anywhere else in 1 John, or the entire New Testament concerning the explicit keeping of Mosaic laws. The ceremonial laws were addressed in Acts 15 at the counsel of Jerusalem, and they are not required. On the other hand, all of the laws of the Decalogue (the Ten Commandments) are repeated in the New Testament in some form with the exception of the fourth commandment regarding the keeping of the Sabbath Day. The New Testament essence of these repeated laws is different. Whereas there was a mandate expressed for keeping God's laws, it was even then stated as being humanly impossible (Deut. 29:4; 31:16–17). To really keep God's commands means the person must understand God's will, know God, not just as a law giver but in a personal manner, and have a heart that desires to please Him. This is the reason Paul expressed the purpose of the law as "a tutor to lead to Christ" (Gal. 3:24). The law was made to reveal man's condition in sin, not to save. In the New Testament Epistles, the concept of obedience and keeping of commandments is given under a context of the finished work of Christ, and the resulting emphasis upon a supernatural rebirth demonstrated by faith, and the indwelling of the Holy Spirit. The transition from the old self to the new self is a transition of reality whereby the recipient is not only enabled by the Spirit of God indwelling, but he also has a change of heart, whereby, he wants to do God's will. This was prophesied under the New Covenant in Jeremiah 31:31, where God Himself takes out the heart of stone (man's sinful heart), and replaces it "with a heart of flesh." In so doing He states: "I will cause you to walk in My statutes" (Ezek. 36:26–27). The idea is that the heart of corruption has been exchanged for a heart that is bent toward loving and following God. The standard of righteousness required by God was clarified in Christ's Sermon on the Mount (Matthew 5–7). Christ said that "unless your righteousness surpasses the Scribes and Pharisees you cannot enter the Kingdom of God" (Matt. 5:20). The reason the requirement must surpass the Scribes and Pharisees is that they were not really keeping God's commandments. They were going through external efforts, but their heart was not right. If the most dedicated religious people could not keep God's commandments, then no natural man could meet the requirement. Only a person "born again" (John 3:3–8) is capable, because of what God has supernaturally provided in a transformed heart.

To **know (2:3)** God, that is, have a personal relationship with God, is the essence of Christianity. To do so places Christ as Lord in the life. The person is truly engaged in God's process of sanctification (Rom. 6:22). This is a key concept of the New Testament, and of the understanding of keeping His commandments. The writers of all New Testament epistles either began their letters, "bond servant of Jesus Christ," or stated in some other fashion their complete devotion to Him as their Lord. The meaning behind this is that the person will no longer follow his old self-will, but will follow God's will. Following God's will is the simple meaning of keeping His commandments.

> ### Pause and Reflect
>
> Man is naturally a sinner, and he is incapable of truly understanding or keeping the commandments of God in the manner required by God. The ability to please God by being obedient to keep His commandments is one of the primary evidences of the reality of the new birth. Only someone "born of God" will be able to keep His commandments. Therefore, there must first be the biblical understanding of the necessity of the "new birth," as a requirement, for the capability of pleasing God, and then the keeping of His Word will follow. Secondly, to rightly interpret what is meant by "keeping His commandments," we must study and be familiar with the Word of God, and have a revealed understanding of God's righteous view of what John means when he states His commandments. One must know God to please Him. Many religious, but unsaved people, have sought to identify with Christianity, thinking that to be acceptable to God is what a person does (Is. 64:6), when the Bible is clear that no one is able to please God by their works. Such concepts fail to understand the natural fallen condition of man, and what is necessary to be pleasing to God. Relationship with God is not made by what we do, but rather what we do is an evidence of a true relationship with God. John is stating that the ability to please God (keep His commandments), is an evidence of the reality of true fellowship. The reason is that the new birth and the indwelling Spirit of God impact the life, direction, and actions of the person receiving it.

b. Our Assertion (2:4)

The one who says, I have come to know Him, and does not keep His commandments, is a liar, and the truth is not in him;

John continues his clarity of division between those who truly have fellowship with God (know Him), and those who do not. Here he uses the phrase "**The one who says**," which refers to an *assertion or declaration that is unsupported.* The person is making a statement that is not seen by the evidence of his life. Census figures a few years ago in America, showed that there are 208 million adults, and of this group 159 million of them claimed to be Christian. Unfortunately, the evidence of those 159 million people being Christian, according to a biblical definition, is simply not real. The biblical definition of **come to know Him** carries with it tremendous ramifications. As has already been stated, **know** is a word that has knowledge components that are experiential, along with a relationship of a kindred nature. To know God in this manner is to understand His greatness, worthiness, character, and sovereign right (among other infinite qualities). In other words, to really know Him means that the person becomes a "God-fearing" person (Prov. 9:10). This God-fearing person is to be distinguished from what Paul says of the unsaved man in Romans 3:18 "there is no fear of God before their eyes." A "God-fearing" person is one who reverences God. It is a person who maintains God in the exclusive number one priority position of the person's life.

> **Pause and Reflect**
>
> The ramifications of knowing God in the manner stated means that it would be impossible to have such a high regard for God in the mind (heart), and disregard Him practically in life circumstances. Once again, John is dealing with reality, the reality that God's sanctification is either taking place or not taking place (Rom. 6:22). The reality of true salvation, which is equal to knowing God, will be seen practically in how a person consistently lives their life in conformity to God's will.

The Bible is absolutely consistent in its testimony concerning genuineness. There is no inconsistency or confusion with God. God has made His moral creatures with a sense of accountability as part of His creation (Romans 1:18–20). The phrase **"The one who says"** refers to the person who has a profession with his mouth. However, a profession of the mouth is not in itself sufficient. He says with his lips, **I have come to know Him**. However, the passage goes on to state that he does not follow it up with his manner of life. He **"does not keep His commandments."** He claims on the one hand that he has his confidence in God, while at the same time he does not live as though he does. Living this way can be a form of personal deception. It is living in a dream world of one's own making. This profession, without living a righteous life pleasing to God, is precisely what Christ was referring to in Matthew 7:21–23. He referred to those who had a profession with their lips, but were practicing lawlessness. It has nothing to do with the past life (1 Cor. 6:9–11), but has everything to do with one's actions after they make a profession of knowing God. In 1 Corinthians 6:11, Paul says, "and such were some of you." Their life style was wicked in the past, but now, it is different. The theme of not just saying, but doing, is consistently found throughout God's Word. The life of the Christian must match his profession of being a Christian, or otherwise hypocrisy exists.

The statement **"is a liar, and the truth is not in him" (2:4)** is an extremely straight forward declaration that cannot be explained in any other manner. John says the person who does not live according to what he professes with his mouth is a counterfeit. He is not genuine. He is a **liar** because he does not speak the truth. This labeling the person as a **liar** places them in a relationship with Satan (John 8:44), and not with Christ. Christianity, at least in the past, has been so pervasive in America that the popular thinking of what constitutes being a Christian is religious acceptance, not a transformed life. Many people with good intentions have assumed their profession alone was sufficient. They have disregarded Christ's statement that "you must be born again." They have, in effect, created a Christianity of their own making, claiming to know a God they do not know. Wanting to have "hell insurance," they have claimed God without really knowing Him. Those in this category are living a fraud. In many cases, the perpetrators are not even aware of their own deception.

> **Pause and Reflect**
>
> Christianity is founded on truth. Unsaved mankind, on the other hand, is akin to Satan, who is "the father of lies" (John 8:44). Even man's own heart cannot be trusted (Jer. 17:9). If there is a difference between what any person states with his lips, and how he practically lives out his life, then his lips are lying. That is the reason John wrote this book. He wrote to expose the hypocrisy, and to bring true assurance of salvation to those who are in conformity to this test.

c. Our Affirmation (2:5–6)

We have been shown by John that it is not merely a profession from the lips that makes one a true Christian. What then is the affirmation of our faith?

(1) Conduct (2:5, 6b)

but whoever keeps His Word, in him the love of God has truly been perfected . . . walk in the same manner as He walked.

The affirmations John offers are found in two clear definitions of true Christianity. The first is a person who **keeps His Word**. The idea of **keeps** is being under *a close watch and holding fast*. It strongly implies the **Word** being known and lived out as a consistent high priority of the life. The point is that the Word of God is constantly challenging life's experiences, and the Word of God is brought into all of the decisions in everyday life. It is brought into life in such a manner that living becomes a process of keeping His Word. "**Keeps**" is in the present active subjective tense, meaning *keeps on keeping*. This is not just living by extracted Mosaic laws externally, as the Jewish leaders sought to do, but by the essence and intent of the Word. This is seeking to understand God's will, in all His Word, as life's priority. Such a way of thinking and manner of life are inseparable and illustrate the definition of what the new person has become.

The second affirmation is that we (true Christians) **walk in the same manner He walked (2:6)**. John's choice of this phrase is interesting. This phrase brings clarity to the concept of **keeps His Word**. Now we are looking at the essence of what is meant to keep **His Word**. It means *to walk as Jesus walked*. This walk is multidimensional. It is not merely keeping certain rules in some mechanical fashion. It is, instead, walking righteously and in holiness in the manner that Christ lived; as our example. Christ first and foremost did everything according to the will of the Father. The summation of what it means to walk in the same manner as He walked is found in Romans 12:1–2. Paul urges the giving of one's self as "a living sacrifice" based on all that God has done in salvation. As Christ was a literal sacrifice on behalf of the Christian, the Christian is now a living sacrifice for Him. So then, this means that just as Christ walked according to the will of the Father, we are to walk according to the will of Christ (as the Father and Christ are harmonious).

Pause and Reflect

The concept of walking in the same manner He walked requires consideration of the characteristics of Christ's life on the earth. How did Christ conduct Himself? There are many things that could be said, but the basics of His testimony are in three specific, supernatural areas. He first of all, walked according to the Word of God (Luke 24:44). By this He showed that His will was not independent from the revealed will of God. Secondly, and in the same general sphere of understanding, He walked according to the will of the Father (John 6:38). Thirdly, He also, walked in the practice of the truth (John 3:21; 8:46). All of these are of the same consistent nature and oneness, but each is from different angles. As this manner of living is required of all who truly have a relationship with God

> (know that we are in Him), it requires the same supernatural work and commitment. The concept of walking as He walked does not demand perfection. The context must always be taken in the light of 1 John 1:8. John is not saying that every Christian will walk perfectly as Christ did, but he is saying the trend of his life will be walking in the same manner that He walked.

(2) Credential (2:5b)

in him the love of God has truly been perfected.

The statement **In him the love of God has truly been perfected**" is a statement connected to the actuality of **keeping His Word** and **walking as He walked**. This statement concerning love once again shows the idea that keeping commandments is much more than merely following rules. The concept of the demonstration of the **love of God** cannot ultimately be counterfeited. The kind of love shown by Christ cannot be manufactured. It cannot even be explained. Christ walked in a supernatural manner. He lived a life above reproach that was the perfect example of love for others. His relationships with others exemplifies a life of giving, demonstrating compassion, and grace. The concept of the love of God is related to the work of God in the heart. This is something the unsaved person cannot do. The essential of God's work in the heart is absolute. Without God moving supernaturally, granting the ability to love as He loves, and thereby being a testimony consistent with Christ Himself, there can be no **walking as He walked**.

> ### Pause and Reflect
>
> Once again we are confronted with a profound principle. To "keep His Word," and to "walk in the same manner He walked," and to do so in a manner that demonstrates that the love of God has truly been perfected, requires something beyond any effort of unsaved man. The best efforts have already been tried and failed. This affirmation supports the understanding of the requirement of God's new birth, and the granting of the Holy Spirit residing within the Christian. These affirmations are supernatural in nature, and show the work of God as their only explanation. What is that work? It is the love of God perfected (matured) and real in the life. The Christian lives in a fashion that is reminiscent of the love of God shown in the life and work of Christ.

(3) Cause (2:6)

By this we know that we are in Him: the one who says he abides in Him ought himself to walk in the same manner as He walked.

John says **by this we know**–by what? We know by the supernatural conduct that cannot otherwise be explained. John lists the **"we know"** as walking in the same manner as Christ, and demonstrating the love of God. John continues to reinforce the clarity of his argument by showing the cause is the power of God manifesting itself in the life. So that there can be no reasonable confusion, he reiterates that **by this we know that we are in Him**. He draws lines that are clear and precise. The concept of being **in Him** means that the Christian has the basis of his standing before God solely on being covered by, and related to Christ. To be **in Him** is to rely completely on His finished work, and to know that Christ has met all the righteous requirements by becoming sin for the person. In Romans 6:1–6, the Christian is spoken of as a person who has died with Christ, been buried with Christ, and been raised with Christ. In other words, Christ is the person's complete salvation and new life. Further, Christ now stands before God the Father as a perfect advocate for His own. This person is **in Him**.

From the standpoint of the Christian, **abides in Him** is an essential. If one is not abiding in Him, then he is not a Christian. **Abides** is the Greek word *menō*, which means "to dwell in Him or to stay in Him." The idea is a *permanent, fixed relationship*. Christianity is a fixed relationship. Whoever God chooses to save is saved indeed. "Nothing can separate His own from Him" (Romans 8:35–36). Christianity is not something flimsy or transitory, but life changing, consistent and continuing. Christ says to His disciples, "without Me you can do nothing" (John 15:5). One who **abides** is the same as one **in Him** by the work of God. One **in Him** will **abide** with Him, producing a life showing His abiding presence, because he is now a part of His true eternal work.

He continues by stating **one . . . ought himself to walk in the same manner as He walked (2:6)**. The word translated **ought** in the NASB does not give the strength of its true meaning. **Ought** is *opheilō,* which actually means "to be under considerable obligation." The word **ought** in the mind of many is "there is a choice involved." However, the same Greek word is more often translated "owed" or "indebted" (Matt. 18:34). It is not a choice but a requirement. It is a *debt* with weight. The idea is that those in Christ are indebted in such a manner that they have no choice but to walk (live their lives in obedience to God), as Christ Himself walked.

> **Pause and Reflect**
>
> Abiding means Christ is the source of power, ability, endurance, growth, and ultimate success. There must first be an abiding in Him, or none of these other things will be a reality. The cause of all positive demonstrations of true Christianity (conduct, actions, lifestyles, love, etc.) occurs as a result of the person abiding in Christ. That is the reason we know we are in Him, when we demonstrate the conduct that results from our abiding relationship with Him. John continues to draw the lines of who is a Christian and who is not a Christian by these undeniable realities.

4. Walking In Love (2:7–11)

We continue under the general theme of "The Requirement of Fellowship with Christ." We are looking at God's evaluation, and determining the definition of true Christianity, so that any person professing Christ can know that he has eternal life. This writing is practical, so that anyone can align himself with this evaluation and come to conclusions. To be a Christian means that fellowship with God has been restored. This restoration is through and with Christ. We have covered tests under "Walking in the Light," "Walking by Confession," and "Walking in Obedience." We now turn to "Walking in Love." All of these present a true picture of working out the new birth in Christ in practical living. The characteristics presented are not given for instruction for the Christian to work on, but to see if they are actually present as proof and assurance of the new birth.

The world system, in which we are all immersed, defines love differently than the Bible does. In fact, the world is so set on redefining terms to justify man's sinful behavior that today there are such words as "gay" for homosexuality, and "addiction" for sexual perversion. In like manner, "love" has been redefined in practice on movie and TV screens as "lust." This has made the concept of love artificial, self-centered, and misunderstood. Love is also shown in our current world to be acting in a "politically correct" fashion. This concept of love is demonstrated in philanthropy and many societal *do-gooders*. It has been redefined as causes for the poor, for animals, and the environment. These things do not define God's love, or real love. They are more often than not misguided, self-promoting, for show, or for means of boasting. Many of these same persons who promote this philosophy, for example, aggressively target the most innocent in our society, the unborn baby, by actively promoting abortion.

God's love is one of the defining issues of the Bible. Cain was the first person born after the fall of man and he, instead of showing natural love, killed his own brother. By this act, we can clearly see that real love has been defective or ruined from the beginning in all unsaved mankind. In Titus 3:3, Paul describes the natural manner of unsaved men as: "spending our life in malice and envy, hateful, hating one another" – the opposite of love. In contrast to this, the Bible brings love into a unique context through God's own demonstration of love through Christ. This love of God becomes an essential in the transforming work of God in the sinners "new birth." Love serves as another of the key evidences of true fellowship with Christ.

a. The Authority (2:7–8)

(1) Expressed (2:7)

Beloved, I am not writing a new commandment to you, but an old commandment which you have had from the beginning; the old commandment is the word which you have heard.

The word **beloved** is *agapētos,* meaning "significant endearment," or "very dear." This same word was used by God the Father when He spoke of His relationship to the Son in Matthew 3:17: "This is My beloved Son in whom I am well pleased." As with the Father and Son's relationship, there is a particular love appropriate for fellow Christians. John does not use this term for endearment toward those in the world at large, but he speaks personally of a special relationship that exists between Christ and His own, and among the brethren. This manner of speaking is most appropriate considering that John's purpose in writing is now turned toward the whole issue of the manifestation of love by the Christian.

He begins verse 7 by telling readers that what he is addressing is not something new. **I am not writing a new commandment to you**. In fact, he goes on to say, **but a commandment you had from the beginning**. The concept of love, as an essential, has been revealed and expressed by God from the very beginning. We know he is writing about love by looking forward to verse 10. Israel was commanded to "love the Lord with all their heart, soul, and might" (Deut. 6:5). They were also commanded to love their neighbors (Lev. 19:18), and to love strangers or all men (Lev.

19:35). These commands were repeated and manifested throughout the Old Testament writings. Therefore, love is an essential to God because He is love (1 John 4:8), meaning it is part of His essential nature, and is therefore, important to Him. It was not only expressed as a command with authority from the earliest revelations, but it has been demonstrated throughout history, especially in the giving of God's Son (John 3:16).

(2) Exhibited (2:8)

On the other hand, I am writing a new commandment to you, which is true in Him and in you, because the darkness is passing away and the true Light is already shining.

This love was not only from the beginning, but continues. In that sense it is not new, but is now exhibited by Christ in the most exemplary fashion. The apostles were direct personal witnesses of Christ, and we, as disciples of their witness, have seen it exhibited before us in transformed lives. It is likened to a **new commandment (2:8)** because we have a true example. Christ expressed the importance of love throughout His earthly ministry (Matt. 5:43; 22:37–39; Mark 12:30–31; Luke 10:27; etc.). He expressed the importance by His own example and by direct command to His disciples (John 13:34–35; 15:17). Why did Christ give this as a precept, and what is the significance?

Anyone even casually following the history of Israel will recognize the general failure of the Jews to follow this command. The essence of love was never realized by most in Israel (Hosea 3:1; Micah 3:2). The concept of love commanded by God throughout the Old Testament is not only missing with Israel, but as time continues, Israel is practicing just the opposite. By the time we come to the New Testament, the Jews have formulated a religion of self-righteous law-keeping. They hated Samaritans, for example (see John 4), all foreigners, and it is no wonder because they even treated one another with contempt (John 7:49). Most significantly, they treated Christ with such hatred and contempt that He was unjustly crucified (although all in the providential planned purpose of God). Therefore Christ reintroduced, and re-instituted the command for love. John is stating that those who claim Christ are expected to be unique in their love just as Christ is unique in His love. This demonstration of love is basic to identification with Christ, "for what communion does light have with darkness" (2 Cor. 6:14). There can be no harmony among people, or no real relationship if there is not genuine agreement on this essential characteristic of God.

This expected love among believers can be seen practically in the greeting section of Romans 16 (see 16:3–4, 6). These Christians loved each other so much that they gave themselves on behalf of one another. This sacrificial love was the example of Paul, and all the Apostles, giving themselves on behalf of others as servants of Christ. Why? Our Lord established the standard by the example of the cross. He demonstrated love in the highest conceivable manner. This love is discussed and amplified in Romans 5 (see 5:6–8). Such giving by human standards is irrational. The only explanation is love, God's kind of self-giving love.

This **new commandment** is also focused on one another. John is addressing the brethren in Christ. The magnitude of this kind of love among brethren is seen in the high priestly prayer of Christ (John 17:23). Christ speaks of this love being of the same quality and magnitude as the love among the Godhead. This statement is perhaps one of the most remarkable statements in Scripture. This love cannot, therefore, be a love that man can simply drum up, or produce in himself. It has to be a supernatural kind of love that God Himself creates within those of His own. This kind of love cannot be measured, expanded, or comprehended. It is shown in its fullness by the complete self-giving for the undeserving and the unlovely. Christ's earthly life is a picture of perfect love that continues to be on exhibit through His Word. He is our exhibit A. John is pointing, from the Old Testament commandments which were largely dismissed, to Christ, and saying, "Look, **the darkness is passing away (2:8)** because the clarity of love in Christ is on display." He says the **true light is already shining** as he points exclusively to Christ. This is the same concept that is stated in Philippians 2 (see 2:5–7), where Paul says, "Have this attitude in yourselves which was also in Christ Jesus." What attitude? – The attitude of exhaustive self-giving. The attitude described is an attitude of love commanded by Christ as a reintroduction, and as an essential. It is to exist among brethren. Nothing else will be able to take its place. Just being religious by practicing religious acts, even beneficial acts, or talking religious talk will not do, if this kind of love is not present. Such things are dead religion as compared to the glory of Christ's love, even when it is exercised piously in orthodoxy. This concept is the same thing Paul said in 1 Corinthians 13:1–2. If I am doing what appears to be great religious works, but have not love, "it profits me nothing."

> **Pause and Reflect**
>
> A right understanding of love is essential for the Christian. The commandment is therefore reiterated, not only because it was from the beginning, but also, because those to whom John is writing witnessed the example of God's love in Christ. As the elect of God, those having a true supernatural relationship with Him by His work done in their hearts, must express this essential characteristic of love in harmony with God's essence. Love then is essential. It is not only essential because God is love, but because God is the sovereign over the new birth of the Christian. That new birth generates love for God and love for the brethren. In order for there to be true fellowship with God, and with God's own, there must be this kind of love. Therefore, love is, and must be manifested in the life of the Christian.

b. The Antithesis (2:9)

(1) Claimed (2:9a)

The one who says he is in the Light

John has already established this new commandment from Christ, which is really an old commandment reiterated; that we should love one another. He has made this an essential. He is measuring realities. Back in verse 4, a true Christian is the "one who keeps His commandments." In verse 6, it is the one who "abides in Him." In verses 7–8, it is the one who "loves." John has established certain realities that must be true of those genuinely in Christ.

John now begins to emphasize the counter determiners of these realities. Continuing on the theme of love, he wants it made clear that it is not simply what we say with our lips, but our actions, that determine who we are. Integral in our actions is this God-kind of love. Simply saying **he is in the light** does not make it so. The concepts of being **in the Light** and being in **darkness** are two extremes, two polar opposites. Light is associated with the holiness, righteousness, and the truth of God. Man is naturally in **darkness**. The idea is that man is not naturally righteous, does not know God, or know the truth. Therefore, man exists in his natural fallen state in **darkness.** On the other hand, the state of being **in the light** is a state of knowing God in a personal way, and being enlightened by a new knowledge, a new perspective of life, and understanding of the truth. Here is a person claiming he is **in the light**, and has moved from the one state of **darkness** into to the new state of **light**. But notice that it is just a claim.

(2) Contradicted (2:9b)

and *yet* hates his brother is in the darkness until now.

The contradiction is very visible. John says that if we claim we are in the light, but really hate our brother, then we are not in the light at all. The outcome of what a person "does" outweighs the word **says** and even contradicts it. The idea is that it is impossible to be in the light, and at the same time hate our brother who has been saved by Christ. This false thinking is impossible because Christ is synonymous with light, and so is His regeneration. The person who is saved by Christ is, by definition, a person who is **in the light** (1 John 1:6–7). If the person claiming to be **in the light** is in actuality hating another person **in the light**, the equation is impossible. Love and light go together, and hate and darkness go together. There is no other mixture possible. It is impossible because of what has just been discussed about the nature of God's love (1 John 2:5–6), and His transforming power. Such a person who **hates his brother** is claiming to be **in the light**, but in reality, he is in **darkness** (the realm of the unregenerate).

This argument is also consistent with the terms of the new birth and the regeneration spoken of in the Scriptures. In our passage, the concept of the new birth is present in all of the discussion of the Christian. If the person has been changed by God in a loving, forgiving, and transforming manner, then hating his brother, who has also undergone the same transition, would be impossible. The true child of God will love what and whom Christ loves (John 8:42), because they carry the same nature as Christ. Therefore, not only what we say, but also what we do, reflects whether we have been recipients of the new birth.

The word **hates** is *miseō*, meaning "to detest or dislike intently." It is associated with a desire to persecute someone. This hate is the same hatred that existed against Christ in His ministry on the earth. It is demonstrated by a person who wants to see harm come to the other person. Therefore, where he can exercise influence over another, he will add difficulty, problems, and even murder against the person being hated. This hatred is not a mere matter of taste or disagreement. This is a matter of a malicious attitude of the heart that, given opportunity, takes radical, detrimental action.

> **Pause and Reflect**
>
> The attitude of hate, addressed in this context, is an evil emotion that has its origin from within the heart of the individual. As God transforms the heart in the new birth in Christ, and thereby transforms the nature, it is completely inconsistent to say that the same heart produces hate, not only hate in general, but also, hate for the very ones who are also loved by God. This inconsistency is not feasible, and thereby, shows the person who has such hate, to be a fraud. Despite what he claims with his mouth, this person remains in darkness; that is, he continues as a natural or unsaved person.

c. The Associations (2:10–11)

(1) Love with Light (2:10)

The one who loves his brother abides in the Light and there is no cause for stumbling in him.

We have looked at the contrasts between light and darkness. Now John approaches it another way. He approaches it according to associations. Love and light are always associated. This association is an absolute and fixed spiritual law.

The first association in this verse is **the one who loves his brother abides in the light**. This is stated as a fact. Any other variation would be inconsistent and impossible. **Abides** (*menō* in Greek) is "to dwell in," or "stay in," with the idea of continuance in a *sphere of belonging*. To be in another place would be unfitting. For example, a fish out of water will not last long because it requires the water and oxygen mixture of that environment to survive. John clarifies the absolute nature of this association by adding **there is no cause for stumbling**. **Stumbling** (*skandalon*, where we get the word "scandal"), means "to not cause others to trip" (spiritually), fall into a snare, or *be an offense*. There are many today who fill pulpits, and claim to be Gospel preachers who are leading people astray. They are causing people to stumble by teaching them to believe false ideas concerning Christ. John is saying that those walking in the light are not represented by this kind of scandalous behavior, behavior that would cause someone to stumble spiritually. Christ spoke of those who would cause this manner of stumbling in Matthew 18:7 (the same word). He stated in that context that it would be better if the person had a millstone placed around his neck and was cast into the sea. To cause spiritual stumbling is a grievous offense. John says **there is no cause** for stumbling in the true Christian. A scandal for those walking in the light would be inconsistent with their character and life practice. This behavior becomes another of those measures of reality. Is there someone claiming to be in the light, while at the same time living a scandalous life that is inconsistent with the teaching and ways of God? According to John, those doing so would be in violation of this reality. This behavior would be a measure of actively living and affecting others in just the opposite manner of what the person is claiming.

(2) Lost Showing Darkness (2:11)

But the one who hates his brother is in the darkness and walks in the darkness, and does not know where he is going because the darkness has blinded his eyes.

John brings the contrast to full understanding by starting the next sentence with **but**. In contrast to what has been stated, **the one who hates his brother is in the darkness**. This hatred is evidence in scandalous behavior. It is so completely out of character for those in the light that John emphatically declares this as a rule or fact. The person who hates his brother (brother here is not physical brother, but a supposed brother in Christ), is not in the light, but is **in the darkness**. False teachers hate those who are teaching the truth. In simple language, such a person cannot be truly saved. He has a profession with his mouth, but it is not a reality because he has shown that his heart and life have not really changed. His heart and life are marked by the actions of those who are still lost. This is seen in the statement **walks in the darkness**. The idea of **walks** is used in Scripture to describe the way a person conducts his day-to-day living, including making decisions, and from that how the person spends his time and energy. John says the manner of this person's walk, in hating his brother in Christ, shows that the person is not walking as claimed in the light, but in **the darkness**.

John further adds that such a person cannot help but be the way he is. This is the doctrine of "total depravity" or inability. In other words, a person in darkness cannot consistently fake or drum up the character of those in the light. John proves his point by adding **and does not know where he is going because the darkness has blinded his eyes**. This is why John can make the defining statements that he has made contrasting those who are really saved (in the light), with those who are not saved (in the darkness). To put the concept in modern day language, it is a black and white issue. This is because the person who is in darkness has no true ability to walk in the same manner, or duplicate the walk, of those in the light. He is saying one thing with his lips, but demonstrating the inconsistency of his profession by his inability to perform the life of love, and therefore, he shows another reality (darkness) with his life.

> ## Pause and Reflect
>
> John, in the process of defining who is saved and who is not saved, brings together all of the elements necessary for a thorough evaluation. As love is one of the characteristics of God, it is no wonder that it must be paramount to the discussion. John reiterates that God's command to love has been from the beginning, but now, with the example of Christ on the Cross, and the provision of the Holy Spirit, it is treated as a new command. This is based on the understanding of God's transforming work by the new birth. When God transforms a person at the new birth, love is present and therefore it is required among brethren, and is manifested in all true Christians. John has clearly delineated that when this love is not present, then the person without such love cannot truly be a Christian. In all of John's dialogue, there is a very clear contrast made between the definition of those saved (walking in light), and those unsaved (walking in darkness). Once the terms are understood, there is no room for error and no gray area; it is black and white. This love among brethren cannot be counterfeited or manufactured in the unregenerate person. He has not the ability to duplicate it of himself. Therefore, true love, or God's kind of love, serves as an absolute basis for recognizing the person saved in contrast to the person who is lost. This is not to say that the love one has for the brethren is perfect or all that it should be, but it is present.

3

The Challenge for Fellowship

2:12–29

Outline context:

II. The Requirement of Fellowship with Christ (1:5—5:12)

    A. The Conditions for Fellowship (1:5—2:11)

B. The Challenge for Fellowship (2:12–29)

1. Absolute Foundation in Reality (2:12–14)

Many people associate religion in any form with that which is speculative or theoretical. These same people have a view of religious faith that provides a definition of someone believing something that is in actuality unsubstantiated. True Christianity is not speculative or theoretical. It is, on the contrary, genuine and real. Christianity is based on reality. We have already seen that the foundation of Christianity is a real Person. That Person is the God-man, Jesus Christ. John has begun to emphasize what Christianity looks like. He told us what it does, and what it does not mean to "walk in the light," and he has begun to define the Christian's "walk in love."

Both of these, however, are broader topics. John wants to make sure this difference is not confused with the maturity process of a believer. Each person in Christ is somewhere along a line of growth (2 Cor. 3:18). This growth process continues until God removes a person from the earth and transforms him into a glorified body (Rom. 8:28–30). This growth process is called sanctification. Associated with spiritual growth in Christ is physical growth and maturity. Even Jesus Christ had physical growth that was associated with His spiritual growth in His humanity, and as a man (Luke 2:52). John now steps aside and reminds his readers that their Christianity is real, wherever one may be on the maturity scale. They have the earmarks of Christianity to prove that something genuine has taken place in their lives. Addressing them in the most affectionate and tender words, John wants them to understand practically that Christianity is a measured change, a reality with every person it touches, whatever their Christian experience or physical age. In so doing, he is reminding us, as readers, of the practical and fundamental reality of true Christianity. Whether a person is very new or seasoned in the faith, and whether a person is young or old physically, at whatever place, he has clear and definable realities that not only exist in the mind of faith, but practically constitute a change of attitude, direction, philosophy, and manner of life.

a. True for All (2:12a)

I am writing to you, little children,

The phrase **little children** translates in the Greek *teknion*, a diminutive of the root *teknon*, an affectionate term that means "begotten ones". The idea gives prominence *to the fact of birth*. The emphasis is upon the "begotten ones of God or children of God." The word also has with it the idea of tenderness. It has thus been translated as **little children**. The idea is that these individuals have encountered a "new birth," are tender or new in that birth, and are being addressed in the most endearing manner of affection because of the relationship. The relationship is likened to a parent and his child. It is a loving and caring relationship of the highest order.

This same word is used in John 13:33 when Christ spoke to John and the other disciples in the most loving and affectionate terms. Just as the conversation that John had with Christ prior to the cross, this conversation from John is very personal, and very exclusive. Christ did not speak to just anyone calling them **little children**, and neither does John. John's appeal pertains only to those begotten of God, God's children, those dear to Him in a particular manner because of their new birth. This exclusive focus is seen in the personal statement **I am writing to you**. Therefore, the basis of the appeal is the reality of their relationship. This is true for all those who have partaken of the kindness of God in salvation. Those he is addressing must be part of the family of God. John builds his appeal based on the solid foundation of it being supernatural, and the otherwise, unexplainable nature of salvation. He does so by reminding them of the reason and substance of their salvation.

(1) Forgiveness (2:12b)

because your sins have been forgiven you

This phrase **your sins have been forgiven** is the most important phrase for any person. John wants his readers to have an assurance of this remarkable fact. The problem with all mankind is that they are separated from God (Is. 59:2) because of their sins. Christ Jesus has purchased a real salvation that forgives sinners (Eph. 1:7). John declares that forgiveness of sins is fundamental for a change of life. To know that God has truly forgiven, and placed the person back into fellowship, is at the heart of Christian doctrine.

(2) Freedom from Doubt (2:12c)

for His name's sake.

This is a bold and immensely important statement. God did not forgive these because of, or based on them. He did it **for His name's sake**. Why should this statement make any difference? If the purpose of salvation is built upon anything related to man, it will fail. Only God and His purposes do not fail. Therefore, there is an absolute assurance of true salvation because it is not based on something movable, but immovable. Isaiah 43:25 states, "I, even I, am the One who wipes out your transgressions for My own sake, and I will not remember your sins." Notice, "for My own sake." It is within God Himself, and therefore, John can proclaim the absolute nature of true salvation because it originates, and comes from God Himself, by His decree, and for His reasons and purpose. It is therefore not theoretical, but actual.

This verse is a repeat of Isaiah 43:25. God does not change, and He is accomplishing His purpose in salvation. John says, you young in the faith, begotten ones of God, your salvation did not originate from you or come because of you, but from God Himself. Therefore, true salvation is eternally secure or, as the older Calvinist doctrines proclaim, it is *"perseverance of the saints."* Those in Christ will overcome all of the circumstances that seek to keep them from God. Although they will not be perfect until glorified, they will be those that are living by faith, and doing those truths described in this epistle.

b. True for Fathers (2:13a)

I am writing to you, fathers, because you know Him

John says that each class of persons "in Christ" has the same assurance, but each has a unique perspective based on where they are in their

Christian life (2:13a, 14a). The process of spiritual maturity (or *sanctification*) places every Christian somewhere along its path. We may correlate it physically with age. The person moves from infancy through childhood, youth, and into many stages of adulthood. In the same manner, spiritually, there is a process of maturity taking place in each Christian's life. In each stage of life, God is present with the Christian in a remarkable way. John addresses **fathers** after broadly addressing the entire group as **little children**.

"**Fathers**" is the Greek *pater*, which means "nourisher,""protector," or "upholder." This is a seasoned person in a responsible position. It is a person with "mileage" on him, and thus experience. This is the standard word for father in the Bible. It is also used of God the Father. In 1st Timothy 5:1, it is used of *older* men, those in a place of *dignity*, with the expectation of wisdom. In Hebrews 11:23, it is used not only of a person who is older, but also of someone who is carrying responsibility. This is a person exercising oversight, serving as a protector, and a person to be respected because of his experience. John addresses the most prestigious time frame of Christian maturity. In addressing these seasoned Christians, he reminds them of the reality of their relationship with Christ in their lives and experiences.

(1) Firsthand Knowledge (2:13b)

who has been from the beginning.

The phrase **who has been from the beginning** reminds these *seasoned* Christians of how having fellowship with God has made a radical difference in their lives. Any true mature Christian can look back and consider how his life has been radically impacted by the caring work of God through his experiences. Also alluded to, is a reminder of the kindness of God through the many circumstances of life. This thought is depicted by John Newton's hymn, "Amazing Grace," when he writes, "Through many dangers, toils, and snares I have already come." There is no explanation for the character and quality of life experienced as a true Christian other than the work of God clearly written on it. John shows the importance of this reflection as he repeats the reminder in 2:14.

(2) Fellowship (2:13a)

because you know Him

When John states that the fathers **know Him**, he means much more than mere information. The word **know** (*ginōskō*) means "to come to perceive, to recognize absolutely or completely by experience," and can mean nothing less than a degree *of personal experience* that indicates a *relationship* based on familiarity. This is the same word **know** used back in 2:3 (see notes), and John 17:3 when Christ is praying for His own. *Ginōskō* is to be contrasted with another word for **know** (*oida*), which appears, for example in John 18:21. This word is "used for perception without relationship." By contrast to mere perception, **know Him** (*ginōskō*) has the significant weight of *relationship*. To know God in this manner is to have a *life changing* experience. No one could know God in this manner and not have an impacted life.

For example, this is the same idea expressed in the accounts of Moses in his relationship with God. In Exodus 33:18–23, Moses desired to see God's glory, and of course, God showed Him an appropriate measure of Himself. As he met with God, his face shone to such a degree the people could not bear it. Or consider also the example of Isaiah (Is. 6:1–7) when the prophet encountered God in a supernatural vision. Wherever we see any encounter with God in Scripture, including the form described here as the knowledge of relationship, it results in an unmistakable impact that changes the life. This knowledge becomes a cherished, personal possession of the most significant value. It is so significant that nothing else really matters, or has a relevant importance by comparison. In Matthew 13:44 we read the parable of the buried treasure. Here, a man found something so valuable that nothing else compared with it. So, when John says **you know Him**, he means you have reached the pinnacle of living. You have come to know God, and, like Enoch (Gen. 5:22), who walked with God—and there is much more to the little phrase than the mere physical—you have God as your Friend. Enoch knew God. To know God in this manner is to find Him, and to know Him in reality and personally. This is the reinforcing reminder John makes to the fathers: you have the reality of the true faith: you know this by the personal experience of walking with God. This is so important that John repeats it twice.

c. True for Young Men (2:14)

We have already seen that John has taken a pause in the midst of his writing. He is writing to show the difference between the saved and unsaved. He is providing a contrast between real salvation and mere profession. In this pause, it is as though he feels the need to express his affection and his concern. He makes a general statement of his affection by calling them **little children**, an affectionate term for those begotten of God, and his children, in relation to him as an apostle and teacher of the truth. He has addressed fathers. Now, he addresses **young men**. It is interesting that he focuses with each age group on certain aspects. He is probably addressing those who are young adults up to around age 40. To understand his thoughts, we should think in terms of what is characteristic of young men. Or, put another way, what is characteristic of young adults in this stage of spiritual life? To answer this, we would point out that youthfulness, because of energy, is usually a very productive time, often the most productive time of the life. It is also a time when some of the greatest decisions will be made. It is a time of growing families, responsibilities, personal education, occupation decisions, and other changes. With all of these pressures and decisions comes the setting of a spiritual tone. How will the person direct his life?

(1) Fight (2:14b)

because you are strong,

John focuses on their strength because that is one of a man's greatest qualities. He says **you are strong**, that is, mighty, powerful, and valiant. Now, we know that all strength ultimately comes from God. He is the giver of life, and certainly in the realm of spiritual life and strength we can do nothing without Him (John 15:5). Even behind the strength of youths must be the energy of God (Eph. 6:10). Unsaved young adults often use their strength or energy in selfish endeavors or evil activities. Here though, John's focus is on the saved using their strength for God. He says that in this strength they have **overcome**, that is, conquered and prevailed (repeats in verse 14) against evil. They have fought and won. Intended by the word "overcome," later in the verse are all the things that entice men in their natural state as sinners. Their actions are contrary to the natural tendencies of unsaved young adults in the world; those loving the world system of immoral thinking and behavior. As John states later (5:19), "The whole world lies in the power of the evil one." But not these young men; they have overcome the world. John will have much to say about this overcoming later, but for now he is encouraging these young men by marking out a characteristic of their testimony. He is convinced that they are truly saved because of their strength being used for God, and overcoming the world.

(2) Faith (2:14c)

and the Word of God abides in you,

Another characteristic of God's true people and their testimony is the presence of **the Word of God,** and the priority it takes in the life of the true child of God. This concept addresses the *how* of the young who have overcome. The word **abides** is *menō*, meaning literally "to stay". John is saying: it is fixed in a person and *remains* in him. It is a part of his life. It is at the core of producing the *thinking,* and flows into the activity of one's life. This **Word** abiding in them is at the root of the overcoming. It is an essential, just as the Holy Spirit is an essential.

This **Word** is the power of God working through the young. The young are generally thought of as gullible, and therefore, easy prey to be influenced by the age in which they live. This **Word** is powerful and alive (Heb. 4:12). It makes all the difference. It provides the truth and light that is contrary to the world's philosophy, deception, and evil. The ability of the **Word of God** and the work of the Spirit can overcome the natural youthful attachment to the world system of evil. This is true even in young men who have so much virility, energy, and desire for living. John again continues the general theme of his writing. Even in this pause, he is exposing the difference between the true child of God, and those who remain in their natural condition. The fact is the **Word** abiding produces faith, a faith that will continue in the one who receives it. That is the encouraging thrust of this powerful statement: **and the Word of God abides in you**. Even for **young men**, there is a radical difference made when the **Word of God** is used of God to transform and take up residence.

(3) Favorable Outcome (14d)

and you have overcome the evil one.

This faith is seen practically and actually in the life of young adults. Often individuals think that the young cannot help but be immersed in the world's ways. Those who have been born again at any age, however, will have favorable outcomes. Those outcomes are overcoming the **evil one**. Nothing is more wonderful than to see a young person who has a godly testimony. A young person's testimony is perhaps more ironic than that of an older person, because we expect the younger persons to be more engaged in the world system. Actually, though, the Bible is clear, the whole world lies under the power of the evil one (5:14–19). This means that all who are outside of Christ are controlled by the evil one. The only explanation for the testimony of a young person, as with any person, is that God Himself has worked in a powerful and supernatural manner. The concept of **overcome** will be a theme throughout this epistle. The person himself could not possibly, within his own strength, **overcome** Satan. The words of Christ in John 16:33 are perhaps the most comforting words spoken. Here He reinforces the supernatural nature of the overcoming power of Christ, and His defeat of evil at the cross. That defeat and overcoming power extends, and is shown through young adults who have their confidence in Christ.

d. True for Children (13b)

I have written to you, children, because you know the Father.

In order to focus on the categories John addresses by age, we skipped over the one titled **children**. The word used for **children** is a different word than that used in verse 12. Here the word is *paidion*, meaning "infant," either a boy or girl, not by his or her spiritual birth (as in verse 12), but his or her actual age. He is therefore addressing actual children by physical age that have a testimony of life in Christ. These children do not have a lot of experience, nor the strength of a young adult, but they know their God. In Mark 10:14, Jesus commanded the disciples to allow the children (those young in age) to come near Him in order to hear the Word of God. He went on to say "for such is the kingdom of God." His meaning was that people had to become as children in their dependence upon others, here, upon God. But it also has a secondary reference to the fact that age is not the issue concerning entry into God's kingdom. This means that children can and do receive the truth, and the kingdom of God is made up of those not only young in physical age, but also characteristic of innocence in the things and ways of the world. The real issue, regardless of age, is that **you know the Father**, meaning that a person has a real knowledge of Him, and a real relationship with Him that is seen in this same, supernatural, overcoming testimony addressed in this paragraph.

Pause and Reflect

John has given us the conditions of fellowship and shown the contrast between the real and the false. Addressing each group, he has demonstrated the reality that true Christianity permeates all age groups, and is not based on maturity, experience, or physical development. There is no merit of man

> with God. A child can be one of His own the same as a father. Each age has its characteristics, but the "new birth" in Christ reaches beyond these. At each age the characteristic of overcoming takes on an obvious reality. And each age has a role in the life that has truly been transformed by the new birth, projecting through the assets and abilities of each one the work of God in their life, and demonstrating the reality of salvation.

2. Appeal Against Loving the World (2:15–17)

John begins a new paragraph, but it must not be considered separate from what has already been proclaimed. He continues his dialogue, separating out those who are truly of God, as contrasted with those who are not. The contrast begins in the form of an *appeal*. This appeal must not be considered an appeal to man's mere energy. We have already seen and understood that relationship with God is a supernatural action. The appeal is to correct the thinking among those who are truly born again, and it comes in the understanding that the power to overcome (presented in verse 14) carries over into this appeal for separation from the world system. The appeal is therefore given to those who can and do overcome, once again contrasting those who are genuine with those who are not. It also seeks to clarify that living in the world, but not as a part of the world, characterizes the true Christian. Although given in the structure of an appeal, it is a part of the overall presentation of the test for those who desire to know their assurance of relationship before God.

The language we often use in common conversation is that a person loves certain things and dislikes other things. One might state, "I love Dairy Queen Blizzards." This saying is a loose expression of love, and should be more appropriately stated, "I like Dairy Queen Blizzards." One could also use terms such as "I strongly appreciate" or "I enjoy." So, in light of our text, is it wrong to love (strongly appreciate) things in this life? What does God state about loving the things in this life, and how does that apply to the context of John's writing? Of course, John is not alone, for Paul wrote, "Demas having loved this present world has deserted me" (2 Tim. 4:10). Paul is obviously troubled by Demas' departure and sees it as placing closure or ruin on Demas' testimony. Leaving Paul, as Demas did, is equivalent to leaving the truth of the Gospel for another love. This is also the idea behind the concept of "**loving the world**" as stated by John. To love (strongly appreciate) a Dairy Queen Blizzard is not contrary to the truth, the Gospel, or the things of God. However, to **love the world** or **the things of the world**, when the definition of **the world** or **things** is understood as something in contradiction to God or usurping the place of God, is quite different. It is therefore exceedingly important to be sure these terms are understood.

The fact that this paragraph begins as a command is strident and very telling of the importance of what it means to **not love the world**. It also shows us that loving the world in this biblical manner is contrary to God's requirement, character, and command.

a. The Command (2:15a)

Do not love the world nor the things in the world.

There is no gray area regarding this command. It provides only two choices. Like all of the contrasts presented in this epistle, this contrast states that either the person will obey God, and love the Father, or the person will **love the world.** The last verse in the paragraph (verse 17) shows us the folly of loving the world rather than the Father, because the world will fade away, while God endures forever. What is meant by the term **world** must be understood.

World is *kosmos*, literally, "a decoration or orderly arrangement." This word *kosmos* is used throughout the New Testament in various ways. In all cases it is translated **world**, but **world** can have *many* meanings that must be determined by the context. For example, in 1 John 2:2, it is obviously addressing a **world** of individuals. In John 3:16, **world** is referring to people from all nations or parts of the **world**, not just Jews. In John 1:10, **world** refers to the actual creation. None of these uses of **world** fit the context of God's command not to love. When John 3:16 says that God so loved the **world**, He would not be telling us not to love what He loves. Or, if **world** in John 1:10 is taken as the planet itself and compared to Psalm 19 where the creation is telling of the glory of God, John would not be saying not to love the planet either since, according to Psalm 19, it points us to God, not away from God.

So what is John commanding us when he writes that we should not **love** using the term **world**? He clarifies within the paragraph itself when he states: **For all that is in the world, the lust of the flesh and the lust of the eyes and the boastful pride of life, is not from the Father, but is from the world (2:16).** We will examine this passage in more detail later, but it is obviously referring to the evil possessing the heart of man (the values, pleasures, inclinations, philosophies, purposes, attitudes, and actions), manifesting itself in what man is about in his fallen state. He is referring to life on earth within and under the system of the curse.

The ramifications of the **world** system under the curse can be understood by looking at the first murderer, Cain. Cain was all out for himself. He was so self-centered, heartless, unreasonable, controlled by jealousy, full of pride, reprobate, and therefore disobedient to God, that he killed his own brother. He also did not even have the excuse of a mentor to lead him in such a path since he was the first murderer. The evil possessing him came from within his own heart. This attitude is something altogether different from the attitude of 1 John 3:17 and 4:17. Here, a **love** is seen that displays itself by pointing in the opposite direction from the self-centered, me-focused, me-first, irrational thinking consistent with Cain and all natural men. "**World**" represents the nature of man in harmony with the system under the curse. It is a system in which man is immersed and naturally a part. It is the system whereby man makes his daily decisions, sets his priorities, establishes his pattern of living, and interfaces with others doing so in a dark and ugly manner. It is the world's effort of rebellion, away from God, as a result of the corrupt nature of man resulting from the fall. Ephesians 2:2 calls it "the course of this world." Its attitudes, logic, morals, standards, focus, are all formed in evil and deception. It is a **world** made up of people bent on disobedience. It is working and moving according to "the prince of the power of the air" (Satan). It is stating the **world** as the place of lost humanity, totally depraved (Rom. 1—3), and hostile to God, His right, and His righteousness. It is a **world** of darkness (the opposite of truth; John 3:19). It is a **world** that has and continues to deny God (1 John 3:1), and refuses to bow before Him. It continues this way because it is a **world** of power dominated by Satan who rules over the fallen natures of all unconverted men (1 John 5:19; Eph. 6:12).

The Greek meaning behind **love** is *agapaō*, the biblical highest form of **love**, or what is often called the "God-kind" of **love**. It has the highest *good* for the object loved in view. On first reading, it appears strange that this word is used in a negative context. It would seem this word would be reserved for God's **love**, or the kind of love that God creates through the new birth. But that is just the point. Whereas this **love** should be reserved for God and for those who **love** God, and **love** one another because of God, it is being purposely abused to show just the opposite: the natural inclination of the unsaved person in his relation with his god (the world system). What should be correctly directed in **love** for God is instead directed at that which is unworthy; the opposite of God and vile to Him. So the **love** that should exist in its highest form toward God is directed exactly away from God. It is directed instead at the **world** system, and is antagonistic and wretchedly repugnant to the holy God who alone deserves this love. This is simply idolatry. For the natural person (those dead in sin), his **love** is fixed on that which is in opposition to God. Instead of naturally loving God, he puts in God's place a different priority that not only usurps God's rightful position, but is totally contrary to Him in every way. Proverbs 6:17–19 lists seven things God hates. All of these things fit the system of the **world**, and they all have to do with behaviors of man based on his wicked, rebellious heart. As God hates these things, they become clear definitions of that which is antagonistic to the "new birth" and "new creature-hood" of the redeemed person.

Often people think that loving the **world** means loving possessions, and rightly so. There is a natural propensity of sinful mankind to **love the world** from the standpoint of possessions. All people have a natural desire to possess material things. Because of sin, this desire has become an inordinate self-centered desire. This desire comes into even clearer focus in the words "lust of the eyes" in verse 16. Possessions are not contrary to God in and of themselves, but they can become so important to the person that they take the place of God, and become more important than knowing and serving God. Therefore in this sense, **things in the world (2:15)** can and do include material possessions.

The wealth of the rich young ruler of Matthew 19 is a good illustration of this very thing. Christ knew his heart, and challenged him directly to make a choice between following Him or his own possessions. Sadly, he failed the test. So do most today, and so do those even in supposed Christianity that are teaching and preaching a prosperity gospel, which is not the Gospel. In 1 Timothy 6:5–10, Paul discusses people attempting to use Christianity for material gain. In that context he contrasts the difference between those who are content and those who are full of greed. All persons need and use money. The issue is not that money is evil. It is merely a medium of exchange, but the person using the money with a heart of selfish greed makes money the "root of all evil" (1 Tim. 6:10). Christ Himself stated, "It is easier for a camel to go through the eye of a needle, than for a rich man to enter the Kingdom of God" (Matt. 19:24). He stated this because the enticements of wealth are strong to the natural person, so that they naturally choose wealth over God. Thankfully, the disciples question, "Who then can be saved?" Christ answers, "With people this is impossible, but with God all things are possible" (Matt. 19:26). He was referring to the necessity of God's intervention into the life of man to transform his heart, and give him the ability to live by faith, and place God before all else. The person who places money or anything above or in place of God is acting as one who **loves the world,** and can make no true claim on knowing God. Once again, the writer has made clear distinctions in his on-going evaluation of who is of God and who is not truly of God. Those who love the **things in the world,** including possessions above God, cannot truly love Him in the manner John defines as essential.

> **Pause and Reflect**
> The **world** and **things in the world** represent that which either takes the place of God in the life or works contrary to God. The world, as we know it, is a system of existence built off of and in the midst of the fallen condition of mankind. It is the system of evil, darkness, deception, and false well-being developed from fallen mankind and ruled over by Satan. Those who place their hope in this system of thinking and living are in reality, loving it, and have replaced appropriate hope in and love for God, with this love for the world. Such a mindset does not fit the truly redeemed of God. It is nothing more than idolatry.

What else does John mean by **the things in the world?** We should be reminded that the Gnostics believed that all matter is evil. This false idea has carried over into various religious circles. For example, the Roman Catholic Church has its monasteries where monks can live with the idea that being separate from all aspects of the material world is more righteous and pleasing to God. Is God displeased with the material world? Consider Job. In Job 1:1–5 and 8, we find that Job is described as a very wealthy man. God's evaluation of Job was that he was also a righteous man. His material wealth had nothing to do either positively or negatively with regard to God's evaluation of his status as a man pleasing to God. In Revelation 21:18–21, 27, and 22:3, we see the condition of redeemed men in future glory in the New Jerusalem. In these future passages are found immense wealth so glorious that it is inconceivable. How then could God be in opposition to mere material wealth when this is, among other things, the future condition in glory? In this same context John provides this statement from his vision, "no one who practices abomination" will enter His future kingdom. The wealth is not the issue, and of itself, cannot be abominable. It becomes abominable by man's lust of the eyes that places it above or in place of God. The Revelation context shows that the central figure of glory to be Christ. The issue is this: the focus and philosophy for living must be focused and have meaning by service to Christ. Like all spiritual matters, it is an issue of the heart and an issue of mastery. The child of God does not place material possessions above His Lord, but instead, has thankfulness to His Lord for every provision of blessing.

"**Things in the**" (world), means "something positional or relational." It means that which is *related* to the world system spoken of, or in agreement with the world system of darkness. These material things are not, as we have already seen, evil things of themselves. These are the things that are associated in some manner with the world system of evil philosophy. Man's heart is the issue. Man's heart, bent on evil, can turn that which would otherwise be good into something sinful. These **things** then become the instruments of man's attitude, desires, and character, which in-turn promote the system that is contradictory to God.

b. The Consequence (2:15b)

If anyone loves the world, the love of the Father is not in him.

If anyone loves is a phrase that indicates there can be no exceptions. **Anyone** means *anyone* found in this category of loving the world's evil system or the things associated with the system. The Scriptures tell us that "If anyone does not love the Lord, he is to be accursed" (1 Cor. 16:22). We can clearly see that the line has been drawn between those who **love** God and those who **love** something else more than God.

John says: **The love of the Father is not in Him**. There is an emphatic measure in those who know Christ and have a right relationship with Him, namely, they do not love that which God does not love. They cannot place something between themselves and God. They might stumble, but ultimately, their love for God above all else will prevail. In contrast, those who continue to love what God hates, or to place "the things of the world" above their relationship with God (**the Father**), cannot belong to Him.

This theme is a consistent theme throughout the Word of God. In 2 Timothy 3:2–7, Paul lists a detailed description of the world system in the last days (the current time), and this description is clearly consistent with this passage. In that context he admonishes Timothy to remain faithful. "You, however, continue in the things you have learned and become convinced of" (1 Tim. 3:14). Paul says, in effect, "In contrast to the mentality expressing the *anti-God direction of the day*, Timothy, stay on track! Do not get pulled into the world system of thinking." In Galatians 1:4, Paul states that Christ died to deliver men from this evil world. This deliverance begins first in the heart, continues in the life, and ultimately results in a physically glorified state.

The structure of this sentence alludes to an absolute choice, a choice that is made by every person who has ever lived. It is a choice so significant that it has eternal consequences. No person will escape without having to make this choice. Moses' choice appears in Hebrews 11:24–26. By the world's standards, it was not an easy choice because he had so much to give up in order to be identified with the people of God. He was not only willing to give up what appeared as the good life, but he was also willing to be obedient and committed himself to hardship in the things of God, rather than the prestige of Pharaoh's government. In the context of Moses, the **things in the world (2:15)** were attached to a government, a political monarchy that denied the true God, glorified man, and fit entirely into the world system of evil. The treasures and possessions of Egypt were not of themselves the problem. They became allurements, **things in the world**, because of their *attachment,* not to God, but to Pharaoh. In order to have the possessions of Egypt, one would have to abandon his allegiance to God, and give his allegiance to Pharaoh. This idea of allegiance and its attachments becomes a type for all who choose. The world system uses the things that would be otherwise good, but are tainted by an allegiance to Satan. How did Moses make such a hard choice? We know the answer because the whole context of Hebrews 11 is about faith. The writer tells us that Moses made his choice by faith. He first had an encounter with God - an encounter that changed his life. It can only be explained as the effectual work of God, and because of God's grace to Moses. He was then by faith able to choose God over the world system.

From this context, there are clearly *only two directions to go*. There are not several choices or some place in between. In choosing God or something else, a person cannot have or serve both. This explanation was the specific meaning of Christ's words in His "Sermon on the Mount" in Matthew 6:24. It is impossible to have two opposing masters going in two opposing directions, and to serve them both at the same time. This same reality is also made clear from the first commandment of the Decalogue: "You shall have no other gods before Me." Any choice that is contrary to God, and placed above God, becomes an idolatrous god.

Not only are there two distinct directions for human love to seek, but they are also not fitted for one another. No honest person can rationalize agnosticism, as if by being in a non-committed position is somehow safer or better than those living in obvious opposition to God. A person that is not seeking to live biblically for God is, by definition, already living in opposition to Him. That person loves the world system of evil and serves it in the place of God. Christ stated in Matthew 12:30: "He that is not with Me is against Me." Therefore, no person can say he is merely living life without offending God—as if rejection of God is not antagonistic to God—for if he is living without God, he is hostile to God.

> ### Pause and Reflect
>
> It is impossible to love what is in opposition to God and to love what He hates, while at the same time having a true saving love for God. Anyone who loves God will love the same things God loves and will hate the same things He hates. John again draws the clear line of separation between those who are of God, and those who are not of God. The definition is a matter of love, either for God, or for the world system. Each person falls on one side or the other, not on both.

c. The Considerations (2:16–17a)

(1) The Singular Elements (2:16a)

For all that is in the world, the lust of the flesh and the lust of the eyes and the boastful pride of life,

In Romans 8:5–6, the apostle Paul makes a significant contrast between those who are living "according to the flesh" and those living "according to the Spirit." **Flesh** in our immediate context, and in Paul's, is referring to someone that is being controlled only by the physical. This is a reference to the instincts of the natural unsaved person. They live and think only in terms of the physical. Unregenerate men cannot know the spiritual (1 Cor. 2:14). These are people walking (living out their lives), only by their sight (what they view without any revelation from God), in contrast to Christians who walk by faith (2 Cor. 5:7). The Christian has the Word of God and the indwelling of the Holy Spirit. Therefore, by contrast, those who are walking according to the Spirit are those controlled by the Spirit of God within them, and influenced by faith in God's Word. They have a mind set on God's glory, authority, and righteousness, and they walk by living out their lives with a view of God's will and purpose. They do not do this perfectly, but none-the-less they are radically different than those of the flesh. Peter states that those who "indulge the flesh" are ruled by their instincts "like unreasoning animals" (2 Pet. 2:10–12). **Flesh** is contrasted with Spirit as two entirely separate directions with different philosophies and attitudes in daily living. **Flesh** stands for those who are spiritually dead, and Spirit stands for those who have been made alive by God's grace.

John makes sure that his readers understand that God is not the author of or does He condone the actions in the world system. He makes it clear that the things which he lists under the general heading of **love the world,** are **not from the Father**. Many people rationalize their actions and sin as acceptable to God. "After all (they say), God made all things, and God allows these things to go on; therefore, He must consider them acceptable." The unregenerate think that God is really like them (Ps. 50:21), but such thinking is rejected by John. The black and white lines of contrast are drawn between that which is from God and that which is contrary to God. That which is contrary to God is consolidated under the general heading of **love of the world**. Man's sinful actions under the heading of **love of the world** (v. 15) are further explained by the writer under the explanation of **lust of the flesh, lust of the eyes**, and the **boastful pride of life**. John's definition of **all that is in the world (2:16)**, or pertains to the world system, is now more narrowly defined. **Lust** is a word in Scripture that means longing for that which is forbidden by God. It is an inappropriate or sinful yearning. When we connect this word with **flesh** and it becomes **lust of the flesh**, it defines itself as the perverted condition of being ruled entirely by natural, sinful instincts. This is the natural condition of all people, as all are born in sin. All people naturally long for that which is evil before God; all are "after their father the devil" (John 8:44), being like him, instead of like God. God changes this condition of lustful slavery by the new birth. Only God can change it, and make it possible for any man to overcome.

Eyes is *opthalmos*, a word having to do with "a person's vision and what he sees." It has an obvious physical orientation that is contrasted with the person who is living by faith. A person living by faith is one who has accepted the truth of God's Word, and has chosen by faith to follow the promises of God concerning His Son. This is having faith in God, hoping in God, and viewing the world from the perspective of knowing God, as contrasted with what a person accepts exclusively by physical sight. When **lust** is connected with **eyes**, the reader recognizes that the gateway of the unsaved person's world is being viewed in a skewed manner. The world is not seen through the eyes of appreciation for God, but rather, with an inordinate manner of corrupt viewing, a manner contrary to and against God.

In Matthew 6:23, Christ addresses this point: "But if your eye is bad, your whole body will be full of darkness; if then the light that is in you is darkness, how great is the darkness!" He is saying that the person who has this bad eye, this lustful eye, this unregenerate eye, has no understanding. Having a corrupt eye affects everything else in his reasoning, decision making, and judgment. He can only see things with a corrupted interpretation that is contemptible, selfish, greedy, philosophically defiled, and in total opposition to God. His eye only serves to feed the beast of sin residing within himself. This corrupted perception affects the entire person, as it directly affects his judgment and thereby his actions. This again is part of the description by John under this heading of **love the world**.

Boastful pride, then, is *aladzonia*, "a braggadocio with a greatly inflated self-confidence." This describes a person living with a vain imagination of who he is, and what he *deserves*. **Pride** represents positioning oneself in the place of God. This is precisely what Satan does (Ezek. 28:17; Is. 14:12), and this is what man does in his foolish sin. The idea of boasting before God is shown to be totally repugnant, wicked, and insane (1 Cor. 1:26–31); yet, this is what man does under the system of evil that consumes the fallen world. James 4:16 speaks against any form of boastful behavior. Among the six things God hates in Proverbs 6, the first is arrogance as seen in "haughty eyes," a face that demonstrates pride. This pride is absolutely contrary to the humble Lord Jesus of Philippians 2, and the broken man who is looked upon with favor by God in Isaiah 66:2. There is no association of man's pride with a relationship with God. Pride is the key sin of Satan (Is. 14:14), and the father of all sin (Prov. 16:18).

(2) The Source (2:16b)

is not from the Father, but is from the world.

The chief consideration of what John describes regarding **all that is in the world**, a reference to the world system of evil under the curse, has as its genesis the *pride of man*. All three components used to describe and sum up what the Christian is commanded not to love in the world system begin their explanation with terms associated with pride (**lust of**, and **pride**). The issue of man's pride is something that should raise a red flag in the mind of Christ's followers and continue to be of special concern. Prominent pastors on many radio and television shows focus, not on Christ, and do not promote reliance upon Him, but on each individual's self-esteem. This philosophy has been accepted by an increasing number of professing churches. It is a philosophy that has been brewed in the secular world of psychology, and has been imposed on Christian thinking by popular preachers. Nothing in the Word of God can remotely justify such a doctrine. In fact, exactly the opposite is true. Such teaching is an enhancement of, enticement to, and justification for man's pride, the very thing condemned in John's writing. One preacher expounding this doctrine said things such as, "You have no idea what you can do, and you have no idea how important you are." Both concepts are contrary to the passage in 1 John and such verses as Romans 12:3. The preacher went on to say, "It is within you; don't listen to negative talk or teaching; you have the power to do whatever you want to do." This is truly "trash talk" of the devil. It is as Paul told Timothy (2 Tim 4:3), that is what individuals will want from preaching in the last days. They will desire to have their "ears tickled."

In this passage John continues separating out that which is of God from that which is not of God. He is emphatically clear that such teaching and philosophy that causes men to boast, to trust and look to men, **is not from the Father, but is from the world (2:16)**. Make no mistake-the source of the message does not matter. Whether it is from a pulpit, a so-called Christian institution, or a popular religion, such a message **is not from the Father**. John is warning his readers to expect this very thing. That is why he declares in verse 26 that he has written these things because there are those who are "trying to deceive you." In clarifying the source of such heresy, he again draws the line between those who are of the truth (of God), and those who practice a religion of deception (of Satan), that is not focused on Christ, but on man.

To make the source a deliberate matter is very important to John's discussion. As he is bringing to light those who belong to God, as contrasted with those who do not belong to God, the root source of the person's actions is significant. Bringing the source to light serves as another means to identify those of truth by how they react to the world's confused dogma. On the surface identifying wheat from tares might be difficult. A true Christian is not perfect and might be in any number of stages of development toward maturity. The tenor of life at any given point might be a combination of what appears as love for God, yet, it may also be mixed with some aspects of wrong connectivity. The same examination of someone who is not really a child of God might bring somewhat similar results. In his depravity, no person is as bad as he can be, and often the unregenerate do act for a time in the realm of moral behavior, and perhaps, even have the appearance of belief. One must be cautious and carefully evaluate.

Real evidence comes not from a flash picture, but from the mosaic of the life. Close association and close listening to a person will bring forth his true belief. Ultimately, the source of the person's belief will be identified during the circumstances of life. The phrase in verse 19, "they went out from us," is critical. They ultimately could not help themselves, and their true colors came out because their source first displayed them as prideful, and then failed them. The same is true for the child of God. His roots in Christ will sustain him, and be demonstrated by his confidence in Christ and by his continuance. All of the connectivity to the source is ultimately and directly proportional to the reality of the person's true identity, that is, of the faith or not of the faith. If the person's source is really **from the world**, then pride will be present and cannot sustain the person.

(3) The Short Span (2:17a)

The world is passing away, and *also* its lusts;

After showing the unreasonableness of following after something that is not sourced from God, John provides another solid argument for not following after the world system. He now emphasizes the contrast between following error and following God as it relates to length of time. Following after the things that are under the umbrella of the world system makes no rational sense. Why?

First, because he says: **the world is passing away**. These things under the world system are only temporary. For a person to invest his soul (the most important thing anyone has) into something that will not last, is more ridiculous than it is for the person to place his money in a bank that he knows will burn to the ground. The Lord Jesus puts it like this: "For what does it profit a man to gain the whole world, and forfeit his soul?" (Mark 8:36). In Psalm 73:18–20, Asaph writes: "Surely You set them in slippery places; You cast them down to destruction. How they are destroyed in a moment! They are utterly swept away by sudden terrors! Like a dream when one awakes, O Lord, when aroused, You will despise their form."

Not only is the investment in the world short term, and therefore irresponsible, but it also corresponds to the insanity of choosing the temporal instead of the eternal. The difference between true Christianity and false Christianity must be seen as the difference between a short term (passing away) testimony or long term eternal testimony.

Second, John adds: **but the one who does the will of God lives forever**. This brings in the aspect of doing God's will with the idea of continuance in that will. God's **will** is to love His Son and to obey His Word. Those who do, and continue to do this, demonstrate the reality of their new nature. This is the very doctrine of *perseverance of the saints*. The true saints (those saved) will continue in the faith no matter what (Phil. 1:6; 1 Cor. 1:8; Rev. 16:14). On the other hand, those not truly saved, those in the church as tares among wheat, are likened by Christ as the seed that fell on rocky places. The seed springs up with joy receiving the Word of God; yet, because it has no firm root (it is not sourced from God), it is only temporary. When affliction or persecution arises, it falls away (Matt. 13:18–21). Those who last or continue are **those who do the will of God.**

> ## Pause and Reflect
>
> John has again drawn the line between those who are truly of God and those who are not of God. Those who are of God do not love the world system of evil. They ultimately are able to delineate that which is purported to be from God, but is actually contrary to Him. They do not listen to those who are proponents of that which is antagonistic to Christ. Those who are not truly of God, even though they are practicing religion for a time, have a binding connectivity and confidence in the world system of evil. The clarity of John's reasoning for not following the world system is that first, it is not of God, and second, it is passing away. Those not of God have no root in God. Their source is of the world, and therefore they cannot stand the test of time and endurance. Like the world that passes away, so does the testimony of those who have no root in God.

d. The Contrasting Promise (2:17b)

but the one who does the will of God lives forever.

God's promise is emphatic, clear, and profound by contrast to the irrational position of following something not only untrue, but also temporary, and therefore with no future hope. "**Lives**" is *menō*, "something that abides in perpetuity." It is the standard word for *continuance* and also *eternity* in the Scriptures. It also relates not just to existence eternally, but in this context implies the highest conceivable quality of life. This quality of life is promised by Scripture: "In Your presence is the fullness of joy" (Ps. 16:11). The living is not just in duration, but in the very presence of God. One only has to turn to the end of the Bible (Rev. 22) to view John's vision of the eternal state for those in true relationship with God. God says that doing His will, in contrast to following the world system, provides all hope, true satisfaction, happiness, and joy not only now, but also eternally.

What is meant here by the **will of God**? The context has already given that answer. In verse 15 John says, **Do not love the world**. The **world** is the system that is contrary to God. Those truly trusting God and sourcing their faith from His Word are the ones who **do the will of God**. All other religious activities, even in the name of Christ, have no true value and will not last. The **will of God** is to abandon what the natural person in sin desires, to not buy into its appeal, to not embrace its philosophies, to not fashion ways after its ways, and to not take on its attitudes or succumb to its attractions. In everything the Christian must walk differently, live differently, think differently, do differently than the world system of deception.

The Christian looking forward to the eternal future is the backdrop of Paul's statement in 1 Corinthians 15:58: "Therefore, my beloved brethren, be steadfast, immovable, always abounding in the work of the Lord, knowing that your toil is not in vain in the Lord." This argument alone is the only reasonable mindset a Christian should have. With it comes the manner of life that trusts in the biblical perspective of those living by faith. But, even when one sets out to keep the ways of God, he cannot do it in and of himself. John says keep on keeping on in the things of God, but the Scripture addresses the reality that perseverance in the way of God is impossible outside of the work of God. Man, left to himself in his sin, has no ability to overcome his own nature, and in spiritual blindness he will always embrace the wrong things. The power for the true state of well-being has its root ability in what Christ stated in John 16:33: "In the world you have tribulation, but take courage; I have overcome the world." Those in Jesus Christ will overcome the world because they are in Him. These are those who do **the will of God (2:17)**, because they embrace the promise of God by faith, and have the expectation of a marvelous future. This perseverance then becomes a major indicator of the blessed evidence of a new birth; conversely, a failure to persevere indicates that the new birth has not taken place.

As John has continued to draw these contrasts mixed with promises, he is providing a portrait of the difference between those who are hopelessly lost and those who belong to God. Here, the lost buy into the world system and are contrasted with those who trust Christ and hate the world system because it is contrary to Him. At the conclusion of Christ's presentation of Himself as the Messiah to Israel, and after showing His glory in numerous ways so that those who continued to reject Him were without excuse, He summed up His plea for belief: "He who loves his life loses it, and he who hates his life in this world will keep it to life eternal" (John 12:25). This is the same reasoning and dividing line. Will the person believe Christ or buy into the world's views, values, and ways? The Christian must give up self and the humanistic philosophy, and instead embrace and trust in Christ alone. Those who have rejected this "world system" are shown exclusively to be those who have a right relationship to God through Christ.

> **Pause and Reflect**
>
> Once again a contrast has been drawn between those who truly have a relationship with Christ (identified as those who do the will of God), and those who do not because they are engulfed in the world system. The point is that one cannot have both. If one is embracing the world system, he is trusting in something that ultimately will not only fail him in this life, but will also lead him to destruction. On the other hand, those who do the will of God, identified as His true children, will abide forever. In showing the difference between those in Christ and those not in Christ, the difference is seen between those who embrace the world's philosophies, and those who embrace God's Word as rightly divided. The difference is further seen by those who are more concerned about the immediate versus those who invest their confidence in a future eternal hope in Christ.

3. Assurance from Abiding in the Truth (2:18–25)

The purpose that God has declared for the church is not unknown. It is presented very clearly in the Word of God. The term "church" is first of all the universal name for all the elect of this age, but it is also a general definition for local assemblies that name the name of Christ. It is this latter definition that John addresses here, although most teaching relates to both. Paul tells Timothy that the church does not belong to anyone but Christ, and that it (each assembly) has an absolute purpose. "It is the church of the living God, the pillar and support of the truth" (1 Tim. 3:15). The church (each local assembly) must be "the pillar and support of the truth." If the church ceases to be this, then it ceases to be the representative of Christ, who is the truth. So the church has an obligation, and therefore each member of the church has an obligation. As John continues to delineate who is of God and who is not of God, he now deals with another essential, namely, the responsibility to abide in the truth. This too, becomes one of the clear indicators of those who truly have a relationship with God, as contrasted with those who do not.

a. Nurturing your Perception (2:18-19)

Children, it is the last hour; and just as you heard that antichrist is coming, even now many antichrists have appeared; from this we know that it is the last hour. They went out from us, but they were not really of us; for if they had been of us, they would have remained with us; but they went out, so that it would be shown that they all are not of us.

Even though verse 18 is a new paragraph and a new theme, there is a connection back to verse 17, where John writes: "The world is passing away." John tells his readers that they are in the **last hour**, (a reference to the timetable of God that is coming to a close), and therefore, each moment and every thought should be held captive to Christ. This is precisely what is meant by the reference **antichrist is coming (2:18)**. John goes on to describe the spirit of antichrist as already being present. This is a message of warning to be wary, watchful, on guard, and not caught by surprise.

John starts this section by affectionately using the term **children** once again. Why does he use it here? Remember that the word **children** comes from the Greek *teknion,* the root *teknon*, means, "begotten ones" as noted in verse 12. The emphasis of his writing is to the "begotten ones of God," or "children of God." John addresses these individuals with the assumption that they are participants of the "new birth," and are tender and new in that birth. John serves as their spiritual father as he addresses them personally. Keep in mind that these Christians did not have the completed canon of Scripture. The apostles, and here John, were their source of precious and needful revelation from God.

John alone in his writings uses the term **antichrist**, even though the same person is obviously referred to in Paul's writings (2 Thess. 2:3), using different terminology. **Anti** means against or in place of, as one who opposes or seeks to replace Jesus Christ. In other writings he is described as the antithesis of the Savior. The **antichrist** is Satan directed and controlled to appear in the last days, and will fool the world into extreme evil prior to the return of Christ. John uses the name of antichrist, not to focus on this particular individual or the event of his appearing in the world as prophesied, but to emphasize the presence of the same kind of evil already manifested. John says **even now**, meaning before this one evil person has come, in time and as predicted, **many antichrists have appeared (2:18)**.

There are many individuals who have the same kind of evil heart set against God and who seek to do as much wickedness and destruction contrary to Christ, as God in His sovereignty will allow. Looking ahead to 1 John 4:3, the reader can attain a better understanding of John's intention in his reference to **many antichrists**. He states that anyone who does not confess that Jesus is truly from God has the spirit of antichrist. These persons, although not "the **antichrist**," have the same mindset of wicked activity, using their power (even though not amplified to the measure of "the antichrist") to be destructive and vile against the work of God. As John calls those to whom he is writing **children**, he informs them that they must not be naive as they evaluate those around them who fit this same criteria. Those who are not of God are not merely neutral. They carry the very same kind of spirit that **antichrist** will bring. Those having to deal with them must recognize the potential danger. Once again, John draws black and white lines between those who are of Christ, and those who do not know God. He uses descriptions of what they are like, both as a warning and a definition.

John goes further and says **from this we know that it is the last hour** from the fact **that antichrists have appeared (2:18)**. He warns that the timing at the end of the age when evil will be intensified on the earth does not happen instantaneously. The world does not merely move through time and history with little change in the climate of evil, and then, suddenly, at the end become radically wicked. No, from this passage an inference is made that there is a gradual acceleration of evil in the world. This is what Christ meant when He stated in Matthew 24:12: "Because lawlessness is increased, most people's love will grow cold." There will be an intensification of the very general atmosphere of evil. This is also seen in Paul's statement to Timothy that in the last days, "difficult times will come" (2 Timothy 3:1–7). There he elaborates a terrible description of the general vile condition of the culture and spiritual degeneration in the hearts of most individuals. This is without question a prophesied intensification of evil. This coincides with Paul's description in Romans 1:18. Those who "suppress the truth" and continue doing so, God "gives them over," that is, withdraws from them His common grace so that they grow more and more hideous in their depravity. Those whom he addresses as types of antichrist (little antichrists) show by their intensified evil that the one antichrist is indeed coming. In stating this, John does not mean that he is just at the door in our evaluation of time, but that the era of this writing has no remarkable manifestation of God before it, except those events immediately surrounding the second coming of the Lord. There is no prophetic supernatural manifestation predicted in Scripture until the prophetic last days referred to as "the day of the Lord" at His coming. Therefore, all the days leading up to Christ's second coming are the last days (or era) leading up to His return, and they are the days of the gradually intensified activity of Satan, and those who act in accord with the coming antichrist.

This intensification of evil activity and pressure against the work of God causes those who have not truly been converted to compromise. This can result in divisions among the people in the church. The intensified difficulty, along with persecution, will ultimately cause those without the Holy Spirit to fall away. John will deal with this in verse 19.

One of the key doctrines of salvation is *"perseverance of the saints."* Some call it *"eternal security"* or *"once saved always saved,"* although the latter is not exactly the same. "Perseverance" has with it the promise of the continuance of the truly saved in their faith, whereas, "eternal security" states that the person saved will end in glory even if he later denies the faith. Perseverance is the more complete doctrine. The idea being that the true child of God will not be deterred from his faith no matter what circumstances or extent of time is involved. This is not because of his personal effort, but ultimately because of the work of God within the person. This doctrine is prominent and clear from the Scriptures (Phil. 1:6; 1 Cor. 1:8; Rev. 16:14; John 10:28; Rom, 8:29–30). With perseverance understood as a basic doctrine of the faith, John says: **They went out from us, but they were not really of us; for if they had been of us, they would have remained with us; but they went out, so that it would be shown that they all are not of us (2:19).** A perceptive reading of this passage brings such clear understanding that little comment is required. However, there are several observations to take note of within the passage. First, note the two contrasting words used to define differing positions: **"they"** is used of those who left and **"us"** for those who remained. This contrast shows immediately that there is a dramatic difference. These are two different classes of individuals. The phrase **out from us** shows that leaving was self-initiated by those who made that personal decision to leave. This is the same phrase in the Greek used for describing the departure by Judas in John 13:30 as he went out purposely from Christ, ultimately to betray Him.

The distinction of these persons is that they departed from the realm of teaching and truth where the apostle John himself was presiding. This is the same as departing from, not just a local church (as some seem to think), but also departing from the exclusive revealed truth, and ultimately the faith. This is the same concept not only of Judas leaving Christ and betraying Him, but also of Demas who not only forsook Paul, but more importantly the faith (2 Tim. 4:10). These are leaving the true fellowship and companionship with Christ (1 John 1:3) because of a love affair with the world. They have made their choice, and they are therefore shown to be apostates, those who have departed from the faith. Like Judas, their interest was not properly placed, nor could it be. The preaching of the Word was ultimately not received, and the temporary general interest that they might have shown could not be sustained in their own strength. Their relationship and love affair with the world, as contrary to Christ, ultimately won out, and they returned to it (2 Pet. 2:20–22).

The statement at the end of this verse, **so that it would be shown that they are all not of us**, indicates that God has specifically built the doctrine of continuance in the faith as an indicator as to who is real and who is not real in their relation to Christ. John is moving through arguments in this epistle providing a defining means of determining who is of God and who is not. Continuance in the faith is one of the chief means of determination. This is the explanation, God's answer through John, of why they went out. This is the answer to what many call backsliding and others call carnality. However, as many believe, it is not a temporary separation of fellowship brought on by sin, as in 1 John 1:8–10. This is a permanent departure from the faith, and the basis for it is that they **were never of us (2:19)**. These only appeared to be saved, but in reality there was no true transformation, no real work of God in the heart bringing about the new birth discussed by Christ in John 3. For a person to obtain true salvation and then lose it (John 6:39), is impossible because God (Christ) is the author and sustainer. Instead, these never had true salvation, and this is the explanation of John's point. Just as in the parable of the soils in Matthew 13:5–6, the *key* was that they had "no root," they had *no reality!* Christianity can be counterfeited for a time before others. It can be mimicked, trumped up intellectually and emotionally, but it will not stand the test of time because as a counterfeit it is not real, and sustaining takes the supernatural work of God. Man has not the strength or wherewithal to maintain a testimony. Maintaining a testimony is something only God can do, and if God does it, it is permanent and cannot be reversed. Its continuance has behind it the promises of God and is backed by His omnipotent power (John 10:27–29).

> **Pause and Reflect**
>
> The church is living in the last times and wickedness, confusion, trouble, and apostasy will intensify. However, these times also have purpose in the wisdom of God. The intensification of evil will cause a greater breach between those who are of God and those who are not. Those who are truly of God will continue in their love of and belief in the truth. Those who are not will become apparent by their failure to be able to continue. God's true elect will and must continue in the faith. They will, in the course of personal history, have moments of weakness, but they will never ultimately abandon the faith. Those who do not have the staying power of God to keep them will ultimately fail. John is not referring to cults, false systems of belief, or apostate ministries that many will cling to with their last breath. But these are those involved in the true work of Christ, and yet, are not saved. As such, they will find themselves, at some point, at odds with the truth and depart from it. John says this becomes another simple, yet profound indicator between those with real salvation and those deceived or pretending. Those without Christ do not have the ability for either stickability or commitment under time and pressure. They will ultimately show their lack of reality by their failure to continue in the true faith

b. Nurturing your Position (2:20–25)

(1) Manifested by Anointing You (2:20–21)

But you have an anointing from the Holy One, and you all know. I have not written to you because you do not know the truth, but because you do know it, and because no lie is of the truth.

The paragraph that began in verse 18 now continues in verses 20 through 25. John is on a theme of continual contrasts. He has just explained why some of those who once followed Jesus Christ and proclaimed faith in Him, have now abandoned that faith. After he specifically addresses the **"us,"** that these who went out, went out from us, he now addresses those who remain. The question should come, why did the ones remain that did remain? What kept them from leaving as the others did? We do not have to wonder, for John tells us: **but you have an anointing from the Holy One**. The difference between the **us** and the **they** of verse 19 is that those who remained (the **us**) **have an anointing from the Holy One**. This is marked by the **"but you,"** indicating those who went out did not have an anointing and never did. Implied is that if they had been recipients of an anointing, they would have remained in the faith.

Anointing is *chrisma*, "an endowment," referring to the *supernatural* work of the Holy Spirit on those whom God has chosen to receive it. This same word is seen again in verse 27. In the Old Testament the anointing of oil was symbolic of the special identification of individuals for service to God and with the reception of the Spirit. For example, Samuel anointed David as God's appointed to be king over Israel (1 Sam. 16:13). At the same time the oil was applied, and more importantly, the "Spirit of God came mightily upon David." Isaiah speaks of the Spirit of the Lord being on him to enable him "to bring good news to the afflicted" (Is. 61:1). This passage has an obvious prophetic reference to Christ, who is the ultimate fulfillment. The point is that God anoints His own with His Spirit, and the Spirit of God is the One that has the power and ability to perform God's will. This anointing is a setting apart, or what is called "sanctification." It is the same word used in Scripture for holy, as the person is set apart, or holy unto the Lord. In the New Testament, following the Day of Pentecost (Acts 2), the Holy Spirit indwells all true followers (Rom. 8:9), just as He was promised by the Savior prior to the cross (John 14:16–17). However, the Holy Spirit was missing from those **who went out** from among the true followers of Christ. As they did not have the Spirit of God (an **anointing**) indwelling in them, they were lacking in ability for true faith.

In this same verse, John addresses the result of the Holy Spirit's anointing: **and you all know. Know** is *oida*, "to have perception." John is saying that anyone with the Holy Spirit has a special instinct, a *special wisdom* from the Lord because of this Spirit. These of the **"us,"** are not pulled away from Christ by being so attracted to the god of this world, and his system, that they leave the faith. In Matthew 24:24, Christ addresses the treachery that will take place in the last days by the tricks of Satan through the antichrist. The masses of people on the earth will be duped by his deception, but our Lord says, "so as to mislead, if possible, even the elect." The idea is that it is not possible to ultimately fool the elect with the devices of Satan because **you all know (2:20)**. The **"you"** have special abilities of discernment, not from themselves, but from the Lord. They are anointed of the Lord and identified distinctively from the unsaved because the unsaved do not have this discernment for they have not been anointed. The Lord Jesus addresses those in the world as those who walk in darkness (John 1:5; 3:19–21; 8:12). This analogy applies directly to the light that is brought as a result of God's **anointing** of the Holy Spirit. Peter says the

Christian has been transformed "out of darkness into His marvelous light" (1 Pet. 2:9). The light is a symbol for truth, wisdom, and discernment. Jesus Christ is the source of all light (John 8:12), and therefore, those in Him have His Spirit, and they **know**.

> ### Pause and Reflect
>
> The reason that "perseverance of the saints," or continuance in the faith, is an essential and an absolutely reliable means of knowing who is saved and who is not is the power behind the sustaining ability. The reason the true child of God (the elect) does not fall away under pressure is that they have an anointing from the Holy One. The ability they have to continue is supernaturally given by God. The anointing provides the strength of guidance necessary to be sustained against all the efforts of evil opposition. This anointing is a reference to the abiding presence of the Holy Spirit that is within every true child of God.

The peculiar statement John now makes is another of his purposeful statements to stir reasoning. His writing to any natural man would be useless: **I have not written to you because you do not know the truth (2:21)**. Those lost in their sin and thereby living in darkness do not have spiritual discernment, and John's statement would be useless to such a person. Paul says in 1 Corinthians 2:14, "But a natural man does not accept the things of the Spirit of God, for they are foolishness to him, and he cannot understand them, because they are spiritually appraised." By contrast, notice what Paul says in 2:16: "For who has known the mind of the Lord, that he will instruct Him? But we have the mind of Christ." That little phrase "we have the mind of Christ," says the same thing John is saying in verse 21: **you do know the truth**. He follows that with what appears as an almost absurd argument: **and because no lie is of the truth**. Today's society is one of relativism, where most people have accepted the idea that truth and falsehood somehow intermingle, and that there is no such thing as an absolute. Instead, John reasons the surety of division between truth and non-truth: **no lie is of the truth**. Something cannot be black and then white all at the same time. Mathematics was created by the same God, and the absolute nature of mathematical formulations is easily seen. So is truth pure, and so is falsehood the absolute opposite of truth. The bottom line that John is stating is that there is no way to intermingle the positions of true relationship with God with having no relationship with God. There are

(2) Manifested by the One Lying (2:22–23)

Who is the liar but the one who denies that Jesus is the Christ? This is the antichrist, the one who denies the Father and the Son. Whoever denies the Son does not have the Father; the one who confesses the Son has the Father also.

John has been using the terms **they** and **us**. The contrasting continues with the use of **you** (v. 24) and **the one**. **You** refers to those to whom John is writing, whereas, **the one** refers to those who have left or departed the faith. The difference between the **"you"** and **"the one"** is seen in the actions of the person. The conclusion is stated: **the one who denies that Jesus is the Christ**. This appears in the form of a question: **who is the liar?** The answer is: **the one who denies that Jesus is the Christ (2:22)**. The lie statement relates back to verse 21: **no lie is of the truth**. Once again, John uses a continuing method of contrasts. This contrast is basic between the truth and a lie. The person denying Christ cannot help but be a liar, as Christ is the truth (John 14:6). Some of these people who had left the church (v. 19) were either still claiming Jesus in some capacity (any other capacity would be inadequate because of who He is), or at the least, continuing to claim a relationship with Jehovah God while dismissing Jesus. This kind of faithless faith is claimed today. Many claim to be Christian but have nothing to do with actually following Christ. Such a claim is worthless because it has not the substance of a true following. They are really denying that **Jesus is the Christ**. If they truly believed with saving faith who He is, they would follow Him. The delusion is like claiming to be obedient while being disobedient.

As **Jesus is the Christ (2:22)**, any denial of Him in that glorious capacity, in any form, is purely a lie. To deny the Lord Jesus His rightful position as Messiah (Christ) is to be placed in the same category of action as the anticipated prophetic antichrist. **Denies** is *arneomai*, "to contradict," "refuse," or "reject." Jesus says, "Whoever denies Me before men, I will also deny him before My Father who is in heaven" (Matt. 10:33). Such a promise makes clear that denial of Christ is a most serious matter. This type of denial was a reference to a public denial or a spoken denial before others. That however, is not the only kind of denial: "they profess to know God, but by their deeds they deny Him, being detestable and disobedient and worthless for any good deed" (Titus 1:16). This verse instructs that Christ can also be denied by indirect actions. In any form of rejection, He is denied the right of His position as Master and Lord. Such a denial carries just as much accountability as a verbally direct denial, for in both instances there is disobedience to the Person of God and His revealed right. The words of Christ, "If anyone wishes to come after Me, he must deny himself, take up his cross daily and follow Me" (Lk. 9:23), shows the pervasive relevance of any form of denial. To say that a person's one time profession of Christ is sufficient, when the same person is now denying Him, is not biblical. Further, the importance of actions that are in conformity to His will proves the requirement is more than lip service, as well as more than a one-time effort. It is a daily and continual placement of Christ as Lord in the life. So the real antithesis of denying Him is to deny self, which means a person puts Christ before his selfish interests, takes up his cross (a picture of the obedience of Christ), and does whatever God has called him to do by *living* first and *foremost* for Him. Anything short of this is a form of denial of Christ. On a broader scale, there are many churches that have orthodox doctrinal statements written years ago that claim Christ in their doctrines, yet they *deny* Christ every Sunday from the pulpit. They do not necessarily deny Him overtly. They do so by denying His right and glory as the head of the church, and by preaching another gospel, which is not the Gospel (Gal. 1:8–9). By these actions, they are denying Christ.

John also notes: **whoever denies the Son does not have the Father (2:23)**. Christ taught that "I and the Father are One" (John 10:30; 14:9). Therefore, John also writes the antithesis: **whoever confesses the Son has the Father also**. This confession, just as with the denial, does not merely mean lip service, but confession that permeates all activities and is displayed before others in the circumstances of life. It is a genuine confession that could be proven in a court of law. So, whatever anyone does with the Son, they also do with the Father. At the time John wrote his epistle, there were those who would deny Christ, and yet arrogantly claim the Father. John says the two are inseparable. Claiming one while at the same time denying the other is impossible. God is One God in three distinct Persons. Being One, no Person of the Godhead can be offended or denied without offending and denying the other Persons. Jews today, who claim Jehovah God and are still looking for the Messiah, are thereby continuing to deny the only Messiah, and therefore, do not have the Father either, although they claim Him. In the same manner, the cults, such as Mormonism, Jehovah's Witness, and Unitarianism, deny the deity of Christ and reject Him as who He truly is as revealed in the Holy Scriptures. Such a denial, no matter how sincere the person is in his faith, destroys any true relationship with God.

(3) Manifested by you abiding (2:24–25)

As for you, let that abide in you which you heard from the beginning. If what you heard from the beginning abides in you, you also will abide in the Son and in the Father. This is the promise which He Himself made to us: eternal life.

John specifically turns his attention to addressing the "**you**," those who have remained in the faith. He states: **Let that abide in you which you heard from the beginning**. What was heard from the beginning was the Gospel of Jesus Christ. His Word brought salvation. One of the blessings of God's precious Word is that it never changes. There is no later addition, no corrections, and no upgrades. It was perfect from the beginning, and John is reminding his audience that what they originally heard has not changed, nor will it. The idea of **abide** is similar to "let the Word of Christ richly dwell within you" (Col. 3:16), or "be filled with the Spirit" (Eph. 5:18). It is a way of saying *love* the Word of God, love truth, *seek* it in every way, and do everything possible to establish and *relish* it in a person's heart and life. The psalmist in Psalm 119 cannot get enough of God's Word. This seeking is the attitude of the Christian. What they **heard from the beginning** is the truth, and the truth cannot be improved upon or destroyed. Instead, it is to be *embraced* with all vigor. This truth serves as the antidote to the previous passage concerning denial of the Son. One of the ways to deny the Son is to deny His Word. He is the Word. Therefore, the Word of God must be the occupation of the true child of God. He must **abide** or continue and remain in it, growing in the knowledge of God, and ultimately becoming more like the Savior. Nothing else can be allowed to take the place of this kind of abiding. The prominent theme in every saved life should be constant attention to the Word of God. Those abiding in it will pass all the issues of life through the grid and spectrum of its wisdom and thought. Those of verse 19, those who "went out from us," actually went out from abiding in God's Word. The *denial* of Jesus is a denial of His Word. To abide in **that which was heard from the beginning** is to remain faithful to the knowledge of Christ and that which is pleasing to Him. Unless His Word is guiding and protecting, it is impossible to remain faithful to Him.

He then sets the condition: **If what you heard from the beginning abides in you (2:24)**. If this Word of God is continuing as the key part of a Christian's thinking, love, faith, and philosophy of life, the Christian has the most incredible blessing. He will not just have those blessing, but **also will abide in the Son and in the Father**. Each of these cannot be separated. So as one has the Word of God, He has the Son, and as he has the Son, he also has the Father. This truth is the other side of verses 22 and 23. If the person is continuing in the truth heard from the beginning, then he has the Son and the Father. He has the true God in all of His full expression of love and salvation. In simple terms, it is a *package deal*, a chain of interlocking realities. The reference to **what you heard from the beginning** is a direct reference to the truth. If this truth is continuing to be the delight of a Christian (it **abides in** him), then he is also abiding in the Son and the Father. Some so-called theologians try to place wedges or differences between them. It cannot be done! This implies a high view of Christ as God, and a high view of the Word of God as it is essential for faith. This truth is not something to be varied from, watered down in the thinking, or relegated to secondary importance. Further, this means that nothing should be allowed to take Christ's place or the place of the Word of God. He, in His Word, must be in the forefront of all worship, doctrine, and practice. Indeed, He must be the prominent theme of life. The idea of abiding means constant focus and attention. This is precisely why Paul used the phrase, "Christ who is our life" (Col. 3:4). This abiding in Christ and His Word is equal to abiding with God the Father. This is why a very telling question among men professing Christianity is always, "What place of priority does Christ have in your life?" A similar and inseparable question is, "What place of priority does the Word of God have in your life?"

Pause and Reflect

John, as he is defining true children of God and not mere professors, wants to clearly state that those who are abiding in the truth, as heard from the beginning, are exclusively the ones who truly have the Son and the Father. Those who have not kept the faith, have not kept abiding in it, and have neither the Son nor the Father. There is always a consistency in the children of God that cannot be broken; they characteristically love the truth and continue in it.

This is the promise that He Himself made to us: eternal life (2:25). With the context being clear, there is no distinction or separation between

God the Son and God the Father. John now reiterates the source of the promise concerning eternal life. Christ made that promise, and since He is co-equal with the Father, the Christian can have absolute confidence in His promise. The antithesis is true as well. Those in cults, who have a view of Christ as less than God, can make no claim to eternal life (John 8:24). If Christ is not co-equal, then He is a fraud, and if He is a fraud, His promises of eternal life are without merit or credibility. Just as John is clarifying who has a true relationship with God and who does not, he further shows that the basis for real faith is founded in the Person and work of Christ, who has the authority to back up every promise. Christ must be real in order to be a real Savior. His followers are real because they are changed and empowered to abide in Him. That abiding will be rewarded with eternal life. Eternal life is a life of endless duration. It is also much more because it is the glorious quality of life with God. John reiterates the final destination, and with it alludes to the idea of how the journey appears in its progress for preparation and arrival of the glorified life with God.

4. Admonition to Avoid Deceivers (2:26–29)

a. Necessity of Being Vigilant (2:26)

These things I have written to you concerning those who are trying to deceive you.

This beginning statement of a new paragraph is typical of John's practical approach. He advises why he is writing what he is writing. In this section he directly addresses the deceivers and their attempt to lead people astray. Much of the New Testament is given over to warning and pointing out the religious lost, who are actively promoting their own gospel, which is not the Gospel of Jesus Christ (Gal. 1:8–9). First note: **They are trying to deceive you**. In the King James, the word "seduce" is used in the place of "deceive." The Greek (*planaō*) simply means "to wander," "go astray," "roam from safety," "lead away," or "from the place of truth to the place of error." Paul in his writings minces no words concerning the *danger* of deceivers. He calls them "savage wolves" that "devour" (Acts 20:29). These then are not just members of God's family with a little different take or slant on truth, or maybe a little different interpretation; they are very wicked and dangerous individuals. They are not to be associated with, not to be communed with, but instead to be avoided. This warning appears in other places of Scripture, specifically in 2 Timothy 3:5 in the context of the last times. This means the flock must always be on the alert and vigilant. Because Satan is crafty, those who are not vigilant will be troubled by these deceivers, which is precisely what we see in our day.

> ## Pause and Reflect
>
> John has been admonishing these brethren concerning abiding in what they had heard from the beginning. These deceivers always vary their message from the true message. There is only one non-varying message that is from the Father and the Son. Those who are of God will "abide" in the truth, the non-varying message. They will not listen to contrary voices (John 10:5). This non-varying message is an admonition, a warning, and a test of true discipleship. There are not many messages; there is only one, and the true children of God will recognize that those who teach a different message are not to be followed. Anytime someone comes up with a new message that is not in conformity with the teaching of the Word, a red flag must go up in the mind of the true child of God. Christ does not change, and neither does His eternal Word.

b. Necessity of Being Selective (2:27)

As for you, the anointing which you received from Him abides in you, and you have no need for anyone to teach you; but as His anointing teaches you about all things, and is true and is not a lie, and just as it has taught you, you abide in Him.

This **anointing** was covered in some detail in verse 20. God anoints His own with His Spirit, who has the power and ability to influence the true child of God from wandering from God's path. The absence of the work of the Holy Spirit in the deceived and *deceivers*, is precisely why they go astray and seek to lead others astray. John is confident that God's true children will not be led astray because of the powerful work of God the Spirit within them. This perseverance in the faith is what is meant by **you have no need for anyone to teach you**. The **"anyone"** refers back to those in verse 26, the ones trying to deceive. He does not mean that those receiving the Holy Spirit should never be taught of God or by sound Bible teachers. Such an interpretation would be contrary to other portions of Scripture, such as Ephesians 4:11–15. The reference is to those trying to deceive (v. 26). The child of God does not need their teaching, not only because it is contrary to the truth, but because they can add nothing edifying to the truth of the Word. The idea is that **you** abide in the teaching that is consistent with the Word, and applied with understanding by the Holy Spirit within. The persons seeking to teach and lead, apart from God's Word must be shunned. They are deceived, and in their deception are seeking to lead **you** (the child of God) astray.

All of those in Christ need to be selective concerning their listening, and then, filtering their reception or rejection by discerning whether what they hear conforms to the Word of God. This discernment must be recognized as both an act of personal accountability, and something that requires the guidance of the Spirit of God. The measure of what the true child listens to and receives is built on the supernatural work of God (the Holy Spirit) within the saved heart of every Christian. God's Word is different and unique and will never be accepted by those who *do not* have the Spirit. First Corinthians 2:14 states: "The natural man (unsaved) does not accept the things of the Spirit of God for they are foolishness unto him." This distinction is between the saved and the lost. The saved feed on the truth, and the lost seek to discredit it. The lost cannot help but do so because they believe the real truth to be foolishness. John identifies that he is differentiating between the truth (**is true and not a lie**), and the teaching that leads astray, that which is contrary to truth or is defined as a lie. There is an infinite gulf between the truth and a lie. There is no relationship at all between them. The reference to **all things** means that the guidance of the Holy Spirit will provide the saved person all that is necessary to keep him from straying. The phrase **just as it has taught you (2:27)** is merely a phrase of consistency. The Word and Holy Spirit are sufficient in themselves to guide the child of God into all necessary instruction. The Word itself teaches the Christian to *trust* it. The statement **you abide in Him** is not a command but a statement of fact for those who are true children of God. Those truly in His will continue in their relationship with God by trusting His Word. Wherever dissenting voices come from, or how they are packaged does not matter practically. The child of God **abides in Him** and will not be drawn away no matter how attractive the voices or the messages, how popular, or even how much pressure comes to bare.

Pause and Reflect

This is a continuance of the contrasts between those drawn astray by the deceiving voices, and those who are not and cannot be mislead. The difference is the indwelling of the Holy Spirit that keeps the true child of God. There is nothing to learn from sources contrary to the Word of God

> and not directed by the Holy Spirit. The Word cannot be a lie, or mislead, and the guidance from God is always sufficient. Those in Christ need not have any concern they are "missing out" on some doctrine or discovery that is not in accordance with the Word of God. The child of God is simply to "abide in Him," or stay the course of continuance in His Word.

c. Necessity of Being Focused (2:28)

Now, little children, abide in Him, so that when He appears, we may have confidence and not shrink away from Him in shame at His coming.

John comes to a summation of this section and wants to make a significant point, and he states **now little children**. This phrase not only highlights what he is about to say, but does so in the form of a personal plea, or admonition, as from a parent to a child. These were his spiritual children, and they were very dear to him. Nothing would please John more than to see all these who have professed Christ to *continue* abiding in Him. In fact, John will later reiterate this idea in 3 John 4. The word **now** brings his plea to a point of special emphasis. The continued idea of **abide in Him** means to maintain a steadfast commitment to a biblical relationship with Christ. This idea of abiding has been the theme of this section, and it has been contrasted with those who abandoned the faith, either by **[going] out from us** (1 John 2:19), by **[denying] the Son** (2:23), or by **seeking to deceive** (2:26). In all of these descriptions, these have failed to abide.

John provides a supreme incentive for abiding. He reminds his **little children**, and therefore us, that Jesus Christ is coming again. He states: **when He appears**, reiterating that His coming is real and that it will occur as sure as the sun comes up each morning. When He comes, His appearance will produce two reactions from those who are on the earth - confidence or shame. John says: **We may have confidence and not shrink away from Him in shame at His coming**. The most important issue of life is to be *prepared* for His coming. This idea is true whether the Christian is alive when He comes, or dies and meets Him before He comes. In either situation, we must face Him (2 Cor. 5:10). Nothing can be more important than readiness to meet God. One of the most horrid descriptions in all of Scripture is seen in the unprepared man when Christ returns in Revelation 6:16. Never has there been a more frightening picture of total desperation.

There is only one way to avoid concern, and that is the theme of this section: **abide in Him**. This abiding then gives another means of discerning true Christianity. Everyone should ask himself: do I long for His coming (2 Tim. 4:8)? The ones truly desirous of His coming are those who are abiding in Him. They are those continually feasting on His Word and expecting His return. Christ, at His coming, will not be an interruption for those abiding in Him, but instead, He will be their anticipation and joy. John's dialogue is obviously directed at those professing a true relationship with Christ. John admonishes us to remain focused on Christ, trust Him alone, and no matter what anyone does or whatever else occurs, do not be distracted. When someone teaches in the name of Christ, but presents anything contrary to what is revealed in the Scriptures, do not allow it to be a personal distraction. When someone teaches in the name of Christ, but presents a man-centered gospel or focus away from the message **heard from the beginning**, the Christian's discernment should move him to the exit. The Christian needs to **abide in Him** with perfect allegiance until He comes. That allegiance means exalting Him, giving Him the glory, and of course, abiding with Him in the manner already discussed.

d. Necessity of Bearing His Image (2:29)

If you know that He is righteous, you know that everyone also who practices righteousness is born of Him.

John now sums up what he has said in this section. He is bringing to a close the difference between those with a mere profession, and those who have true possession. John begins his argument with **if you know that He is righteous**. He uses simple reasoning. John will use the matter of likeness to Christ as an issue for true fellowship. The character of Christ is **righteousness**. John declares the obvious that those **born of Him** will also practice righteousness (a full discussion of the practice of righteousness by the child of God will follow in chapter 4). The phrase **born of Him** addresses the supernatural activity of God in saving a person, and reminds us that something radical takes place when a person becomes a true Christian. With this new birth comes the *ability* to practice righteousness. This ability is something unavailable in the realm of the unsaved. Their realm is "dead in trespasses and sin" (Eph. 2:1). The change in the child of God provides a new nature to live for Christ. In a very practical sense, all that has been stated about abiding will result in practicing **righteousness**. Righteousness is often thought of as being free from sin. Certainly this is true, but the idea of practicing righteousness includes not only what the Christian does not do, but also what he does do in the general manner of his life. Practicing righteousness in this life does not mean perfection, or even being entirely free from sin (see discussion of 1:8). Practicing righteousness is directly associated with abiding in Christ, which keeps the Christian focused on Him, and growing more in likeness to Him in the sanctification process. It means that with a new *ability* to live for Him, the Christian is so influenced that he is doing what pleases Him, and what is righteous, that is, what is right! Abiding must first be true within the Christian's thinking because of his relationship with Him by the new birth. The Christian must be one who is continuing in what was **heard from the beginning,** and not varying from the truth. The thinking of the new person from his abiding with Christ will be projected into his daily walk. When righteous character is seen, the Christian demonstrates that he is born of Him. A physical descendant, a child, shows the characteristics of the parents. The child of God shows Christ's righteous character because he is born of Him.

The term **practices righteousness (2:29)** must take into account 1 John 1:8–10, where John teaches that a radical change does not mean that a Christian is completely free from sin. But, the trend of the life is different, and the means of fellowship is by the mode of dealing with remaining sin through a brokenhearted confession to Him who is faithful and just to forgive. The one who **practices righteousness** in this context, is the person *walking* or abiding with God as the *trend* of his life. The conclusion is that the "abiding" enforces righteous character, and thereby, provides evidence of the new birth, and relationship with the true God. It is not the cause of the new birth. It is the evidence of the new birth.

Pause and Reflect

Abiding has with it the necessity of bearing Christ's image. If anyone is truly His, and has experienced the new birth in Christ, there will be radical changes seen in the life. The concept of abiding is particular, and it is real. An equation is made here that is not unlike a mathematical equation: being born of God equals practicing righteousness. The person practicing righteousness will be effectively abiding in His Word, focused on it, and staying away from false teaching. This concept of abiding is so important that it is reiterated over and over by John. John even brings in the coming of Christ. The necessity of abiding (continuing), is seen by the person so living that they are not be ashamed at Christ's coming. This is in contrast to those of the world (that have no relationship) who have foolishly spent their time and energy living for sinful and useless endeavors. John has gone full circle. Abiding in Christ produces righteous living that is pleasing to God, and prepares the person for the coming of Christ.

4

The Characteristics of Fellowship

3:1–24

Outline context:

II. The Requirement of Fellowship with Christ (1:5—5:12)

   A. The Conditions for Fellowship (1:5—2:11)

   B. The Challenge for Fellowship (2:12–29)

C. The Characteristics of Fellowship (3:1– 3:24)

1. Practicing Moral Excellence (3:1–10a)

John's arguments to identify those saved from those who do not know God has been a journey of distinctions from various angles. John continues to highlight such distinctions between the unsaved and the saved. The new distinctions are elaborated from the characteristics of fellowship with God. John delves deeper, and in more detail at what is true of the person having fellowship with God.

Pressured by worldly compromise, weak theology, misapplication of grace, and wrong focus, many churches have fallen into the deception of the world. The world offers, not the testimony of the Bible's narrow road—the exclusive way, but a way that will pacify and satisfy the world's philosophy and darkness. To adapt the world's ways into the supposed Christian life rather than stay on the unpopular, often criticized, and more difficult path of the narrow way, is certainly easier and more attractive to the eye. Indeed, as has already been discussed, the Christian life can only be maintained by a supernatural work of the Lord. All other efforts, no matter how seemingly powerful or sincere, will fail. Other means do not have the foundation in themselves to take on the "the cares of this world" (Matt. 13:22). The understanding of any person on his Christian journey, and the testimony of the person on the journey are very revealing.

In verses 3:1–10, the word "practices" appears six times. This is a word that means to do continuously by agreement. It simply means that what someone is doing follows what he believes. Again, this is the general tendency of his life. It does not mean that this is all he does, or that he does it perfectly, but it does characterize his life. The major understanding is that what a person does in the primary manner of his life is reflective of what that person believes in his heart. John begins this new chapter by providing the Christian's bearings. He refers to Christians, or at least professing Christians, by using the word **us**.

a. Our Prospect (3:1–2)

See how great a love the Father has bestowed on us, that we would be called children of God; and *such* we are. For this reason the world does not know us, because it did not know Him. Beloved, now we are children of God, and it has not appeared as yet what we will be. We know that when He appears, we will be like Him, because we will see Him just as He is.

John first uses the word **see**. This word literally means "to stare at," with the idea to *discern* while being in awe as one observes. What is it that a person is to see? John states, **how great a love the Father has bestowed on us (3:1)**. The **us** refers again to those who are truly of God (His elect). "Greater love has no one than this, that one lay down his life for his friends" (John 15:13). The deepest, most infinite explanation of this love is in the words: "For while we were still helpless, at the right time Christ died for the ungodly. For one will hardly die for a righteous man; though perhaps for the good man someone would dare even to die. But God demonstrates His own love toward us, in that while we were yet sinners, Christ died for us" (Rom. 5:6–8). By any stretch of man's understanding or reason, such love is irrational. It is *incomprehensible* and cannot be fathomed. This is a supernatural love that speaks of the infinite God and His character.

Later in 1 John 4:8, John shows that God is spoken of as love. Since this description does not define Him in all aspects, it means that the hallmark of God's infinite characteristics is seen most prominently in His love. Love is the supreme eternal bond and that which is completely missing in the natural man in his relation to God. God provides the true meaning of love. It further reminds Christians who they are by comparison. Here is the great God, who incomprehensibly made everything from a galaxy 13.3 billion light years away, the furthermost known at this time, to the atoms in a shellfish at the bottom of the sea. He not only made them, but He rules over them, and holds all the destiny of every creature and object in absolute sovereign, purposeful control. He has all of this glory and infinitely more, and yet, here, John states that He loves **us**, the creatures He determined to create and save in such a wondrous manner. The weight of the statement is to *magnify* this love as *supernatural* and not explainable from the standpoint of reasonable reflection.

In this passage, God must be addressing "particular love." God does not love those He has not chosen to save in the same manner as His elect for whom His Son died. This particular love is the importance of the **us**. The love that God has for all mankind is related to kindness, fairness, and generosity. For even though God "sends rain on the righteous and the unrighteous" (Matt. 5:45), He does not redeem the unrighteous through the blood of His Son. Nor, is there definitively any statement in the Word of God that proclaims equality of God's love for all of His creatures. The world's form of religion likes to believe that God loves everyone equally and will make statements along the lines of, "we are all the children of God," intimating the equality of all men in the eyes of God. This equality is true from a creation perspective, but not from a redemption perspective. *Arminian theology* (originated with Jacobus Arminius), believes that God loves all men the same, and is attempting to save all men. This theology cannot be true, for all that God has intended to save will be saved (John 6:37). From a creation perspective, all people belong to Him, but only the redeemed belong to Him from a higher level of love that took the life of His own Son. The love that is meant here is that same love that is spoken of in the high priestly prayer of Christ (John 17:9; 22–23; 26). Love is spoken of for Christ's own in terms of the same quality of love that exists among the Godhead. This statement is perhaps one of the most amazing in the Bible: "So that the world may know that You sent Me, and loved them, even as You have loved Me" (John 17:23). The phrase "even as" speaks to the same love that exists between the Father and the Son.

Pause and Reflect

It is no wonder that John states here to discern and be amazed. Christians are to look at, and consider realistically, as much as able, His infinite love. They are to look at the manner of love He has displayed for His own, and then build upon it with everything else John will reason out in this section. Love must be placed in its proper light in order to deal with what else John

> will reveal as he makes distinctions among mankind and their relationships to God. The idea is that God has invested much in those He has redeemed through His Son, and the ramifications of His investment of love are shown in the distinctions John is drawing in this epistle. The distinctions are real, living, and unique because God, by demonstrating His love, will see that His chosen are indeed ultimately changed to be like their Lord (glorified), but even now, are in a process of sanctification (becoming more like Christ) to testify of their relationship to Him

(1) Actual Standing (3:1a)

See how great a love the Father has bestowed on us, that we would be called children of God; and *such* **we are.**

The distinction is highlighted when John calls the **"us"** the **children of God** and then adds the reinforcement **we are**. Is John saying that every one of these for whom he is writing is a child of God? That is not his intent. He would not be writing an epistle under inspiration that deals with defining who is of God and who is not if everyone reading the epistle was automatically of God. The emphasis on **such we are** is an emphasis to those who are, and this emphasis upon what **we are** becomes part of John's logic for *distinction*, as he will show. The emphasis is on the immediate for those truly in Christ. This same emphasis is repeated in verse 2. John goes on to say **that we would be called the children of God**. Those he is addressing who are in this position before God have been begotten of God. It speaks of the new birth in Christ, the very work of God in His supernatural intervention in changing Christians' natures, so that through Christ, Christians are not only justified, but changed to become His children. The very idea of using the language **children of God** shows the nature of God in kinship to Him. Christians are His by adoption (Rom. 8:15; Gal. 4:5; Eph. 1:5), but this must also mean that Christians are by nature changed. The first sentence states the Father has **bestowed on us**; this is a work of God from beginning to end. This, of course, does not mean that Christians are merely adopted as wayward children to continue in their sin and likeness to their previous father, Satan (John 8:44). God deliberately and purposely *initiated* a relationship to those–the: **us.** There was no treachery in it; nothing forced Him to do it, and no obligation on His part. He created a relationship by grace, and made them true sons of God. With that amazing work of God, radical change comes in the recipient. Christians, the recipients, now bear His image, have a new nature (2 Cor. 5:17), and have a new Master (Col. 1:18).

(2) Ambiguous Identity (3:1b)

For this reason the world does not know us, because it did not know Him.

He goes further to make this distinction clear: **For this reason the world does not know us**. Had Christians been changed only in position, there would be no distinction from the world. The idea is that the world cannot understand those in Christ. Paul speaks of this in 1 Corinthians 2:15. The Christian is an offense to the unsaved because he is not only different, but he is also changed in his attitudes and actions. Simply put, his nature is different and in diametric opposition to the old nature. Christ spoke much about this difference to His disciples prior to the cross in John 14–16. Looking ahead in 1 John 3:13 he states, "Do not be surprised, brethren, if the world hates you." The **child of God** is the one who has become "the alien." John provides the explanation by stating **because it did not know Him**. How could a true Christian who is a son of God be identified with the world instead of God? Christ, who was the only begotten (by physical birth) Son of God, was not identified with the world. In the same manner, those who are adopted children of God, and have experienced the new birth, cannot be identified with the world; they are instead identified with Christ of whom it is stated that the world **did not know Him**. Practically, the world did not know Him because those in authority in the world (that is, controlled by the system of evil in the world), not only denied Him His rightful place, but also, even put Him to death.

(3) Assured Revealing (3:2)

Beloved, now we are children of God, and it has not appeared as yet what we will be. We know that when He appears, we will be like Him, because we will see Him just as He is.

John has been calling the saints "little children," but now he calls them **beloved**. The word **beloved** is a form of the Greek word *agapētos*, expressing "the highest form of love." He is again addressing the saints in the most *affectionate* terms. This idea is also clear from what he says next: **Now we are children of God**. The idea is that the Christian is indeed attached to God Himself in this glorious description of being His child. This relationship is not something that will happen someday; it is true right now. Christians physically look like anyone else, although in many cases, their lots in life are of poorer or they have worse dispositions than many others. This reminder of the current status with a look to the future does two things. First, it should give understanding to Christians that their current situation is not purposed by God to be glorious for them. It is purposed by God for them to be faithful. They should be faithful, knowing that even now they are **children of God**. Second, it should give them a *heavenly* perspective. This current, fallen, world is not their eternal state or destiny. They are sojourners looking by faith at what God will yet do. What John is building toward is the clarity of another reality of the true Christian. The true Christian is not living for this world, but living by faith for what God has promised.

John next states: **it has not appeared yet what we shall be**. That statement does not mean the Scriptures do not address the glorified state of the righteous, but John is addressing it from the standpoint of the Christian's actual understanding. The Christian is looking by faith through a glass darkly; he is confined to what he sees naturally around him and limited in his thinking and understanding (1 Cor. 15:35–42). A great illustration is given in the Gospels by Christ. He uses a seed, which by all appearance is insignificant. The seed dies by entering the earth, and in the same manner everyone's body must die and enter into the earth. The seed produces a beautiful plant with fruit or a mighty tree. The natural illustration is perfect to realize the same is true for those in Christ, who appear as worthless seeds, but will have a glorious result in Christ. Think from the standpoint of a person that had only seen a seed, but never the end result of the plant or tree it produced. That is the position of the **"us,"** who are now children of God in seed form. Those in Christ are somewhere along the road of sanctification, but will not be seen in fullness until glorification. This idea is that **it has not appeared yet what we shall be (3:2)**. In other words, the Christian cannot begin to imagine the glories of what God has in store for His adopted children for whom Christ died.

He goes on, though, by stating what we do know; that **when He appears**—that is, when He is seen in His glorified state, either at His second return (which seems to be the implication here), or when believers join Him by death and enter into His presence (2 Cor. 5:8)—**we will be like Him for we shall see Him as He is**. This is wonderful truth. When the time comes for the person in Christ to enter into a glorified state to meet the Lord, he will go through a complete supernatural transition. God, who made the body in the first place, will remake it, and He will remake it into the fashion or manner of Christ's glorified body. When Christ comes in His glory at His second coming, those called **beloved** will come with Him (in their interim state) and receive glorified bodies, but for those unrepentant on the earth it will be too late. All of God's own will be physically identified with Him because **we will be like Him,** and have a glorious future. This is the promise of God, and the hope of every true Christian.

> ### Pause and Reflect
>
> Those who are truly of God have the love of God. This idea does not merely mean that God loves them, but they are already living out the characteristics of the difference in a moral, radical change that has taken place within them. This difference is not seen (now) externally, but internally. The world (the system of evil controlling fallen man) does not correspond with this internal change anymore than it embraced Christ when He came veiled as a mere man. By physical appearance, the person appears as anyone else, but something major has happened internally. As a result of this change, the person is misunderstood. Because the person is in contrast to the system of evil, and even a rebuke to it, he is unknown and ultimately hated. John says this misunderstanding will be cleared up when Christ appears. For when He does appear, all those who are truly His will also appear with Him in transformed bodies like His. Knowing his future, the child of God lives by faith, not for the immediate, but with anticipation of the promises of what God will yet do. The work of God then begins first on the inside, and John conveys that the work on the inside must be real. If there is no work now on the inside, then there can be no expected work on the outside when Christ appears.

(4) Attention on Him (3:3a)

And everyone who has this hope *fixed* on Him

Where the hope is fixed is very important. This hope leads to action, but the hope is not fixed on action, but on Christ. This hope is an extremely important aspect of Christianity. The hope spoken of in the Bible is always fixed exclusively on Christ. **Hope** (*elpis*) is a word connected with faith. It means "confidence mixed with expectation and anticipation." Here, the context concerns Him in relation to His return, and the glorious *expectation* of all the wonderful promises coming to fruition. It is the apex of salvation. If the same kind of hope is applied to anyone or anything else, including things one might regard in the place of Christ, even religious practices, that is idolatry. Christ is God, the jealous God, who will have no other god's before Him. Many people under the name of Christianity hope in their denominations or aspects of religious activities that they perform, such as: the sacraments, attendance, membership, or works associated with the efforts of a religious institution. Other people have a hope in their sincerity. Others have a hope in their faith. Some people even have their "faith in their faith." But again, if anything is inserted in the place of hope in Christ alone, no matter how innocent it may appear, it is a form of idolatry. Christ is "all in all" (Col. 3:11), and "I determined to know nothing among you but Jesus Christ and Him crucified" (1 Cor. 2:2), are the kind of statements made in the apostolic writings to show the exclusiveness of the fixation on Christ alone. This is the basis of true Christian faith.

(5) Actions Affected (3:3b)

purifies himself, just as He is pure.

Anytime there is a meaningful, genuine focus of the kind of **hope** in Christ that is described, there must be associated with it activities or actions that demonstrate the **hope**. How then is the genuineness of this **hope** (anticipation by faith) seen? In other words, if the hope described truly has meaning to the person, then it will unquestionably make a difference in the person's actions. Notice that John makes no exceptions. He says **everyone**, meaning that if any person has this kind of hope, he will be affected in his actions. The action that the person will have is defined as **purifying himself**. The word **purifying** (*hagnizō*) means "to make ceremonially clean." This purification is a reflection back to the Old Testament sacrificial system and fits with the words of Paul in Romans 12:1: "present your body a living sacrifice." The idea is to make a conscious and powerful effort for one to be presentable to Christ. The doctrinal role of sanctification spoken of by Paul (Rom. 6:22; 8:29–30) as a part of the whole process of salvation serves to identify the children of God. The mood is right now. The person is not waiting, not *hesitating,* but has such **hope fixed on** Christ that he is taking immediate action to do what he can to be prepared to meet Him. This focus of his faith takes top priority in his actions. This priority does not mean the person believes he can purify himself by his own power. What it does mean is that there is a priority to "work out your own salvation," while at the same time recognizing, "it is God who is at work in you" (Phil. 2:12–13). The person is being sanctified, set apart, in Christ. God is at work in his life.

Referring back to the **now we are children of God** of verse 3:2, John again places the emphasis on the actions taking place for the child of God in the present. Salvation is never something in the *"sweet by and by."* The person who has truly been touched by God, and transformed as His own child, starts on a different road than the one on which he was previously engaged. The action begins at the moment of change. Here John states: **And everyone who has this hope fixed on Him purifies himself, just as He is pure (3:3).** The passage is very specific to the action of the one who is in Christ with his hope on Him. For someone to have his hope fixed on Christ, and yet continue to live as he has always lived, would be impossible. The people of the world have no concern to purify themselves in the likeness of Christ. The word **purifies** is *hagnizō*, meaning "to make properly clean," with a *reflection* back to all the ceremonial washing ordinances necessary to enter the holy places under the Old Testament laws. Just as the priest entering the holy place (in the presence of God), had to purify himself physically, so must every Christian be working toward this likeness of Christ whereby he is dealing with personal sins and traits of sinful behavior that are contrary to Christ. The change of the true Christian from his old self to his new self generates a concern for the desires of his new Master. This process is sanctification. He sets out to know God in His Word, and prepares himself to meet Christ, not just because he is commanded to do so, but because his entire perspective has changed since his conversion. He is now focused on Christ, and Christ is the most important person in the new life.

Pause and Reflect

To think that a person changed in Christ and having his hope fixed on Him, would someday stand before Him in judgment with a history of continuance in the same sinful mindset, inappropriate behavior, and disobedient patterns that characterized them prior to conversion, would be illogical. From the standpoint of the test that John is administering, he is stating that there is a focus on Christ where true conversion has taken place. With this focus, an obvious effort and energy is being spent toward growth in the likeness of Christ, and with it, a life characterized by genuine concern to please Him. This growth is the earmark of God's work in sanctification of the person. This is the evidence of the work of God.

> Where it is not seen, we see the converse, that is, the evidence that no true conversion has taken place.

b. Our Propriety (3:4–6)

As we have noted, the priority for those who have a true relationship with God is changed. With that focus resides a natural conformity to new standards of behavior. As sin is the dominating factor in the life of all people born under Adam, the change to a relationship with God must affect this dominating factor. How or to what degree is that domination affected?

(1) Association to Sin (3:4)

Everyone who practices sin also practices lawlessness; and sin is lawlessness.

John first uses the word *pas* (**everyone**), which has two basic usages: "the entire number of" and "those of every sort." The NASB has appropriately translated the word here as **everyone**. The opposite of this would be Romans 3:23: "All [*pas*] have sinned and fall short of the glory of God." The idea is that it includes **everyone**, and there are no exceptions.

The next word in the sentence brings a qualifier. **Practices** (*poieō*), means "to band together with and make or do in a continuous manner." The idea is who the Christian is in his *manner* of life. It is something dear to him, and that he is seriously enjoined with so that he is willingly participating by deliberate action. The person practicing sin in this manner is being mastered by it, and his desire is so affected as to be controlled by it. He has a strong association with sin, so much so that it defines him.

When **everyone** is placed in front of **who practices sin**, any possibility of exception is eliminated. In other words, John says that **everyone** who practices sin as the standard and continual manner of his life, without exception, is practicing **lawlessness**. The word **lawlessness** (*anomia*) means "violation of the law" (here it is the laws of righteousness that God has decreed, or that which is different than His character), so that it is every form of wickedness or unrighteousness that is *contrary* to God. It cannot be considered innocent because it is that which is opposing God. In 2 Thessalonians 2:3 and 7, it is used as one who stands in direct *opposition* to Christ. It can also be thought of in the context of 1 John 2:18 as those who function as "antichrists." John goes on to say **and sin is lawlessness**. In Matthew 7:23, the Lord on judgment day denies those claiming they did things in His name by stating that they were those who "practiced lawlessness" (same word again); such are the unsaved. John wants to make clear that sin is absolutely and completely an offense against God. The weight of sin is such that it cannot be excused or smoothed over, and those engaged in sin are described as those who **practice** it and cannot, therefore, be born again.

> ### Pause and Reflect
>
> John wants us to know that everyone who practices sin is offending God in total culpability. He is working contrary to and against God as his enemy. His inclusion of everyone focuses on the fact that all people are either in one camp or the other. There is no neutral ground. All those who are under the yoke of being mastered and controlled by sin to the degree described as its practice are in the opposition camp. There is no comfortable position, according to this one verse, of those who love their sin, and continue in the practice of sin, while claiming they are Christians. Therefore, the idea that the Christian and sin go together does not fit. What John goes on to say will make this practical understanding even clearer.

(2) Antithesis of Sin (3:5)

You know that He appeared in order to take away sins; and in Him there is no sin.

John has stated that everyone who practices sin as a manner of life demonstrates his opposition to God. So what is the antithesis of sin? Christ. He has no association with it, nor can He have any kind of association with it ("In Him is no darkness at all," 1 John 1:5), except for His one-time occurrence: **He appeared in order to take away sin. He appeared** (came to the earth as a man), and although He was innocent Himself, He took sin in His own body on the cross (2 Cor. 5:21). He became sin for those He would save. The sin He bore did not remain with Him, but was defeated as He physically suffered and died—He **[took] away sin**. The idea of taking away sin means that He eliminated sin altogether, and thereby the consequences of sin (death, eternal separation from God), are also eliminated. He did not come to make sin acceptable—some claim that the extended meaning of grace is a form of indulgence. Nor did He just take away the ramifications of sin so that the person "in Christ" is merely by position only in Christ for eternity, but not necessarily changed. John states **in Him there is no sin**, and the previous passage states "we will be like Him" (3:2). Ultimately, the person who is truly a child of God will be "sinless."

This sinless state cannot be referring only to a positional redemption, but a complete removal of sin, or the complete elimination of sin. However, in 3:3, this idea is spoken of as a **hope**. This idea means that the ultimate sinless condition is real, but is also future in the glorified state. The argument John is making is not, therefore, an argument for being "sinless" in this life, but an argument for a radical change in this life that points expectantly and longingly toward a sinless condition in the glorified state.

On the one hand the position of man hopelessly attached to and in love with his sin is seen in verse 4. The contrast in verse 5 shows that Christ was sinless and came for the very purpose of taking away sin. This fact has ramifications in the immediate, and the future. It is verse 6 that ties these two ideas into the relevant now; the life of the Christian fighting the good fight of faith.

(3) Antagonistic to God (3:6)

No one who abides in Him sins; no one who sins has seen Him or knows Him.

John says **no one**, which is again a regulatory term of complete exclusion. **No one who abides** (see comments 2:6) **in Him sins**. This is a present indicative in the Greek, which carries the idea of on-going activity or the perpetual, deliberate habit of continuance in sin (as defined by "practices" in verse 4). This one who sins is someone continually doing that which is contrary to God and His nature. John is emphatically stating, in a manner that cannot be disputed, that for the person in this category to really be a Christian, is impossible. The person who **abides** is the one continuing in the faith of Christ. The person who has **seen Him** carries the idea of really understanding and perceiving who He is. The person who **knows Him** is one who has more than information, rather, real knowledge that can only come through relationship. These terms provide no room for anything but true salvation, the new birth, and the regenerative work of God in the person resulting in a life that is in a disassociation with sin. As already seen in verse 1:10, and elaborated on by the Apostle Paul in Romans 6:3–18, this life is not a life that is sinless, but one in which the Christian exercises an overcoming degree of power over sin.

> **Pause and Reflect**
>
> John has shown that Christ is sinless, and those who claim Him as their Savior must in their actions demonstrate a change from their natural association with sin to an association that is likened to Christ. This difference is seen in the manner of the person's life. This is their sanctification process. The characteristic of those who do not have a relationship with Christ is habitual sin. Christ came to eliminate sin, and He will make all of His children sinless in glorification. For now, though, there is a radical change. Those who truly know Christ are not practicing sin in the same manner as those who do not know Christ. Those who have come to faith in Christ act and react differently toward sin than they did prior to their conversion. To be truly associated with Christ, while at the same time being unchanged, is impossible. The mark of the true Christian is seen in his changed life, a life that no longer drinks in sinful behavior, or practices sin as if there has been no encounter with Christ. John states that another of the proofs of true Christianity is how a person handles sin in his life. If the life continues to be ruled by sin, then there cannot have been a true conversion. The person ruled by sin is not engaged in God's sanctification. If one is not involved in sanctification, then what evidence is there that he has been involved in justification, or ultimately will be engaged in glorification? Sanctification is the process of Christ-likeness that is to take place in this present life in every Christian (Rom. 8:29–30). If it is not taking place, then there is no basis for thinking there is justification or there will be future glorification.

c. Our Production (3:7–8)

(1) Association with God (3:7)

Little children, make sure no one deceives you; the one who practices righteousness is righteous, just as He is righteous;

In contrast to those who practice sin, which has been his focus on the negative side of the argument, John now addresses the positive side or righteous side of the saved. The phrase **little children** has already been discussed (2:12) as a term of those "begotten of God," the truly elect. It is a term of endearment for those new in the faith, those seeking, learning, and understanding the things of God. This phrase fits the concern of the writer as he says to **make sure no one deceives you**. The world is filled with deception, and even the professing church is a place where deception often takes place. The word for **deceive** (*planaō*) means to seduce or roam from safety. Satan (the prince of this world) is called the deceiver (Rev. 20:10), for deception is what he is about, and his end is to be cast into the lake of fire (hell) along with all those deceived. Deception, then, is a very hideous thing to be shunned with all effort. John is deeply concerned, and knows that the remedy for deception is precisely what he is doing under the inspiration of God. The Bible, rightly understood, is the antidote to all the deception that comes from every other source. Here, the deception refers to the fact that someone can be a true child of God, and continue to practice unrighteousness as though it makes no difference.

Not only does the one who is truly of Christ act *differently* in his relation to the practice of sin (vv. 4–6), but from the positive side he practices **righteousness**. Whereas, the general trend of the life of the person outside of Christ is the practice of sin, the general trend of the life of the Christian is the practice of **righteousness**. The basis of this is the fact that **He** (Christ) **is righteous**. While the person outside of Christ is associated with sin, the person truly of Christ is associated with Christ, who is **righteous.** Those who are truly of Christ cannot possibly be attracted to Him if there is not at least some affinity toward **righteousness.** John is merely making the reasonable argument that no person can lay a claim to Christ unless he also demonstrates a desire for, and appreciation for righteousness. Christ and righteousness go together, and therefore, true Christianity and righteousness go together. To put it concisely, those who are in the family of the living God act like it. Paul puts it this way in Galatians 6:17: "I bear on my body the brand marks of Jesus." He shows his kinship to Christ by what he does and how he lives. What the true Christian produces in his life is righteousness. That is the trend of the life in conformity to the revealed will of God. This, again, addresses the sanctification process in every Christian. The Christian wants to live pleasing to Christ and makes pleasing Him the priority of his life. To believe otherwise is to be deceived.

(2) Association with Satan (3:8)

the one who practices sin is of the devil; for the devil has sinned from the beginning. The Son of God appeared for this purpose, to destroy the works of the devil.

John continues to elaborate on the production of activity in the life as being very telling. Christ also stated, "You will know them by their fruits" (Matt. 7:20). Not only does the Christian produce fruits unto righteousness, but also, those who habitually practice sin are **of the devil**. This statement is a most damning and clarifying statement. Everyone is either, by association, with Christ or with the devil. There is no neutral position, person, or place of association. According to Christ, "He who is not with Me is against Me" (Matt. 12:30). Christ told the unbelieving Jews that they were of their "father the devil" (John 8:44). A person's associations, or who a person is most comfortable being around, is reflected with no real surprises by the person he most acts like. Each person is either prone to act like Christ, or to act like the devil.

John states that Satan **has sinned from the beginning**. His nature is evil, and he practices every form of sin. Those who act just as he acts belong to him. In contrast, **the Son of God appeared for this purpose, to destroy the works of the devil (3:8)**. This statement is very revealing. The modern movement in Christianity is to create new theologies that accept man continuing in the practice of sin, and taking lightly the vileness of man's behavior, even though Christ's purpose is to **destroy the works of the devil**. Paul clearly makes this same argument in Romans 6:1–4, where he explains the relationship of works to grace. The person under grace is transformed by the defeat of sin on the cross. By contrast, the works of the devil continue through those unsaved. The vileness of sin demanded that the Son of God die in order to facilitate its defeat. Therefore, there is nothing in Christianity about being saved *in* sin, but instead, being saved *from* sin. There is a radical change of direction by those in Christ. Their life is not one of perfection, but it is a life that reflects change. The true Christian demonstrates this change. How can one who has experienced true conversion keep *wallowing* in sin? He cannot. If he continues in sin, he clearly demonstrates that conversion has not taken place, and his real association is still with Satan.

Pause and Reflect

There is nothing unclear here: either a person is practicing a life of righteous behavior (not perfection, but a trend or general direction), or he is living the habitual practice of sin that is contrary to God. How he lives is a personal demonstration of the reality of his faith and the reality of his sanctification, or the absence of both. A true Christian is seen manifesting a general defeat of sin, and therefore, manifests an association with God. By contrast, true Christianity is absent if what is seen in the life is the habitual practice of sin. If the latter is true, one's association is not with Christ but with Satan.

d. Our Proof (3:9–10)

(1) Affiliation in God (3:9)

No one who is born of God practices sin, because His seed abides in him; and he cannot sin, because he is born of God.

The Christian life is depicted in the Bible quite differently than in many of the popular churches and prominent Christian (so-called) movements of modern time. Most of Christianity has moved the focus of the Bible from Christ to personal interests. Preaching against sin has virtually become a non-issue, as it simply does not fit the pattern of self-indulgence and ear tickling characteristics of the modern church message. The challenge to find mercy with Christ has been replaced with the challenge to find happiness, success, and prosperity. The modern theological view of God is that He loves everyone, and wants foremost for people to be happy. The picture is painted of God as a genie who wants to bless everyone, but cannot because it is a matter of *so-called* right thinking. This thinking has replaced true biblical faith. Thinking right begins by believing that happiness can be found by ridding oneself of negative thoughts, and by believing that a person can have "his best life now." Included with this thinking is the ability to gain the world as it now exists. This kind of belief, however, is absolutely contrary to the Word of God. This commentary began by assessing the modern church movement. Now the text arrives at a place that is diametrically opposed to the "prosperity gospel," which is not the Gospel, but is prominent and is thought of by many as the gospel in these last times. John does not bring *a person's current happiness* into the argument, but his affliction is identified as a mark of the true Christian.

In Matthew 5 are the beatitudes of the Lord Jesus. "Blessed are the poor in Spirit, for theirs is the kingdom of heaven; blessed are those who mourn, for they shall be comforted" (Matt. 5:3–4). Christ pictures those who are blessed as the poorest, sickest, most afflicted, and most troubled. Why are they the most troubled? They are the most troubled because they do not fit with the world's philosophy, goals, and ideals. They do not fit the world system because **His seed abides in (3:9)** them. These are associated with Christ, not with the world. Thus, because Christ was a man of sorrows and acquainted with grief (Is. 53:3), they are associated with the same. Christ suffered as a man because of sin. Those who are poor in Spirit and mourn are those who do so because of sin. Sin is the powerful opposition force against the Lord's people. John has already shown that those who practice sin are of the devil (1 John 3:8). They are associated with Satan and therefore act as they do; they do not mourn over their sin, but drink in sin like water. John says the same in a positive way: **No one who is born of God practices sin**. This statement is one of the most emphatic statements in all of Scripture. It effectively eliminates the modern idea of the "carnal Christian." The "carnal Christian" theology, accepted as fact in most churches, states that one can be a Christian and live indefinitely as if he is not a Christian. He can live as a Christian in a state of practicing sin. This belief is at the root of the modern doctrines that focus on having "a person's best life now." Righteousness under such theology is not important.

In the phrase **born of God, born** is *gennaō*, "to make,""conceive," or "bring forth." The concept is found in John 3 where Christ is speaking to Nicodemus. The exact phrase is repeated in 1 John 2:29; 4:7; 5:1; 5:4; 5:18; and Acts 13:33. It is also translated "begotten," the idea of a unique, *supernatural* work of God. Theologians call this *regeneration*. The affiliation is that this one spoken of is **born of God**. The ramifications of this birth are shown in verse 10 where John states: "By this the children of God . . . are obvious." Why are they obvious? It is because something supernatural has occurred in them. They were once affiliated only with Satan because of sin, but now, they have been **born of God**. For this reason they cannot practice sin. God does not sin, and therefore, those born of Him therefore cannot practice sin. Remember that **practices**–(*poieō*) means "to band together with, and make or do in a continuous manner." The concept is not that Christians never sin, but that sin is not the *rule* of their life. The idea here of practicing sin (band together with sin), is to be in union with sin, in effect, carrying on a love relationship with sin, and thereby being controlled by sin.

The Christian, however, is in union with Christ. John gives this reason: **because His seed abides in him (3:9)**. **Seed** is *sperma*, "the male side of conception". It is associated with the production of life. Here the life of God is, therefore, within this person. Some theologians dispute whether this is referring to the Word of God or the Holy Spirit (James 1:18; 1 Pet. 1:23). In these passages the seed is the act of sowing, referring to the work of the Word. The Word is *essential*, but what John is referring to is what is stated by Christ in John 3:7–8: "born of the Spirit." *Both* the Word of God and the Spirit of God are essential in the new birth. This concept is stated in Ephesians 1:13–14, where the Holy Spirit seals believers after they have listened to the Word. In Romans 8:9, the fact that the Holy Spirit lives within the true Christian is a reality for all who are **born of God**. John states clearly that anyone who is really born of God will lead a lifestyle unidentifiable from the lifestyle of those of the world, which is a life characterized by sin. In this regard, the one **born of God** has no affiliation with the world system.

As if to reiterate the emphatic statement, John further expresses **and he cannot sin, because he is born of God**. The reference to **cannot sin** must refer back to the **[practice]** of sinning, not the fact that sin will be an intermittent part of life as long as the person is in the fallen world and not yet in a glorified body. **Cannot** is *ou dunatai*, which literally means "not able." John concludes that the ability to continue practicing sin is *impossible*. Because God has done a work in the person (a work continuing in sanctification), it is not feasible that someone born of God would be able to continue to practice sin.

The word **abides** (*menō*) is also a key to understanding this passage. The word means "to remain or to continue." God's seed (the Holy Spirit) does not produce a regenerate life, and then walk away or become lazy or unconcerned within the person. If there is a true new birth whereby His Spirit has entered, then the Spirit remains within and continues with vitality in the person. This understanding is related to the doctrine of *perseverance of the saints* (Rom. 8:29–30; Phil. 1:6; 1 Pet. 1:5). This concept is a practical reality in the Scripture. For example, after David sinned, he was in complete misery (Ps. 32). Why was he miserable? His sin was contrary to his nature and totally disagreeable to him. Even if a person could sear his conscience, and grieve the Spirit to such a degree that for a time he acts like an unbeliever, there is still the issue of God's discipline to His wayward child (Heb. 12:4; 14). He will not allow continuance in sin.

Pause and Reflect

A lifestyle of sin does not fit a true Christian. For a true Christian to continue in sin in the same manner as a non-believer is impossible. The lack of continuance in sin is not because the Christian tries harder, or merely disciplines himself, but instead, because the Holy Spirit of God resides within him. Because the Christian has undergone a new birth, he is now a new creation in Christ (2 Cor. 5:17). He is set apart by God and actively engaged in God's sanctification process (Rom. 6:22). The Christian's union is with Christ, not with sin. The lifestyle of the Christian will not be perfect, but it will become increasingly more like Christ.

(2) Activity of God (3:10)

By this the children of God and the children of the devil are obvious: anyone who does not practice righteousness is not of God, nor the one who does not love his brother.

By this (by the actual fact of a lifestyle that the person is practicing), **the children of God and the children of the devil are obvious**. The proof, therefore, of kinship to the Father (God) or to the devil is made obvious either by the lack of the practice of sin in the life, or by the practice of sin in the life. In this passage there are only two possibilities. Either, one is a child of God, or he is a child of the devil. The word for **children** is *teknon*, meaning "offspring or family relationship." The determination of the family *kinship* is demonstrated by the actions of the children. When children are observed, their strong family resemblance to parents is often obvious. In this passage is the same kinship. **Obvious** is *phaneros,* which literally means "to shine." The kinship is apparent and manifested to all - the children are of God or the devil. Kinship can be determined through observation. Phillips Petroleum Company has had a slogan for years that sums up this idea: "It is performance that counts." A person's performance or actions eliminate all pretenses, tricks, smokescreens, or hustlers, just as Christ stated, "by their fruits you shall know them" (Matt. 7:16, 20).

Ultimately, this idea points to the work of God in a person's activity or lack thereof. If the person is of God, that is, born again, and has God's seed abiding in him, the fruit of that reality will be shown in the life and be obvious to all. This concept is so emphatic and absolute that John repeats it to show this is always a consistent reality: **anyone who does not practice righteousness is not of God (3:10)**. He introduces something of a new element. Not only does the one "born of God" not practice sin, but now John says the one who is of God is not in some sort of neutral position. He must practice righteousness. The **"anyone"** shows the inclusive nature of this statement. There are no exceptions, not even one. Making the statement in a negative fashion (**who does not practice righteousness**) shows the *power* behind the work of God in the heart. No person who has had a work accomplished in his heart can be living life without the practice of righteousness. Again, be reminded that John is addressing the general trend of the life, not necessarily the life at any given moment. A true Christian is not identifiable as a Christian at one specific moment anymore than a non-Christian is identified by one particular moment. Rather, he is identified by the overall trend of his life. Observing a righteous trend will clearly identify him as belonging to Christ.

At this point, one might bring up Judas. Judas was not seen, except by Christ, as a false brother from the beginning. There were earmarks along the way, such as John 12:4–5 (anointing of Christ by Mary). In this situation, Judas pretended he was concerned about Mary's extravagance and the poor, insisting that the proceeds from selling the oil could have been given to the poor. This was a smokescreen for his greedy heart. But the lack of genuineness of Judas in comparison to the other disciples was still not clearly seen. This was true because the other disciples were generally in a state of confusion and error about many things that Christ was doing. Keep in mind that these accounts were before the giving of the indwelling Holy Spirit. The Holy Spirit working in the life of every true believer is producing the life of sanctification (Rom. 8:9), and thus, the evidence of which John is addressing.

John does not stop with the practice of righteousness. At the end of verse 10 he introduces **love**, which must also be present in the same manner as righteousness. In the activity and work of God, righteousness and love always go together. The word for love is *agapaō* (noun *agapē*), the highest form of love, "sacrificial love." John writes: **nor the one who does not love his brother**. That statement builds on the impossibility of one being a genuine child of God, and not practicing righteousness. John states just as emphatically that if one does not love his brother, then that person cannot be born of God. One might argue that to practice true righteousness love must always be included. This theme of love, as an undeniable indication of the activity of God, is fully developed in the verses that follow.

Pause and Reflect

As the reader continues to look carefully at an epistle that is intended to bring to light, and to define who is of God and who is not of God, John draws a distinct line between those who practice righteousness and those who do not. A Christian cannot move through life practicing unrighteous behavior in the manner of the unsaved. Nor can a Christian move through life being in a state of neutrality to his life's activities. John proclaims that practicing righteousness is an undeniable indication that a person is born of God. By contrast, not practicing righteousness is an undeniable indication that a person is not born of God. This can be expressed as a mathematical

> equation or maxim. This equation carried out shows that God must be producing righteousness in the person. God's activity makes it a reality. The converse to this reality is also true. If no practice of righteousness is seen, then the evidence indicates that God is not present in the person.

2. Practicing Love (3:10b–24)

a. The Distinction Exemplified (3:10b–16)

A professing Christian with good intention once told me that he really did not know why a person needed the entire Bible. He thought only one verse was necessary, and that verse was John 3:16. He reasoned from this verse that all that any person needed to know is that God loves him and that he must simply believe in God. Many people oversimplify, not only John 3:16 but also, the understanding of God's character, purpose, plan, and work. This kind of shallow thinking has moved into the church and affected the understanding of the Gospel, as well as the whole counsel of God found in the Bible. Sufficient glorious truths concerning God are given in the Bible, and all are essential for our understanding (cf. 2 Tim. 3:16). People will spend eternity growing in their knowledge of God.

Christianity is the only religion that has **love (3:10b)** as a core value, but the problem of addressing love is to really grasp and develop what is actually meant by God's love. After all, if just ten people were questioned on the street about their definition of love, each definition would be different from the others, and different from how the Bible defines it. There are in most minds ideas pertaining to love as emotion, preference, sentiment, kinship, patriotism, romance, sex, and so forth, and all are mixed with each person's experience. Later, John writes that "God is love" (that is, part of His character, 4:8). He further describes love in 4:10 by the sacrifice of God's own Son. Only by looking seriously and in depth at the crushing of Christ on the cross, can anyone begin to soberly grasp the real meaning of God's kind of love. Christ's death on the cross was the greatest act of love ever expressed, and it bears the power and standard of God's love. It also challenges the reader to view His love as a complete, self-sacrificing of that which is dearest and most precious. The objects of Christ's love are undeserving sinners, even enemies (Rom. 5:10). Everyone must prayerfully consider this concept to truly begin to see biblical love. God has this kind of love as a necessary essential for His children. God does not merely love sinners, but He changes sinners to love as He loves. The presence of love is another mark of the sanctification that must be taking place in every true child of God.

The idea of brotherly love is personified in Romans 14:15, where Christians are disputing with one another over incidental matters of the conscience. One Christian (a brother) is concerned about what he eats, and another is not. The one who is not concerned is required to be more concerned about his brother's feelings than his own feelings or rights. Because of love, he should be more concerned about not troubling his brother than having his personal comforts or preferences. In thinking on this concept, the reader must measure everything against the clarity of to whom it was written. In Romans 14:15, Paul is focusing uniquely on those, as he states, "for whom Christ died." The weight of the argument is built on the relationship between God and those specifically *for whom* Christ died. This statement is one of the strongest in Scripture for understanding particular atonement in the Bible. If the argument were that a person should be concerned about how he treats just anyone (not a brother in Christ), then this statement "for whom Christ died" would not be applicable. Particular atonement means that Christ died for a specific people, His elect (all who would demonstrate true faith or be born again). God, for reasons known only to Him, determined to save some out of all humanity (Eph. 1:3–14; Rom. 8:29–30). Christ did not pay the penalty for all people on the cross (as many think John 3:16 declares); otherwise, all would be saved. However, He is moving in history to save every soul He predetermined to save (John 6:39; Eph. 1:4). Particular atonement makes God's love special for all of His own (John 17), and better defines the specific nature of the Christian's own relationship, not only with God, but also with the brethren.

The uniqueness of love in a particular manner is also seen in the relationship between a husband and wife. If the nature of spousal love is what it should be, the husband has a greater love for his wife than for any other woman, and the wife for her husband more than for any other man. That relationship of love is special. So is the relationship between Christ and His church (Eph. 5:25). Therefore, if anyone claiming to be a Christian acts in a manner that could be described as hate for someone for whom Christ died (the evidence being by the manner he is treating the other person), he is working against God, pitted against God's plan, His church, and His glorious work. Therefore, as John states, the lack of a demonstration of love becomes a witness as to whether someone is born of God or not.

The word **brother** (*adelphos*) literally means "a community relationship based on identity of origin." **Brother**, in this context, is not speaking of physical siblings, but by origin of life within the family of God. The same is true of all persons in the family of God, whether male or female. Males are often used as a metaphor for all mankind. These are spoken of as persons who are born of God. They are now brothers spiritually because of their new birth. Their new birth is evident because, as Romans 14:15 states, they are those "for whom Christ died," and **His seed abides in them**, showing that they are loved of God. As they are loved of God and kindred through Him, John therefore, emphatically proclaims: **nor the one who does not love his brother** (as defined) cannot then be truly of God. The reality of God's **"seed abides in Him"** (1 John 3:9) is a seed that accomplishes a heart change resulting in loving God and the brethren. By this change, hate co-existing with the love described, is impossible.

(1) Critical from the Beginning (3:11)

For this is the message which you have heard from the beginning, that we should love one another;

The concept of love for the brethren is not new. It was a critical command of God from the very beginning. It has decisive importance to God. When Cain killed Abel and God asked him, "Where is Abel, your brother?" (Gen.4:9), God was granting opportunity for repentance. Love was in the question as God knew what Cain had done. The phrase **from the beginning** reminds us that God revealed, in the earliest of revelations, that He was to be loved (Deut. 6:5), and He commanded Israel to do the same to neighbors, aliens, strangers, and sojourners (Lev. 19:18; Deut. 10:18–19). Christ clarifies this requirement of love as an identifying mark in John 13:34–35. Christ states it as something ne, because Jews had twisted their understanding that Israel was to be identified with Jehovah through ritual and laws, when in reality they were to be known as *lovers* of God, and their fellow man. Paul states in Titus 1:5: "The goal of our instruction is love." Therefore, if there is no *transformation* of heart whereby love is truly shown, the instruction has not met its intended purpose.

(2) Contrasted (3:12)

not as Cain, *who* was of the evil one and slew his brother. And for what reason did he slay him? Because his deeds were evil, and his brother's were righteous.

John goes back to the very beginning to show that the true depth of man's condition is not one of natural love, but of sin. The first man born of a woman was a murderer. John makes a contrast with what he is referring to as the love of Christ compared against the attitude and action of Cain. Cain showed not even the least glimmer of love. He was not just a murderer, but a murderer of his own physical brother, and one who murdered for selfish, jealous reasons.

When John writes **not as**, he provides a negative example so that there can be no excuse or misunderstanding of his words. What is the explanation? Cain **was of the evil one**; his affiliation was not with God but with Satan. He showed the same vile nature of hideous sin, and the irrationality of extreme hate, by jealously destroying his own brother. What is Satan like? Christ states in John 8:44 that he is a murderer. Paul says he is constantly "scheming" evil (2 Cor. 2:11), and is "blinding minds" (2 Cor. 4:4). Peter says that Satan goes about "seeking to devour" (1 Pet. 5:8). He is a deceitful monster (Rev. 12:9). There is no good in him. So, the first description of Satan is by the example of the first man born in mankind, and he demonstrates the same nature as Satan. Not only did Cain commit the act of murder (as Satan), but his reason for doing so was because **his deeds were evil and his brother's deeds were righteous**. Instead of a motive of love, his was jealousy. Abel was slain for *no real reason.* One could state that Abel was slain by a negative definition of "grace" completely contrary to God's form of "grace," not in love, but in hate. The motive for killing Abel was simple hatred, the opposite of love. It is easy to see the constant friction between **evil** and **righteousness** throughout fallen human history. Here, also, **from the beginning,** is the first indication that sinful man hates the light just as Satan. He also acts as Satan hating the truth (John 3:19–20). Just as mankind from the fall became a vessel of **evil** instead of **righteousness**, so Satan is a vessel of hate, evil, and not of love.

Pause and Reflect

There is a dramatic contrast between the natural man, as viewed by looking at Cain and his hatred motivated by jealousy, and Christ's complete sacrifice of love on the cross on behalf of the undeserving. Because of the work of Christ, the Christian, bearing the name of Christ and His seed within himself, will and must bear the same kind of love as his new Master. John makes the distinction that these differences between love and hate are obvious and revealing. The person who knows Christ because of the

> "new birth," will love his brother. The person who does not really know Christ will be like Cain, capable of hating his brother.

(3) Corrupted Expectation (3:13)

Do not be surprised, brethren, if the world hates you.

Do not be surprised, brethren, if the world hates you. Why would John make such a statement? First, it follows on the heels of the example of Cain and Abel. Cain hated Abel because Abel's deeds were righteous. Cain's reaction was irrational, but that is the condition of man in sin and it has not changed. If it was so from the first child born, and since man's nature is unchanged, why should we be surprised about hatred against true Christianity that existed then, and continues today?

John is continuing to prove his point concerning who is of God and who is not. One of the chief consistent marks of the saved is love, while one of the chief consistent marks of the unsaved is hate. The Lord Jesus Christ addressed this very issue to John and the other disciples in John 15:18–19: "If the world (a metaphor here for the unsaved in the world) hates you, you know that it has hated Me before it hated you. If you were of the world (still held captive by the system of evil under the curse), the world would love its own, but because you are not of the world, but I chose you out of the world, because of this the world hates you." Further into the text, Christ states: "They hated Me without a cause" (15:25). This hatred of the world towards the Christian is not because the Christian has done something worthy of offense, but solely because of his attachment to Christ and His righteousness. Christ made this statement so that those chosen of Him would understand that the world will not naturally appreciate or love them. Instead, the world will naturally hate them. He said this to prepare them for what would lie ahead in their ministry. The same is true today.

Pause and Reflect

Only the Christian who is taught from God's Word can understand why the unsaved of the world act irrationally by living in destructive sin. They are enemies of Christ and of His people. They naturally envy and hate the righteousness of God. This animosity is one of the reasons there is so much counterfeit in many mainstream churches. These churches are trying desperately to get along with unsaved people and with their agenda. The

> problem is that the unsaved agenda is contrary to God and His truth. These churches focus on the idea that God loves everyone equally, which is a twisting of several passages. This satisfies the conscience of the unsaved to convince them that God loves them, despite their hatred of Him and their defiance of His revealed ways. Even sinful perversions (Rom. 1:26–27; 1 Cor. 6:9–10; 1 Tim. 1:10), are ignored and accepted under the guise of love. The thinking of those taking compromising positions is; had God told Cain that regardless of his rebellion, He loved and accepted him anyway, Cain would not have been as envious, and likely would not have murdered his brother (Gen. 4:5–6). Such perverted thinking is promoting an effort to have the church get along with the world. However, God does not love evil, nor does He excuse the workers of evil (John 3:36). Christian love only belongs to the person who has received the new life in Christ. Love will not be present except where God has worked. Hatred of God, His Word, and His people is natural and consistent in the unsaved man. This hatred for God will show itself in every form of disobedience. Not every unsaved person will show his hatred or opposition of God to the same degree, but it will always exist.

(4) Contrasts Providing Proof (3:14–15)

We know that we have passed out of death into life, because we love the brethren. He who does not love abides in death. Everyone who hates his brother is a murderer; and you know that no murderer has eternal life abiding in him.

We know is a strong phrase expressing the absolute assurance indicated by whether one loves the brethren. This phrase indicates a *settled conviction*. It has appeared before in 2:3 and will be seen again in 5:2. Love of the brethren in this context is the evidence, not the basis, for being a Christian. The Christian does not try to love the brethren so that he can prove he is of God, rather, he loves them because of God's work in him (sanctification). John makes this clear by the statement: **we have passed out of death into life**. Something supernatural has occurred in the Christian. He has moved from one realm to another. He has moved from the realm of spiritual death into the realm of eternal life with God. How does one know? John answers: **because we love the brethren (3:14)**. The evidence for God's courtroom is love for the brethren. This means love to all manner of brethren and that without exception. Christian love is just as natural to the converted heart as hatred is to the unconverted natural heart born under the curse.

By contrast, **he who does not love** the brethren is the antithesis of the evidence of life in God, for John says: **he . . . abides in death**. As love is an absolute evidence of true Christianity, so the absence of such love is evidence of spiritual deadness. There is no *wiggle room* here; these are both absolutes. If there is no love of the brethren, then the person is lost. This person is still dead in sins as indicated by the statement **abides in death**.

John continues his argument in verse 15: **everyone who hates his brother is a murderer (3:15)**. This is the practical common sense of the Bible. Christ Himself explained this in His *Sermon on the Mount* (Matt. 5:21–22). Not only is the actual killing of a brother physically considered murder, but a hatred carried and festering in the heart is also considered murder to God. God looks beyond the externals and at the motives of the heart (1 Sam. 16:7). The idea is that of someone harboring hate. He wishes in his heart for the other person's demise, and not his good. He therefore, has the same attitude as the person who actually commits a physical murder. Christians are to be reminded that God is not concerned with merely the keeping of externals, but He deals with the heart. The "new covenant" is a radical change of heart (Ezek. 36:26; 2 Cor. 5:17). John reasons that if this heart change has not taken place, then a person is prone to hate, and when put to the test, he commits murder in the heart. John goes on to add: **and you know that no murderer has eternal life abiding in him**. That someone with a truly changed heart would still be harboring a murderous attitude, is inconceivable and inconsistent with the work of God.

This difference between the saved and unsaved person is defined in Galatians 5:19–24, where the "deeds of the flesh" are contrasted with the "fruit of the Spirit." In speaking of the "deeds of the flesh" in verse 21, Paul states: "those who practice such things will not inherit the kingdom of God." This is an emphatic statement, and corresponds to the clear evidence that John is contrasting between love and hate, with love defining the brethren. Paul further addresses this contrast in 1 Corinthians 6:9–11. At the end of verse 10 he states again that they "will not inherit the kingdom of God." However, he is not talking about those who at one time might have had these attitudes, or committed these terrible acts, but he is referring to those who have not been changed, and are continuing to think and act accordingly. In 1 Corinthians 6:11, he states: "such were some of you; but you were washed, but you were sanctified, but you were justified in the name of the Lord Jesus Christ and in the Spirit of our God." The issue is *not what someone did in the past*, but whether or not he has experienced the "new birth." Therefore, what matters is *what he is now*. If there has been no true change of heart, then he is a murderer (in the heart), and therefore for him to have **eternal life** is impossible. **Abiding** is the same prominent word we have seen before (2:24, 27, 28). It is the Greek word *menō*, meaning "dwell with," "continue with," or "endure with." The idea of **abiding** is something lasting and real; the point being that eternal life (the life of God) *cannot* possibly dwell in the same place and at the same time as the evil attitude of murder.

> ## Pause and Reflect
>
> In making the case for who is of God and who is not of God, John continues to define issues of the heart that produce living evidence. The attitude of those who have the new birth is love for their brothers. There are no exceptions. By contrast, those who do not love the brethren show they are still dead in their sins. They have not experienced the new birth. He narrows his argument to show that love and hate *cannot* coexist. The one who does not love is not merely neutral, but hates, by degree. Hate is associated with murder, and no murderer can inherit God's kingdom. Again, there are *no exceptions*. John's words are not an admonition to love, but rather, a statement of fact defining who is truly a Christian and who is not by the evidence of his love, or hatred for the brethren.

(5) Christ's Right Example (3:16)

We know love by this, that He laid down His life for us; and we ought to lay down our lives for the brethren.

Now that John has shown that love must be present if one is to know that he is a true Christian, he now moves to specifically define what he means by love. The key phrase here is: **we know love by this**. How does the reader know the kind of love that John is referring to as necessary from all the superficial ideas of love that are being portrayed in society, and even in many churches today? The definition of love must be taken from the example of Christ. Christ's real life example shows what is intended by the love stated by John, and the difference between the love of God for the saved, and the love of God for the unsaved. The Christian's *measure for love* must be the standard set by God. It cannot be the standard set by anyone else, or in any other manner.

What then did Christ do? **He laid down His life for us**. The magnitude of who He is, being the Son of God, adds infinite weight to this simple statement. However, the aspect of His deity does not appear to be John's primary focus here as it was in his Gospel. Taken at face value it is the idea that Christ *put Himself last*. He did what He did on behalf of the brethren. The **us** must, in context, refer to those who have true saving faith (1 John 3:1; 2 Pet. 1:1). He placed all of His own prerogatives, rights, comforts, and what He deserved, aside on behalf of others. He laid these aside in order to benefit others. He received nothing in personal human benefit from the suffering of the cross. Yes, He benefited in the sense of honoring the will of God (Heb. 12:2), but the actual event of the cross could not be seen in any manner as reasonable in terms of personal benefit. He allowed Himself to be sacrificed on behalf of others.

This example of love becomes the standard for every Christian in relation to every other Christian. This is the opposite of Cain's actions, and of man's natural, selfish nature, being born in the same sinful mold as Cain. In order for a person to be like Christ in his manner toward others, he must have received an outside supernatural work to "become partakers of the divine nature" (2 Pet. 1:4). To act like Christ, instead of like Cain would be impossible in man's natural condition. First, to act like Christ *is not desired* by the natural man any more than it was by Cain. Second, it cannot be *manufactured* as it is contrary to the natural sinful *nature* of all men. Man must understand that he cannot of himself manufacture and carry out this type of love. Recognizing this helps one to understand the magnitude of what is stated next.

We ought to lay down our lives for the brethren (3:16) is John's statement on how we are to love. The word **ought** has confused many commentators at this point. In the usual interpretation of **ought**, one would think this is something that is optional, and the statement thus becomes an admonition. This interpretation is stated like this: a Christian should, even though he often does not, put himself second to the brethren as Christ did. However, a closer examination of this passage shows that this is not an admonition, at least in its primary use. The word **ought** in the Greek is *opheilō*, which means "to owe" or "to be under obligation." It is translated most often "owe" in the New Testament. It is also translated "indebted." Because of what Christ has done, and the example He has set, John is saying that *the Christian is indebted*, and is obligated before God to lay down his life on behalf of the brethren. This owing is not an option or admonition to reach a higher level of love, but instead, it is a necessity based on the reality of Christ's work; it must be paid. It is a requirement within the context of the "new birth" that the Christian is changed, not perfectly, but is growing in Christ's likeness. Christians have taken on the new nature and the Holy Spirit as an enabler. Therefore, the Christian can and does have an obligation to love as Christ loved. John is saying that this will be seen in the true Christian, at least in some measure, by how he deals with the brethren.

The **lay down our life** clause, also, must be understood from the Greek, and in relation to what Christ's attitude was in setting the example. **To lay** is *tithēmi*; to "kneel down" or to "become prostrate." The word **life** (*psuchē*) has to do with "the breath and spirit." It has reference, therefore, to the person in his *entirety*. It means that the Christian cannot merely go through the mechanics of "putting others first" when his heart is not in it. It is the idea of *placing others before self* from the inside out. This is real love. God's kind of love is sacrificial from the heart. Exercising this kind of love is not just an option for the Christian, any more than the cross was an option for Christ. Christ had to state: "not as I will, but as You will" (Matt. 26:39). He, because of His nature and heart, had no real choice. His nature, being merciful, righteous, and conformed to the will of the Father, gave Him no option. He, alone, could do what He did, and He did so because of who He is. The same is true of the real Christian doing the will of Christ instead of fulfilling personal selfish desires. This then, is the impossible standard that only God performs through those who have His Spirit. This is the *required standard* of every Christian as stated at the beginning of the argument (3:10). Again, the indication is not that the Christian will love others in perfection, but that the Christian will be moving in the same direction (or living in the general sphere) of demonstrating the same kind of love as shown by Christ.

Pause and Reflect

Our example for determining whether a person has true conversion is Christ. His example is established according to His work on the cross. One cannot merely speak of love, but know what love really means by definition when he understands Christ's sacrificial love on the cross. The weight is not on the Christian performing a glorious act such as He performed—no person could do what He did in that sense—but is on the Christian having the mind of Christ (Phil. 2:1–7; 1 Cor. 2:15–16). This state of love is presented as a means of determining whether or not one is truly born again. John says that Christians are indebted to this kind of love

> if they are in Christ, because God has performed a work for them and in them. This kind of love must be, to a significant degree, replacing the Christian's past natural selfishness.

b. The Distinction Examined (3:17–24)

After establishing parameters of whether or not a person has a relationship with Christ based on the possession of God's kind of love, John now seeks to elaborate in a personal manner these distinctions practically in the reader's life. Christ told His disciples in John 14:12 that they would do the works that He did: "He who believes in Me, the works that I do, he will do also; and greater works than these he will do." This could not be referring to the works accomplished on the cross, or even miracles, for no other person could do more miracles, and certainly not greater ones. He was obviously referring, and certainly the context bears this out, to the *work of building and ministering* in His church. The church has *expanded* greatly since His ascension, and this expansion has been done by God through the spreading of the Gospel by His followers. Christ had relatively few actual converts. Through the work of witnessing, Christ's followers have been used in the adding of significant numbers of the elect to the church. Ultimately, the Holy Spirit is the One who must enlighten the heart, but God has chosen to use people to communicate His Word. Those who believe (His church), in this sense, have accomplished greater works than Christ. Further, God's people minister to one another. The supernatural work of God in the heart changes the heart from selfishness to love.

(1) Challenge to Our Heart (3:17–18)

But whoever has the world's goods, and sees his brother in need and closes his heart against him, how does the love of God abide in him? Little children, let us not love with word or with tongue, but in deed and truth.

In verse 17, John addresses a practical scenario. To talk about love in some kind of theoretical sense is easy, but to put it into action is difficult. John informs the reader how this God kind of love is manifested by God's own people. Already discussed is man's greatest need–the Gospel. The saved of God are the ones who proclaim the Gospel. True love is this: telling people what they need to know and hear. John goes even further: **whoever has the world's goods, and sees his brother in need and closes his heart against him, how does the love of God abide in him (3:17)?**

John asks a practical question, a question that backs the reader into the corner. Notice that John does not ask the proclaiming Christian to do something that he is not reasonably able to do; **whoever has the world's goods** leaves the impression the circumstance is not necessarily a significant sacrifice. There is no indication that the Christian would have to personally go without, or his family without in order to give. Such a sacrifice, however, for the moment is not the issue. Also, not at issue, is whether or not this person with the need has led an undisciplined life (2 Thess. 3:10–12). John is not discussing the person's worthiness outside the boundaries of seeing that he has a real need, a need that the professed Christian sees, but **closes his heart**.

This Christian has *no excuse* not to meet this need. But he shows no pity or mercy for the brother in need. If this concept is applied back to Christ on the cross as our example, then no person would be saved if Christ Himself had not exercised mercy. The lesson is evident that Christians who bear the heart of Christ are expected to exercise the *same* kind of love shown by Christ. Christ had the resources to rescue man, and He sacrificially did so. The argument, then, is from the greater to the lesser. If Christ would do that for His elect, and He and His work are far greater, how then can the elect not do so for others of the elect, the lesser? How practical and providential this is! It shows the *reality* of either selfishness or love. The question is rhetorical because the answer is a given. If the Christian is truly a Christian, and has the love of Christ as has already been discussed by John, then how could he practically **[close] his heart?** The clause **how does**, in fact, shows the improbability of a true Christian as one bearing the heart of Christ, closing his heart. It is a staggering contradiction. If God's work is abiding in the heart, *love will be manifested* in righteous action.

The phrase **little children (3:18)**, is the term of endearment used repeatedly by John. The word *teknion* literally means "begotten ones of God," and its appearance here shows that John expects growth in his readers. He is bringing their conscience to bear in this telling argument. The Bible does so to expose to the readers when fraud is present. The reader is convicted when he sees that he is not measuring up to what he should be. A possibility exists that there were true Christians who had momentarily sinned in this regard, although that sin was inconsistent with their Christian lives in general. Remember, John wrote initially, "If we say we have no sin we are deceiving ourselves and the truth is not in us" (1:8). Again, John is not addressing perfection, rather *the general trends* of life, or the basic overall evidence of life. The Christian moves in one direction, and the lost person in the other.

John adds a further admonition: **Let us not love with word or with tongue, but in deed and truth (3:18)**. For one to just *theorize* or *talk* big is not enough; real love must be put into *shoe leather*. God places each person into providential tests throughout his life. These interfacing situations that appear along one's pathway are the evidences being discussed. The question always comes to mind, if any person reading this writing, were to be put on trial for being a Christian, would there be sufficient evidence to convict him? And what is the sufficient evidence? It is the manifestation of his love.

(2) Confidence within Our Heart (3:19–20)

We will know by this that we are of the truth, and will assure our heart before Him in whatever our heart condemns us; for God is greater than our heart and knows all things.

John says in verse 19: **we will know by this that we are of the truth**. Notice the same phrase that has been repeated often before: **we will know** (2:3; 2:5; 2:18; 3:2; 3:14; 3:17). The idea is to avoid deceitful thinking or foolish speculation. The Bible is the truth, and we must conform to the truth through understanding. Nothing is more important, for it is not just useful and necessary in his testimony before others, but it is also useful to convince his own heart and conscience of the reality of his profession, and thereby have assurance.

This phrase actually goes to John's stated purpose for this writing (1 John 5:13). God has provided a book to study and the reader can know for certain that he has eternal life. Here, John clearly states: **we will know** if this kind of love is present that his profession of being a Christian is real. He has *passed* this aspect of the test. John goes on to state: **and will assure our hearts before Him**. The word here for **assure** is *pithō,* which means "to convince" or "to pacify." The word for **heart** is *kardia,* having to do with "the place of reason," "feelings," or "conscience." The direction of this assurance is **before Him**. Standing before Christ and hearing His verdict is all that really matters. The weight of this clause is the idea of *judgment day honesty*. This person is not one who is speculating about his faith, but is one who has *confident* assurance. The reason provided for confidence is that the profession of the mouth is consistent with the actions performed in the circumstances of life. These actions indicate as nothing else can, that real love is present.

In verse 20, John takes another step in explanation. He brings in the conscience. The clause **in whatever** is comprised of three Greek words that cover everything to do with the contents of conscience. Conscience is God-given (Rom. 2:15). If something is nagging a person's conscience, **in whatever our heart condemns us**, means that his conscience is troubled and must not be ignored. Conscience is a means of correction. John goes on to add that **God is greater than our heart (3:20)**. This is meant in two ways. First, God is the author of conscience and uses a man's conscience to *direct* him as a moral being (Rom. 1:19), and this conscience control is something authored in each person as God's moral and accountable creation. One can derive from this and other texts that God *speaks* through man's conscience, and therefore his conscience must not be ignored.

Second, one can say that if his **heart** (conscience) **condemns him**, he knows that God, who made him, is greater than his conscience (more discerning and omniscient); therefore, if his conscience condemns him how much more is God going to condemn. The idea is that God's people are those who must be living in a manner that follows a *clear conscience*. This too, is part of the sanctification that must be present. It becomes another of the gauges to testify as to the reality of a man's relationship with Christ in the new birth. Speaking metaphorically, there is this little *meter* inside each man that is very telling. If a person, therefore, lives in such a manner that his own heart (conscience) condemns him, and brings no real peace because of his personal hypocrisy, how then can he expect to know true peace with God?

Pause and Reflect

No person can hide from his own conscience, and he certainly cannot hide from God. If the kind of love that is spoken of in 3:16–19 is not being acted upon, and a man's heart is right before God, his conscience will convict him. If the love spoken of is not real, it is a wickedness that cannot be hidden. In Psalm 32:3–4, David attempted to hide his evil, but his conscience would not let him. In Isaiah 57:20, the wicked are compared to the troubled sea. Someone might say, "What if the conscience is seared or hardened" (1 Tim. 4:2)? In such a terrible state, a person might deceive himself, but under no circumstance will God be fooled. The admonition is to use the conscience to guide, while recognizing that because of the new

> birth, only the person honestly desiring God's will can love the brethren, and thereby fulfill righteous obedience.

(3) Confident Action (3:21)

Beloved, if our heart does not condemn us, we have confidence before God;

The idea in this verse fits with the overall theme: "That we might know we have eternal life" (5:13). It not only serves as another means of determining the reality of a man's relationship with God, but also in the context, provides a man's confidence in prayer. The phrase **before God**, coupled with "whatever we ask" in verse 22, clarifies that John is now speaking specifically about prayer and how our prayers relate to our involvement with others. This prayer continues in the context of love for the brethren (3:16). Our love and prayers for the brethren *will be continuous*. Personal prayer life and prayer life among brethren is a *fact* in the Christian's life. It is consistent with faith and love. Paul's prayers for the brethren are seen throughout his epistles. That this love exists in the Christian's life, making him active before God in the priority of prayer, is therefore related to a clear conscience, a conscience that is acting according to God's will and especially in relation to others. The role of maintaining a clear conscience is also seen in Acts 24:16 and 1 Corinthians 4:4, where Paul addresses its *necessity* in relation to honesty before others. Clearly, John is not saying he has confidence because of what he has done in his own strength, or by the mere mechanics of expressing his love to others through prayer. What he is stating is that he has confidence because of the work of God within him making him what he is as a new creation in Christ, engaged in God's work in the attitude of love that is pleasing to Him, and being a blessing to others. Because God is working through him, his conscience is clear and he has confidence. *Only* as the Christian is functioning in righteousness before God can he have any assurance, and thereby, ability and confidence in God's work.

(4) Complementary Association (3:22)

and whatever we ask we receive from Him, because we keep His commandments and do the things that are pleasing in His sight.

The thought in verse 21 is carried forward to complement love and effectiveness with prayer. Prayer is one of the *greatest acts of love*. God's people pray, not only for themselves, but for one another. Prayer is also an *act of faith*. However, people cannot be effective in prayer without confidence, and they cannot have confidence unless they have a clear conscience before God. The request being promised with an answer—**and whatever we ask we receive from Him**—is a prayer according to the will of God that is in harmony with the Christian's love for others, and is in accordance with the chief command to love God and others. It is a prayer according to God's will, or otherwise, there would not be a clear conscience. The prayer is prayed in complementary association with a person in right relationship with God. Clear conscience and answered prayer go together. With this association, John declares **and whatever we ask we receive from Him**. As evidence of a clear conscience, the person is praying with confidence because he is *walking* with his Lord. This prayer is not something mechanical, but spiritual. John says that access to the throne of grace before God is marvelously available to those in this relationship. God always bids His children to ask, and to depend upon Him. This asking is always in the context of accomplishing the will and work of God (John 6:26–29; 9:30). The manifestation of consistent praying serves as another evidence of salvation both by its continuance and the presence of answered prayer. Answered prayer takes many forms, but one thing is certain - God answers in wisdom in ways that cannot be anticipated. Answered prayer, as a special work of God, is repeatedly seen with no other explanation than God's intervention. The glorious activity of answered prayer brings blessings, not so much in the manner the world perceives of blessings, but in the evidence of God's presence in action through effective prayer.

John continues: **because we keep His commandments and do the things that are pleasing in His sight**. The correlation between having a clear conscience and doing what God has commanded makes a full circle. Each works hand-in-hand with the other. The commandment that is immediately in the context is showing love for the brethren, and looking out for them, including praying for them. This action pleases God, provides a clear conscience, grants confidence in praying, and serves as a testimony to the reality of *true relationship* with God. As a result, God's presence of grace is promised in hearing such prayers.

(5) Commanded Expectation (3:23)

This is His commandment, that we believe in the name of His Son Jesus Christ, and love one another, just as He commanded us.

John wrote in his Gospel: "This is the work of God that you believe in Him who He has sent" (John 6:29). A man's belief is evidence that God is working and that there is genuine faith. Faith is also never alone. As James says, "faith without works is dead" (James 2:26). This could be stated in reference to Christ's own words: "If you love Me, you will keep My commandments" (John 14:15). There is a consistent relationship with the reality of the new birth, and the *practice* of all of the elements of the new birth. Here, the **commandment is that we believe in the name of His Son Jesus Christ, and love one another, just as He commanded**. This is another complete circle. John is saying that a person cannot have one without the other. A man cannot say he believes in the Son, and is obedient to Him, *without* being obedient in the matter of love to the brethren. This love of the brethren is the *expectation* of everyone born of God, and with the love is further evidence of spiritual reality.

The phrase: **believe in the name of His Son Jesus Christ** carries with it the idea of believing in the *totality* of our Lord. By using the phrase **believing in the name**, John intends to convey *everything* essential about Jesus in His work and Person. Saving belief is not a mere assent to facts, but it is a belief that is an inclusion of all that Christ is as God, Lord, Savior, Sovereign, Judge, and altogether Lovely One. The aspect of His authority over us is seen in the requirement of belief that issues forth in obedience to His commands and will. This obedience is true saving faith, and is consistent with the context of the compounding proof required by John in making his case for those who "know they have eternal life." The proof is wrapped up in doing what He commands, and specifically, the command to believe in Him, and show the belief by loving the brethren.

(6) Conclusive Evidence (3:24)

The one who keeps His commandments abides in Him, and He in him. We know by this that He abides in us, by the Spirit whom He has given us.

John now provides a reiteration of two final evidences for assurance. First, the one who exclusively abides or continues in the faith has a relationship with God. Second, whoever **keeps his commandments** shows his relationship with God. These two things must coincide. Included in this keeping of the commandments is also the greatest of the commandments– *to love*. This abiding and keeping are interconnected, and serve naturally because of the reliance on Christ as stated **"abides in Him."** Also, notice the connectivity goes both directions, **and he in Him**. There is nothing more valuable than Christ in a man and a man in Him. This is unity. In this unity with Him, He is the power and the source that makes one *able to do those things* he ought to do in obedience to Him. That He is the power and source is shown by the phrase **by the Spirit whom He has given us**. The Spirit is the power that controls a man in this new walk. It is the possession of every true child of God (stated in Romans 8), and gives one the universal consciousness of God. John writes (John 15:5) that "without Me you can do nothing," but with Him Christians are "overcomers" (Rev. 2:11). The fact of the overcoming is the basis of the evidence John is addressing (1 John 5:4). It shows again that Christians are engaged in God's sanctification. John is reminding believers that a relationship with God changes their *affections* and *desires* in the heart. It further *enlightens* their minds. It also *elevates* their resolve. The same work of the Spirit *sustains* them in trials. It also *stimulates* them to Christian service by giving them the very mind of Christ (1 Cor. 2:16). This mind of Christ in believers *produces* the fruit of the Spirit (Gal. 5:22–23).

John continues, **we know by this that He abides in us, by the Spirit whom He has given us (3:24)**. In other words, the presence of His Spirit is the reliable proof that God is working in a heart, and that presence is seen in the evidence of the life (Eph. 1:13). It explains why the unsaved are going in one direction, and Christians are going in a profoundly different direction. This evidence is overwhelming because it shows that no other explanation is possible. The direction of the Christian can only be explained by the presence and work of God. The evidence is compelling. All of this is because Christ is our Lord and our new Master. He is within us, and is making all the difference. The glory belongs to Him. There will be times when the life of Christ is seen more in the child of God than at other times, but it is always present. The evidence is consistent.

Pause and Reflect

The key verse of this section is verse 21: "Beloved, if our heart does not condemn us, we have confidence before God." This section is all about the heart. A Christian is a new creature (2 Cor. 5:17), and that new creation means an internal change has taken place in his heart. That change is demonstrated in how he lives and by his love. With both, it is a matter of living in a manner pleasing to God and loving what God loves. Just as Christ demonstrated love by going to the cross, the Christian in a similar obedient manner will exercise genuine love if he is abiding in Him. Genuine love must be defined by God's kind of love. A Christian has a special conscience. If his conscience is troubled, he cannot get away with neglecting its voice, for God Himself is greater than his conscience and will not allow it. Assurance and confidence are attached to his prayer life. He cannot come to God with unresolved disobedience and expect real communion. Being obedient, on the other hand, will bless his prayer life and provide the ability to accomplish God's testimony through him. The whole of his obedience in carrying out true love can be summed up in simply trusting God. This obedience is the relationship of a Christian to his God, and this will issue forth in Christ-like love, and bring compelling evidence as the Christian does His revealed will.

5

The Cautions for Fellowship

4:1–21

Outline context:

II. The Requirement of Fellowship with Christ (1:5—5:12)

    A. The Conditions for Fellowship (1:5—2:11)

    B. The Challenge for Fellowship (2:12–29)

    C. The Characteristics of Fellowship (3:1– 3:24)

    D. The Cautions for Fellowship (4:1–21)

        1. Practicing Cautions (4:1–6)

Everyone is expected to make reasonably discerning choices about the items he selects on the menu at a restaurant; his choice of clothing, toothpaste, how he combs his hair, where he purchases his groceries, and everything he does. But the idea of being discerning as it relates to knowing God or true Christianity is often irrationally considered unacceptable. It borders on being a crime. An example can be seen in a recorded conversation of the late Dr. Jerry Falwell arguing with a conservative news person over Christ being the only way to God. The news person became very agitated and angry over Falwell's narrowness.

That attitude is common in today's politically correct world. Interestingly, the same concern over the rigidness of Muslims in their beliefs is largely accepted, while the truths (real truths) of the Christian faith that cannot be compromised are not. This harshness against traditional, exclusive truth, has led many Christians to either hide in silence, or compromise under the pressure. Other supposed Christians have mixed truth with error in the name of tolerance or acceptance, and have redefined Christianity as being without righteous boundaries or definitive doctrines. The problems with these erroneous compromises are numerous, but at its root, Christian beliefs that are *essential* to the faith, and reveal God and His plan, have been practically disregarded. The destructive nature of this is seen, for example, in man's lack of biblical comprehension of himself as a sinner without hope, and as a natural truth suppressor. Man further lacks the knowledge of who God is as a God of truth and righteousness, and he lacks the understanding that Satan is actively deceiving the world. Such biblical ignorance leads to a denial of the central role of the church as the custodian of the truth (1 Tim. 3:15). Additionally, it also escapes notice that compromising the truth leaves whatever remains without substance or power. This "compromised position of non-truth" that is left is something that cannot save, cannot help, and actually *leads* people into *false* conclusions that support the march of lost humanity to hell. God declares through John that the Christian must be a person of wise discernment and non-compromising conviction.

a. The Caution concerning False Prophets (4:1–4)

(1) Command to Test (4:1a)

Beloved, do not believe every spirit, but test the spirits to see whether they are from God,

John begins by using the term **Beloved** (2:7; 3:2; 3:21), *agapētos*, meaning "significant endearment or very dear," which is referring to the particular love that interconnects those who belong to Christ. John does not express such a term of endearment to the world at large. He says **do not believe** in reference to every spirit. **Believe** is from *pisteuō*, meaning "to entrust oneself," or "to put one's faith" in **every spirit**. John warns us to be cautious and use wise judgment or discerning judgment in what a Christian accepts as the truth of God. The idea is not to be naive or accepting of things with a shallow mindset. The world is full of all kinds of voices, and whether they are misguided, destructive, deceived, or purposeful in falsehood, they all share one thing in common: they are wrong! They are not the truth, and therefore, are not to be brought into the belief system of the one professing Christ. To purchase soap, for example, that does not effectively clean is one thing, but it is quite another to buy into a religion or belief that *will not save*. One is temporal and of little consequence; the other is eternal with infinite consequence.

What is this test's ultimate purpose? John says, **to see whether they are from God**. This is always the issue. When dealing with spirits, there can only be *two choices:* God or Satan. Keep in mind what Ephesians 6:12 states: "We do not wrestle with flesh and blood." The point is that superhuman evil forces are behind false, deceitful teaching. To ignore the warning is not only to be naive, but is also to be living as a fool, because the person is not listening to what God has said in His Word. He has *warned* man in many passages and by examples throughout both Testaments. This testing of spirits is essential, and the concern and ability to test is implied as defining the truly saved from those who are deceived.

The word **test**, *dokimazō*, means "to test thoroughly" (Luke 12:56), "to analyze" (Luke 14:19), "to try them out" (Rom. 2:19), "to approve," or "to examine" (1 Cor. 11:28–29). To illustrate, no one who is thirsty would go into a science lab and start *indiscriminately* drinking the liquids present in the lab. The person, no matter how thirsty, would want some assurance that what he is drinking is not harmful. By application, would not such testing be even more reasonable with that which is spiritual and eternal? The idea of course is to *be sure* and *thorough.* There is no room for assumptions or good intentions, because the consequences of being wrong are too horrific.

Note further that this testing is *commanded.* This is not something to do only if a person is merely inquisitive. The weight of the word **test** requires it. All the **beloved** are responsible and accountable for this testing. No true Christian can embrace every religious doctrine or preacher claiming to use God's Word. This means that every Christian sitting in a church that is *not testing* what is being said is disobedient. How does one test? John 17:17 has the answer: "Sanctify them in truth, Thy word is truth." Everything must be tested by a careful and honest alignment or evaluation with the Word of God. The idea of testing **every spirit** *is to look below the surface,* and to take nothing for granted. What is to qualify acceptance? Could the one teaching lead people astray? The test is not always what someone says with his lips, but rather, really getting to know the person. What is that person's testimony? **Spirit** (*pneuma*), "rational soul," is used of "the reality of life within" that drives a person. The test is not so much a matter of perfection as it is a matter of seeing that there is indeed a *true relationship* between the person and God. Does the person really have a heart for God? To evaluate the **spirit** of a person, to the measure intimated, is appropriating the skillful understanding of the *entirety* of this writing by John. This writing not only gives the skill to evaluate ones self, but also, to evaluate others. John says this testing is *essential,* because of the nature of the seriousness of the subject.

(2) Composition of the World (4:1b)

because many false prophets have gone out into the world.

John says that the reason one must test is that **many false prophets have gone out into the world**. The word **many** (*polus*) is always used of "an abundant number." The word for **false**–*pseudo*–means: "spurious," "pretender," or "imposter." A prophet means one that provides information from God or a declaration of His divine will (past, present, or future). The thrust is pointed at those claiming to speak for God, but do not, and they are *abundant* in number. Each Christian needs to be fully aware of what he is up against. Churches today that are built around false teachers are prominent and well-attended. One must be reminded of Christ's words at the end of the Sermon on the Mount when He said: "Many will say to me in that day, 'Lord, Lord' . . . But I will say depart from me for I never knew you" (Matt. 7:22–23). There will be *many* deceived, and those deceived are without excuse, because all who claim the name of Christ are warned repeatedly in the Word of the active presence of deception (1 Cor 6:9-10; 2 Tim 2:19; Titus 1:10; 2 John 1:7).

(3) Confession as a Means of Examination (4:2–3)

By this you know the Spirit of God: every spirit that confesses that Jesus Christ has come in the flesh is from God; and every spirit that does not confess Jesus is not from God; this is the *spirit* of the antichrist, of which you have heard that it is coming, and now it is already in the world.

The initial question that should be asked is: why did John choose for his argument the idea of confession to distinguish a Christian from a non-Christian? To **confess** means to embrace with words from the heart. To confess in this biblical sense is something that truly defines the person. It has to do with allegiance and not just words. There are two spirits that are always active. The Spirit of God always glorifies the Son (John 15:26; 16:13–15; 1 Cor. 12:1–3), and conversely could never not glorify the Son. The other spirit, of Satan, cannot possibly be honest in glorifying the Son, but can only do the opposite. The same reality is seen in 1 Corinthians 12:3: "Therefore I make known to you that no one speaking by the Spirit of God says, 'Jesus is accursed'; and no one can say, 'Jesus is Lord,' except by the Holy Spirit." Paul makes a contrast showing the necessity of the Holy Spirit for true confession. Where the Holy Spirit is present, a true confession of allegiance to the Son will be made. Therefore, John is saying that no one can utter a confession "Jesus is Lord" (in the sense of a life transforming manner), except by the presence and power of the Spirit of God. Such a confession is not natural, and *impossible for the unsaved* because they are devoid of the Holy Spirit. This confession is a parallel thought and passage to the confession that John will describe by the essential understanding of the identity of Christ–that is Christ **has come in the flesh is from God (4:2)**.

Many people claim Jesus. The real issue, though, is whether or not the Jesus they claim is the real Jesus. John has added, **has come in the flesh is from God**. John is specifically addressing the "incarnation." He is dogmatically identifying who Jesus Christ really is–God! The message of the incarnation is that God, as the Second Person of the Trinity, became a man. Just as the command from Christ that "we love God with all our heart, mind, and strength"(Deut. 6:5; Matt. 22:37), is the command that encompasses all other commands (meaning if this kind of love is taking place, all of the commands will be met), so the confession that Jesus **has come in the flesh (4:2)** carries the same encompassing ability with regard to His person. It encompasses that He is the "God Man," the *only* Savior, and therefore the *Lord overall*. All is *owned by* and *owed to* Him. Ultimately, He must receive all glory. It further means that He is the center of all. He is the only hope as the Savior and the exclusive way.

If a person studies the theology of *New Age* beliefs, he will find missing any reference to Christ being God. Christ will be acknowledged in some capacity as a teacher, leader, prophet, angel, or good example, but not the person shown in the Gospels. Such people have devised a Jesus not defined from the Bible, but by their own *imagination*. In a less obvious fashion, people deny Jesus Christ in His right to rule over them. In 2 Corinthians 5:13–14 is the example of Paul. Paul says that in his relationship with Jesus Christ, he is no longer the same. The people observing him might think he has lost his mind. He goes on to say "the love of Christ controls us" ("us" referring to all who are saved), meaning that he has a different guide in his life. It is no longer himself, but the Spirit of God. In fact, he goes on to add in verse 16 they: "no longer live for themselves, but for Him." Therefore, *believing* that Christ has come in the flesh *encompasses* His death for sins, His teaching on the necessity of the new birth, and His coming again to establish His kingdom. These are all life changing descriptions. This was His message that was to be proclaimed by His church. True conversion is interconnected with the understanding of who He is by the confession phrase **come in the flesh** (2 Cor. 5:17–20). By using the doctrine of His incarnation, John has been able to separate shallow, non-saving faith from true saving faith. Those who belong to Him must *embrace Him fully*. This embracing includes the essential embracing of Him as the God-man Savior with all of the ramifications of His Person and His authority as Lord.

"Every spirit that does not confess Jesus is not from God; this is the spirit of antichrist" (4:3). John expresses the truth that there is no middle ground. Everyone who does not confess Christ, as discussed above, is in the same position as the coming antichrist. They are, and will be susceptible to every deception and lie that issues forth from Satan's coming religious leader- the antichrist. The attitude and spirit of such are **already in the world.**

(4) Capability to Overcome (4:4)

You are from God, little children, and have overcome them; because greater is He who is in you than he who is in the world.

What is the reason that one person believes and demonstrates transformation in the life, and another continues consumed by worldly actions and activities, even though he may make a profession of faith? The answer is clear. The Spirit of God *is working* in the one individual *but not* in the other. This work, too, becomes a means of examination of the reality of true Christianity.

John says: **You are from God, little children, and have overcome them**. The idea **you are from God** means that a person's salvation is sourced from God, and not from himself. It is a work of God, and not a work of man. If anyone's salvation is not sourced from God, then he does not have true salvation. The **"them"** in this verse is a reference back to the previous verses (4:1–3) referring to "false prophets," and the "spirit of antichrist." John also uses the phrase that he has used before, **little children**. This phrase not only demonstrates John's endearment to them as his spiritual children, but it also helps to maintain a proper perspective. Like **little children**, all Christians must and will demonstrate practical dependence, not only as learners, but also as dependents in their thinking. Salvation is not a means of boasting because the recipient is valiant, strong, capable, or special, but only because of the work of grace being accomplished in him. This is also true of overcoming ability. Therefore, the term **little children** is appropriate to keep and direct the mindset in proportionate humility.

As powerful as Satan is—his being crafty, tricky, full of plots, and scheming—God is infinitely more powerful. Therefore the definitive statement can be made that if a person truly has the Spirit of God: **greater is He who is in you than he who is in the world**. That statement not only makes all the difference, even to the point of clarity as an indicator for who is of God and who is not, but also shows the catalyst for the power of the Christian life. The **"in you"** is a clear reference to the Spirit of God that *must be* resident in all the elect, or they are not true believers at all (Rom. 8:9). This indwelling is why the elect cannot ultimately be deceived (Matt. 24:24), or fall away from the faith, or denounce their God; because they have the Holy Spirit of God within them, and thereby, have **overcome** all the powerful assaults of evil.

> ### Pause and Reflect
>
> God's people must be overcomers, not because they are anything in themselves, but because the all-powerful Holy Spirit of God resides within them and makes them overcomers. The converse is also true. If there is no overcoming, there is no true relationship with God. Practically, there are many people with good intentions expressing themselves as Christians, when in reality their lack of overcoming reflects no faith or ability to please God. Such persons are deceiving themselves and confusing others about true Christianity. A Christian can and does sin (1 John 1:8–9), but he is not immersed in sin, or indifferent to the revealed will of God. There must be a demonstration in the saved life of the overcoming power of God. It cannot be concluded that these are merely confused or immature if they are denying the fundamentals. Such individuals are not overcomers, and therefore, not Christians by John's definition. Every child of God is an overcomer. They overcome because they truly believe and confess Jesus Christ as He is declared in the Word of God.

b. The Caution regarding listening (4:5–6)

(1) Communication (4:5)

They are from the world; therefore they speak *as* from the world, and the world listens to them.

They are from the world is a practical argument based on people showing their natural origin by their actions and words. When people who originate from Massachusetts, for example, engage in conversation with those who have their roots from Alabama, the difference in dialect is obvious. Their speech is a red flag to their background. In the same manner, when we listen to others teaching or presenting what is claimed as God's Word–what they teach is very telling. Why do so many preachers teach what has become known as the *prosperity gospel,* which is not the gospel? Why do many not focus on Christ? Why do many disregard the doctrines of the Bible, and instead, teach the precepts of men? Why do many compromise the Bible, torture it, twist it, disregard it, or teach contrary to it? John answers: **They are from the world**. John makes no apology in drawing yet another clear line of distinction. If a pastor or other person has taken on the role of a teacher of the Word of God, and is not communicating the real Gospel, but another gospel, he is *false and a deceiver*. What is implied by John's statement **they are from the world?** If they are not communicating the real Gospel–get away from them! This warning coincides with Matthew 7:15: "Beware of the false prophets, who come to you in sheep's clothing, but inwardly are ravenous wolves." John says, **they are from the world, therefore they speak as from the world**. They are to be recognized by their connectivity to what they speak.

Now he adds: **and the world listens to them (4:5)**. If the false teachers had no stage and audience, they would have little impact. But the fact is that the world does listen to them. The word **listens** (*akouō*) means "to come to, give audience to," or as shown in Acts 4:19 "give heed." It means *to listen with action* in view. This is shown in reverse in Matthew 10:11–14, where Christ states: "whoever does not receive you, nor heed your words" ("heed" being the same word as **listens**), the idea of hearing with action, is commanded to "have nothing to do with them." This has a double meaning. Implied is that Christians listen to God and take action, and false prophets or teachers do not listen, and therefore, do not take action. No one can have a real claim to be a Christian if God's Word is not important to him. On the other hand, those who are listening to that which is false, with no regard to the Bible, are identified with the false teachers. Neither the false teachers, nor their listener's are of God.

The idea of **the world** here also has a double meaning. **World** generally means the lost or unsaved people. The **world** in this sense is the system of evil under the curse. All of the unsaved belong to this sphere described in Ephesians 2:2: "the course of this world, according to the prince of the power of the air, of the spirit that is now working in the sons of disobedience." In this case, **world,** refers to the evil spiritual realm ruled by Satan (see discussion in 2:15). John is saying that the lost people of the

world listen to false teachers or the spirit of disobedience. Secondarily, the idea of **world** here also alludes to the masses of people in humanity, or the majority of people in humanity, meaning the lost, blind, unsaved mass of humanity destined for hell.

> ### Pause and Reflect
>
> Because 1 John is a book about reality, it brings several practical tests from John. He tells his readers how to identify a false teacher, and by implication, how to discern those who have embraced Christ. The Christian must always be analyzing what he is hearing, and apply only that which is beneficial. It is a critical matter because of the two spirits at work. There is the Spirit of the truth coming from the Bible, and being applied by the Holy Spirit through God's spokesmen, and there are the false teachers who are giving out the spirit of lies and deception fostered by the evil one. John provides a two-fold exam. First, he tells the readers that they will know true teachers by their confession of the truth, that is, by whether the person teaching is able to overcome the pressure of compromise and is teaching the true Gospel of Christ. Those that speak from the world (the false religions sourced from Satan), are deceptively counterfeit and sourced from evil. No matter how well received, sincere, or appealing, they do not belong to God. There is a clear delineation. Second, however, not only are the teachers being identified by what they say or represent, but also, the listeners are being identified by their participation in listening. Those who accept and appreciate worldly philosophies are of the world, and not of Christ. Those who hear and accept God's truth are of Him.

(2) Communion (4:6)

We are from God; he who knows God listens to us; he who is not from God does not listen to us. By this we know the spirit of truth and the spirit of error.

The last portion of the cautions for fellowship that John provides deals with communion with the truth. He begins by reminding his readers that he is an apostle **from God**. The apostles spoke providentially with the authority of God, and their writing carries the same authority. The Word is God's revelation to man ("men by the Holy Spirit spoke from God," 2 Pet. 1:21) and therefore, it is the only authority with a sure foundation to be trusted in the matters of faith (the 66 books of the canon of Scripture).

John says that **he who knows God listens to us**. The belonging is stated by the term **knows God**, meaning a real or genuine knowledge or relationship with God. By definition, these are those who are truly being sanctified by God. **Listens** (*akouō*) means "to give audience." These who "know God" are genuine Christians because they *give audience* to the apostles. Therefore, a mark of a genuine Christian is that he *listens* to the apostles or, in modern day meaning, he accepts, appreciates, and devotes himself to the Word of God. This behavior, along with others covered in this writing, are identifying marks of a true Christian. The idea of **listens** not only carries with it attention to the Word of God, but also implies the exclusion from contrary words. These listeners of the apostles will not listen to the false beliefs of the world. They do not listen because the Word that they do listen to warns them to stay away from false words. True Christians are very *careful* about whom they give audience; they will not listen (will not make the message a part of their belief system) to those presenting something *contrary* to the Word of God. In Acts 4:19, akouō is translated "give heed," meaning to listen with action in view. This means that those to whom John is speaking will not merely pick and choose certain portions from the Word of God, as if attending a buffet, but the emphasis is on obedience and adherence to all the words. The Bible takes precedence over any personal rationalization or outside contrary voice. No person has a claim to be a Christian if God's Word is not important, and so important, that it is believed to the detriment of anything and everything else. For this reason, in Matthew 10:11–14, Christ states that those who will not listen are not worthy of Him, and He informs the disciples to "shake the dust off your feet," that is, have nothing to do with those who will not listen.

John adds: **by this we know the Spirit of truth and the spirit of error (4:6)**. The reader should note that John uses the phrase "**by this**" repeatedly. It is a statement of definitive separation, clarifying knowledge from speculation or truth from error. The phrase "**by this**" is related to those giving adherence to God's Word in contrast to the voices that do not. Love, respect, and appreciation for God's Word, to the exclusion of all contrary voices– is the indicator. This response is God's measurement and that is why it is so important. It is *absolutely necessary* in a world of darkness and false teaching. In Ephesians 4:14, after defining the purpose of the various gifts given to the church (Eph. 4:11–13), Paul indicates that they are given to mature us to the fullness of Christ: "As a result, we are no longer to be children, tossed here and there by waves and carried about by every wind of doctrine, by the trickery of men, by craftiness in deceitful scheming; but speaking the truth in love." He goes on addressing coming to maturity. Maturity is one thing, and giving audience to false doctrine or heresy is another. The children of God might not agree on minor matters of lesser consequence, but on essential doctrines, because the Spirit of God dwells in every true Christian, they will only give audience to the truth. This adherence to truth is seen by what Christ states in Matthew 24:24, which speaks of false Christ's and false prophets arising. He states that if it were possible, these would fool even the elect. To ultimately fool the elect, however, is not possible, for they possess the truth and the Spirit of God.

Pause and Reflect

John continues his test of who is real and who is not real in his relationship to Christ. He uses the phrase **by this we know.** All who **listen** (give audience) consistently to the truth of God's Word are from God. Those that claim to listen, but really do not, are shown as those who do not listen to God by how they live contrary to what God states in His Word. Hearing and doing are joined together as inseparable realities. James 1:22 says that those who hear, but are not transformed in their behavior, are deluded (deceived). This test is God's measurement and is critically important. Not only does John tell who is of Christ by their giving audience to the Word of God, but he shows how to identify false teachers as well. Those who speak the Word of God are from God, and those who might claim to speak the Word of God, but really do not, are not from God. This verse exemplifies the extreme importance of discernment. This world is one of falsehood, deception, and darkness. Christians are to be in a constant mindset of analyzing all that is taken in. They are to give special attention when discerning those who claim to speak for God. The standard of measurement for all discernment is the Word of God. The Christian must know the Word and never stop studying it personally, and in helping others to know it. The Word of God is integral in the relationship one has with God. It cannot be separated from the relationship. Those who have communion with God have that communion through the understanding and appreciation of His Word.

2. Production of Love (4:7–21)

a. The Caution of an Unloving Spirit (4:7–14)

When a person shops at a store using a large denomination of money such as twenty dollar or greater bill, he will often encounter clerks using a special pen to determine if the money is real. They test the money because counterfeits are everywhere. Using the right means, the genuine can be determined. In the same way, there are many counterfeits in the world of Christianity. God has given His children a means of determining counterfeits from His Word. To receive bogus paper money because it is worthless is a poor practice and might cause a financial hardship. But taking bogus Christianity is far worse, for doing so has eternal consequences, and can damn a person's soul.

This section instructs the reader that one of the telling evidences of true conversion, distinguishing true believers from false professors, is love. John has already discussed love (3:11-18). Now, he addresses from yet another angle. Most people have a poor concept of what is meant by biblical love. Is it sentimentality, social expression, something romantic, sexual affection, or the possession of a gracious demeanor? It is none of those things. In fact, today's Christian must put aside modern American television ideas of love. These are artificial and do not match the Bible's definition of love. Whatever love is, it is shown throughout the Word of God, as well as here, to be an essential. When asked, "What is the greatest commandment?" Christ stated: "You shall love the Lord your God . . . and your neighbor as yourself" (Matt. 22:37). In 1 Corinthians 13, Paul explains that even if Christians were able to do great acts of faith, but do not have love, "it profits nothing." John reminds his reader once again: love is one of the essential testing factors regarding true Christianity. There must be the presence of real biblical love in the Christian.

(1) Call for Indispensable Love (4:7–8)

Beloved, let us love one another, for love is from God; and everyone who loves is born of God and knows God. The one who does not love does not know God, for God is love.

Beloved (*agapētos*) means significant endearment or very dear, a sense of connectivity and obligation that goes beyond the bounds of mere affection. This is a type of love that is seen between the Father and the Son in the Godhead. This word is used in 1 John 2:7; 3:2; 3:21; and 4:1. Once again in this context, it means that John is speaking only to Christians. John defines what he means by love by putting it into five categories: its command, conception, character, conspicuousness, and connection. The words **let us** are not in the original Greek. They were added because of the tense of the word for love, which means the love expected is to continue.

First, its *command*: **love one another (4:7)**. Similar to the command to test the spirits in verse 1, the focus now is testing the spirits according to love. Part of the work of the Spirit is the development and proliferation of love. This is seen by looking forward to verse 12: "If we love one another, God abides in us." Wherever God abides, there will be love. The next verse (v. 8) tells the reader that **God is love**. Therefore, because God abides in Christians (who are in the process of sanctification), Christians have the capacity to love in the same manner He loves. Love in this context is not the cause of spiritual birth but the effect from the birth. The command to love one another is nothing new (Matt. 22:38). To claim to love God, and yet, to be continually disobedient to Him is impossible. The amazing thing about true biblical love is that when it is shown, all other commandments follow. Love is the summation of all commands (Matt. 22:40). As a command, it is essential because God is worthy. Love serves as an identifiable and obvious bond of the connection between the believer and His Lord. At the least, when a professing believer does not demonstrate love, he instead demonstrates disobedience to the Savior. From previous contexts, that continued disobedience brings into question the reality of the person's profession.

Second, its *conception*: **for love is from God**. The source of love is vitally important. The kind of love to which John is referring is not already in a person, waiting to be let out or expressed. The natural man (unsaved) does not have this kind of love, or even a potential love within him (Titus 3:1–3). Romans 8:7 states that in a man's natural condition he is "hostile to God." Romans 5:5 states that "had not the love of God been poured out within our hearts through the Holy Spirit," no Christian would have love. Any love that a person has is dependent upon God, and is a derivative of the new birth (2 Cor. 5:15; Gal. 5:22). The only explanation for this *God kind of love*, which is distinguishing love, is the new birth. Love, in its conception, has a direct correlation with the reality of salvation.

Third, its *character*: **and everyone who loves is born of God and knows God**. This is a clear statement of fact and is true Christianity. It speaks of genuineness. The reader is reminded that a Christian is not someone who attends church, who is religious, who does certain mechanics, or merely who expresses his adherence to certain doctrines; rather, he is someone who is manifesting this God kind of love. This passage is a direct reference back to the Gospel of John chapter 3. Christ defined the new birth to Nicodemus as a supernatural and special work of God. Those that are deceived will show no evidence that God has done a supernatural work, and no indication of the manifestation of His love. Having this kind of love is not something a person can manufacture, but it is something that God does for and in a person. There are two essentials here: **born of God** and **knows God**. Taken together, no one can **know God** unless he is **born of God**. However, that is not all, for a third characteristic is also added, stated as: **everyone who loves**. All three of these are obviously inseparably linked. The idea is that **everyone who loves** (in the form of God's love) is **born of God** and **knows God**. There can be no exceptions. If one is true, so must the others be; if one is missing, all three are missing. The word "**know**" is *ginōskō,* which speaks of "knowing intimately" and is always related to relationship. All of these unique terms require God's election in order to exist. The "**everyone who loves**" does not have reference to the one that loves his wife, children, friends, and dog as being a child of God, for it is not talking about natural affection. But God's kind of love is a *special love* that can only be defined in the context of God's Word, and it identifies the real Christian as distinct.

Fourth, its *conspicuousness*: **The one who does not love does not know God (4:8)**. This is one of the plainest, simplest, and clearest statements in all of Scripture. No one can claim Christianity who does not show the kind of love spoken of here, God's kind of love. Indirectly shown by John is that the absence of true saving faith serves as evidence against both false professors of Christianity, and false professors of love. One must keep in mind that love is always consistent with truth (1 Cor. 13:6). John is really saying that this true love must exist, and that it will be manifestly obvious. It must be real because it is part of the fruit of the Spirit (Gal. 5:22). It is the first mentioned and is also the definition for all that follows. Love has been sourced from God, and purposed by God to reflect Him and what He is like. Christians, after all, are ambassadors for Christ. They are set apart (sanctified) for the very purpose to love God, and love His people.

Fifth and finally, its *connection*: John can make a dogmatic statement because of the idea of the word **know** being a relationship term. The explanation of this connectivity is that **God is love**. God cannot help but love (biblical love), as it is His very nature (Eph. 2:4). His love has no explanation outside of Himself, for He loves the unlovely (Rom. 5:8) and this simply true because of His nature. This love is a great source of supreme comfort through sorrow, trouble, and anxious times. The Christian can **know** that God loves him, and therefore, has a *supreme purpose* behind all situations, for He always will act in love.

A major point here in reference to the reality that a Christian must possess the *God kind of love*, is that no one can separate true Christianity from God's character. Since part of God's essential character is love, so all who are truly converted will manifest a measure of that same kind of character. The simple idea is that all of God's activities are done in love, so then will His true child's activities be *done with the motive of love*. Just as children reflect the physical characteristics of their parents, and act in mannerisms consistent with the parents, God's spiritual children must carry His characteristics. They will not do so perfectly, but they will do so essentially because of their connectivity to Him.

(2) Commencement of Love (4:9)

By this the love of God was manifested in us, that God has sent His only begotten Son into the world so that we might live through Him.

By this (another of the clarifying statements), John explains, **the love of God was manifested in us**, meaning Christians were the objects of His love, but not only the objects, but the recipients of the same kind of love. Therefore, John can say **that we might live through Him**, so that Christians can show their possession of real spiritual life, the new life of love. They are now different because they live a life that is characteristic of Christ. This is the love of God that is manifested in His children as recipients of His love. *This is real life in Christ.*

(3) Conveyance of Love (4:10)

In this is love, not that we loved God, but that He loved us and sent His Son *to be* the propitiation for our sins.

John goes on to show, based on the connectivity just expressed, that the quality of this love is infinitely meaningful. How does one know or measure the quality of this love? John tells the reader that **God sent His Son,** and so the Christian *begins to see* His love when he looks at Christ's coming and dying on the cross. His coming and actual dying on the cross is the apex demonstration of the kind of love that John is addressing.

What is God's love like? Man's carnal ideas of love are mixed with sexual attraction, affections, and selfish motives. Man's idea of love is sadly tied up with *taking* instead of *giving*. God's love, in contrast, is in two parts. The first part is sacrificial. God does not look to see what He can gain, but what He can give. The second part of His love is something done to *benefit others*. The Scriptures often speak of Christ's compassion (Matt. 9:36). This compassion was a chief motivation. No person was looking to love God or appreciate Him (**not that we loved God**), but instead, all people were His enemies (Rom. 5:10). Men because of sin naturally hate God. There was no reason for God to look at men and say, "I will respond to their love." Not even a spark of love for God existed from man toward God. In fact, there was only the opposite. Yet, despite no one loving God, **He loved us and sent His son**. Not only this, but He was sent **to be the propitiation for our sins**, that is, to be the satisfaction of God's wrath toward sin. This love is the infinite love of God that is glorious, supernatural, wonderful, and not explainable. It is not explainable by reason. It can only be seen as an *act of immeasurable* love. This is the kind of love conveyed that must become a part of the person in true salvation.

By contrast, the testimony of many who talk of love, instead demonstrate hatred, wrath, malice, and all manner of evil behavior that is absolutely contrary to God. Man can truly only understand the God kind of love by looking at the cross. True love cannot sacrifice holiness anymore than God the Father sacrificed holiness by crushing His Son. While demonstrating His righteousness, He also demonstrated His incomprehensible sacrificial giving of Christ. He looked on man with the eyes of compassion and sent His son. Therefore, as **God sent** and conveyed that kind of love on His children, and transforms them with the new birth, they must possess something of the *same quality*; such love becomes a part of the reality of the true believer. The credibility of God's love spreads to His children, and becomes something of the credibility of their relationship with Him, and also with others. *My how they love one another,* often described the early Christians. This demonstration of love is another mark of the one engaged in God's sanctification.

(4) Conclusive Call for Love (4:11)

Beloved, if God so loved us, we also ought to love one another.

John once again uses **Beloved** –*agapētos,* "significant endearment" to convey the sincerity, intimacy, and importance of what he is writing. It is personal and particular for those who claim Christ. **If God** is not a "maybe" or "it could be." It is emphatic and could be translated "since God." Verse 10 helps in the translation where it is stated that **He loved us**; an action by God in the aorist, active, indicative, that addresses our incredible well-being. John is addressing Christians whom God loves with a *particular* saving love. The conclusion that he is making, as He loves His children and they have partaken of His nature, is that we are to continually (present tense) **love one another.** This is appropriate and reasonable. Since God loves His children (so much that He gave His Son), the only rational conclusion is that God, who is perfect in reasoning and love, has established the exclusive standard. How can one who claims Him, do something contrary to what He is doing? The word **ought** *opheilō* is "something owed, bound, indebted, or under obligation." This is the same word used in 3:16, and the word translated "indebted" in Romans 15:27. The word is not a suggestion. It is instead an *insurmountable* debt, or obligation. It is something required. This verse brings the believer to a conclusion that as a Christian–he must love who Christ loves. This verse is also connected to verse 12.

(5) Chosen Portrayal of Love (4:12)

No one has seen God at any time; if we love one another, God abides in us, and His love is perfected in us.

No one has seen God is a true statement with a practical concept and solution. The world (meaning people living physically in the world), does not see God because He is not physically visible. God told Moses that "no man could see God and live" (Ex. 33:20). The emphasis of this verse is that God is holy and man is unholy. This separation is why man cannot see God and live. What then, can the world know of God, or how can they receive some understanding of what God is like? While God can be seen in a general sense by what He has created (Rom. 1:20), He can be known only through His Word (John 5:39), and the Word provides all that is needed for faith and godliness (2 Tim. 3:16–17). This context, however, deals with the love shown by His children. Christians are to be bearers of, or reflecting His likeness. He can be seen practically, in day-to-day action, as **He abides in us** (His true children). The Christian's love likeness to Christ can only be explained by a supernatural work of God that has affected the heart. Each Christian is chosen to be a portrayal of God's love to the world. In this regard, he is showing the world what God is like.

The words **if we love** can be translated "since we love," demonstrating once again a definite reality. This same concept is seen clearly in 1 John 5:15: "if we know" shows that John is not addressing speculation, but a fact, "since we know." The Christian has the love of Christ if he belongs to God. Putting it another way, through the work of God and the resulting obedience in doing His will, the Christian reflects the very love of God. People cannot see God, any more than they can see electricity, but the effect of electricity can be seen, and the effectual work of the Spirit of God can also *be seen in a changed person.* As God's love is shown by that person, others will see the effect.

Christians are to be the portrayers of the *likeness* of God. We are His ambassadors (2 Cor. 5:20). We bear His name and are to bear His brand marks (Rom. 12:1; Gal. 6:17). **His love is perfected in us**. The word **perfected** is *teleioō*, "to complete", to "accomplish," or "to consummate" (Luke 13:32). In Acts 20:24, this word is translated "finish." The idea is that the Christian accomplishes his full purpose in relation to love when he loves God, and loves others. This love is the Christian's *target, goal, and purpose*. In so doing, he displays to the world the likeness of God. People do not see God, but they do see those who profess the name of Christ. By this love, the Christian's association is bearing a testimony. Therefore, as he displays what God is like to the world, he should be displaying His kind of love, instead of scams, shams or mere talk. The world should see something that is *different* than anything else, and can only be explained as belonging to God. They should see God's love. This love is what Paul meant when he told Timothy: "The goal of our instruction is love from a pure heart" (1 Tim. 1:5). This displaying of love is both an evidence of the Christian's true relationship with God, and a challenge to express it to the world in a meaningful way, as a representative of Jesus Christ.

(6) Confirmation from Love (4:13)

By this we know that we abide in Him and He in us, because He has given us of His Spirit.

By this we know is a repeated phrase used by John for his test of true relationship with God. This is the benchmark statement already seen several times (2:3; 2:5; 3:14; 3:24; 4:6), and is now repeated to confirm another discussion of assurance. Religious people make up their own manner of confirmation. They take ideas that might be included in the Word, and yet, have another purpose, or they add their own ideas. Such things as baptism, aisle walking, card signing, church attendance, good works, sacraments (Roman Catholic), professions of faith, and all manner of religious activities which may be honorable and sincere, but they are not confirmations of a true relationship with Christ. The love described in this context reflects the work of God, not mere *religious activity*. Love shows that God is at work in the sanctification of the person. Love cannot be fabricated. It requires the work of the Holy Spirit.

John therefore says, **by this we know**. What is known? What John has just stated in verse 12: "if we love one another God abides in us." Christians can only reach the target of God's kind of love if **we abide in Him and He in us**. This love can only be true **because He has given us of His spirit**. This love is union with God and the testimony of His sanctification. This is the same kind of possession of the Spirit that is spoken of in Romans 8:9: "If anyone does not have the Spirit of Christ, He does not belong to Him." If a man's relationship is real, the reality will be shown because of the possession of the Holy Spirit, and with His presence will be the God kind of love. If a union with God exists, it will be obvious, real, and not explainable in any other way. This love will not always be manifested perfectly, for John has given room for growth, development, and even a target, but it will be present in the person. The magnitude of its presence depends on where the person resides along the process of sanctification.

Paul reminds us in 1 Corinthians 13:1, that someone can have all manner of doctrine, talk from the Bible, and exhibit manifestations of faith, but if he has not this kind of love, then all else is worthless. This manner of love is an essential confirmation.

(7) Convicting Testimony of Love (4:14)

We have seen and testify that the Father has sent the Son *to be* the Savior of the world.

The word **seen** is *theaomai*, "to look closely or perceive" (1:1; 4:12), and carries with it the idea of a *personal encounter*. The person who is saved has an encounter with God. He has seen the true God and knows Him because the Spirit of God has revealed Him personally (4:13). As a result, **we abide in Him and He in us**.

Testify then, is *martureō*," to be a witness" or "bear record" (John 1:7; 1 John 5:6). Believers can testify because the Spirit testifies through them. The idea of these genuine testimonies is their integrity or reality because they are the result of the work of God (sanctification). **That the Fa-**

ther has sent the Son to be the Savior of the world is not a statement of *universalism*. This very epistle delineates between the saved and the lost. The idea here is the same as with John 3:16; Christ is the only Savior, and the Savior for persons all over the world of every race, tribe, kindred, and tongue (Rev. 5:9). Those who are part of the new birth are the only ones who can testify in truth of this great Savior. The obvious outcome is that those who have encountered God–will testify. This testifying becomes a part of the evidence, or reality, of salvation. The believer's testimony is not merely from his lips, but from his life, how he lives, and here, with special emphasis on *demonstrating love*. This dramatic transition is seen when matched with passages such as Titus 3:3–5, where, before conversion, persons were once engaged in "malice, envy, hateful, hating one another." But, when the supernatural work of the "washing of regeneration and renewing" brought a massive change, they now love those they once hated.

This section began with "test the spirits" (1 John 4:1) and that was in specific reference to whom a person listens. In our day it would be a reference to where one attends church, and particularly where pastors or teachers are embraced. John then goes on with the detail of that testing. This testing was addressed (see 4:1-14). Why does he place so much importance on this? It is obvious from the wording "many false prophets have gone out into the world." This "testing of the spirits" is eternally important. It will have a direct relation on the spiritual well-being of all under the influence of those claiming to preach and teach God's Word.

Pause and Reflect

This paragraph emphasizes the telling evidences of love as an indicator of relation to Christ, and especially for those teaching. A sweeping, all-encompassing, dogmatic statement is made at the very beginning; all who truly know God possess God's kind of love. This must be so, because God is love. With this setting, John makes his arguments for how love is an essential characteristic of being a Christian, and for how those not possessing His love cannot be Christian. This love is initiated entirely by God Himself, and therefore cannot fail to exist within His own. Everyone who is truly born of God must have this love, without exception, and such love will be obvious. This kind of love should be manifest by those in places of Christian authority and influence. No one has seen God, instead, what he can see is the evidence of God's work in the lives of His children

> who are representing Him. As ambassadors for Christ, His children are to be witnesses demonstrating His love. The love of Christ that is within His children, is directly associated with the fact that God the Holy Spirit resides in and enables every true believer. The Spirit testifies through the believer that Jesus Christ is the exclusive Savior of the world. There is no other Savior or means of true transformation. Only in Christ can a person be rescued from his fallen and hopeless position of separation from God. Those with God's love testify to the truth of God, and His great salvation.

b. The Caution against False Presumption (4:15–21)

(1) Causes Genuine Peace (4:15–18)

Whoever confesses that Jesus is the Son of God, God abides in him, and he in God. We have come to know and have believed the love which God has for us. God is love, and the one who abides in love abides in God, and God abides in him. By this, love is perfected with us, so that we may have confidence in the day of judgment; because as He is, so also are we in this world. There is no fear in love; but perfect love casts out fear, because fear involves punishment, and the one who fears is not perfected in love.

Many attending church will admit that they do not have confidence in the reality of their eternal destiny. They hope their destiny is okay, and might presume that it is. They will often say something such as, *I am a good person who goes to church and seeks to do the right things. I have done everything I know to do. I have lived a good life, and I believe in God.* Such testimonies would be considered normal in most of the religious communities, but they are presumption only. Many think that absolute assurance of salvation cannot be known this side of the grave. However, the Christian should be reminded of passages such as 2 Timothy 4:8 and 18 where confidence is spoken of in terms of loving Christ's appearing. In that same passage, Paul indicates that the same attitude of assurance is for all of God's own. In this context, John continues describing true Christianity from false Christianity, only now he adds a Christ-centered form of assurance as another means of testing.

The reader was told back in verse 4:1 to, "test the spirits," to see whether they were from God. This test was a particular reference to a biblical test; looking under the surface of things with the understanding there can be false assumptions. If he is not listening to the right spirit, he can be presumptuous, and *presumption can lead to great tragedy*. In Nathaniel Hawthorne's "The Celestial Railroad," a parody following up on "Pilgrim's Progress" (John Bunyan's classic), the time had come when a railroad had been constructed from the city of *Destruction* to the *Celestial city*. The people riding on the railroad thought that they were going to end up in the *Celestial City* (heaven). The railroad was preferred to the old, hard road that the pilgrims were traveling, and claimed to end in the same place. There was only one thing wrong: the railroad was a deception and really did not lead to the *Celestial City*, but to hell. Nothing should be more sobering than being deceived about one's eternal destiny. Nothing is more important to know than the truth, and to know it now; for after this life, it is too late. Assurance for God's people bears a most important place in this passage.

First, its *significance* (4:15): a new paragraph begins, but it carries the same line of thinking. John elaborates the activity of the residence of the Spirit of God within every true Christian, and the testimony of love that the Spirit generates into outward confession and inward peace. First discussed is that there is a confession: **whoever confesses that Jesus is the Son of God, God abides in him (4:15)**. This is not only a reality in the true Christian, but is also a statement of fact that whoever confesses, in the manner stated, has God abiding in him and he in God. This again relates to those of whom we listen. The word: **confess** (*homologeō*) means "to be in agreement with God." It is a verb in the aorist tense, which means a fixed, definite attitude. It therefore cannot merely be *lip service*, but obedience and surrender. This thought, carried to a logical conclusion, is a life changing confession that shows the person has been revolutionized.

Second, it *signals* the *presence* of God as **God abides in him. Abides** (*menō*) means "to be present with, remain with, dwell with" (always referring to the actual presence of) either physically or spiritually. This is the same word used by Christ in John 15:6 where He commanded His disciples to "abide in Him," stating that "without Him they could do nothing." This abiding is a union, for the passage goes on to say **and he in God**, indicating the reality of the presence of God in those that are truly confessing Christ in saving faith, from both their lips and their life. The nature of the abiding can be seen elsewhere in Scripture as an *inseparable union* (Rom. 8:31–34; John 10:27–29). The knowledge and experience of the inseparable union makes a considerable difference in the attitude of the recipient.

Its significance is so very important that by comparison nothing else matters, and this significance provides a sense of peace and satisfaction beyond anything the world can provide.

Third, its *sanctification* (4:16): **We have come to know** expresses the idea of growth or progress. It is a realization of **the love which God has for us**. As noted before, **know** (*ginōskō*) is often used by John, and has the rich meaning of "to know absolutely, and by experience." It is always associated with a *relationship*. John is saying that the one who has this actual confession (4:15) experiences the presence of God in his life. How is that presence seen? It is evident in one's own trust. **Believed** is *pisteuō* which means "faith," or trusting in the truth that God has special love for His people. This word has the idea of growth in the sanctification process, and this growth has brought a sense of well-being (**come to know**) by experience, not just facts, but in a relational sense; a type of *internal peace* under the scope of God's love. Nothing could bring a greater sense of joy or well-being.

John again writes that **God is love**, one of the premier characteristics of God. As has been previously stated, the definition of this love *is the cross* of Jesus Christ. Its purpose in being added here goes beyond just the setting of this premier characteristic of God. A real Christian is a person who **abides in God, and God abides in him (4:16)**. There can be no exception (Rom. 8:9). Therefore, this person also **abides in love**. Again, there can be no exception, for when one receives true salvation he also receives God and His love. There can be no diminishing of the one without diminishing the other. If one has God, he has His love, and that love will make a *radical difference* in his attitude and perspective in life. John states that the presence of God and His love have an effect upon the believer's peace in the words, **the love which God has for us**. Knowing this fact and believing it with all of a believer's heart, brings *contentment* like nothing else. The unsaved, including those who are religious but lost, will not experience this sense of joy or contentment.

This work in salvation is supernatural and reflects God in the life of His children. The church, in general in these later days, has cheapened the quality of God's love by incorrectly applying it equally to every person. The Bible applies it *particularly*, and in the sense of saving love, exclusively to God's own (John 17). Particular love is another means of clarifying that there is a difference between *presumption* and *possession*, and the difference is the tangible love of God in the life. The work of God in the Christian naturally produces the character of God's particular love. The nature of particular love, loves God, His Word, His brethren, and what God loves.

Fourth, its *solace* (4:17–18): John now carries the product of God's presence in love further into the practical. Not only does love produce peace, but with it assurance. **By this**, he writes–by what? This abiding work just described, results in love and is in the process of being **perfected with us**, maturing the Christian and growing him in Christ-likeness (sanctification). The effect of this real love is so significant, so manifest, so real, that it influences all that the Christian does and thinks. It results in a different life, a life that could be called *the love life*.

One of the benefits of this love life in sanctification is assurance. John explains: **so that we may have confidence in the day of judgment (4:17)**. The **"day of judgment"** is the most important personal event for any person. Whatever else is important in each of life's events, it all pales by comparison to this one event. When a person stands before God, nothing else will matter. There are several occurrences in the Bible where men come face-to-face, at least in some measure, with God when His glory is being exemplified (Job 38–42; Is. 6; Rev. 1). In each circumstance, even righteous men are terrified and broken. Here, John says that **we may have confidence in the day of judgment**. The word **confidence** (*parrēsia*) refers "to boldness or frankness in speaking." It carries a measure of assurance, for the person's described that they will not shrink back (Rev. 6:16). The issue is readiness, and as this sense of readiness is so beyond the ability of man, there is nothing that man can do of himself to prepare for judgment. God Himself must be the *Preparer*. Therefore, what John says again speaks of the supernatural work of God. There is only one way to be ready, and that is to be ready in the manner that John describes. The soberness of this time of judgment is shown at the return of Christ when He separates the people in Matthew 25:41. That is also why "every knee will bow, and every tongue confess that Jesus is Lord" (Phil. 2:10), even the unsaved. With this sober reality looming, John boldly states, **we may have confidence**. How can this be so? It can only be so because of Romans 8:1: "There is now no condemnation to those who are in Christ Jesus." If a person is in Christ Jesus, condemnation is impossible; so says God Himself through Paul (Rm. 8:34). His standing, by position in Christ, is a glorious truth, and having a peace about it when he actually stands before Christ is a supernatural additional benefit. This confidence will come as we "test the spirits" now, grow in Him, love as described, and are abiding in Him.

John adds credence to the understanding of this confidence: **as He is, so also are we in the world**. To know in the mind what the Scripture states is one thing; to be able to apply this *practically* and *experientially* when standing before God is another. What is John really stating here as the ground of such confidence? **As He is, so also are we** is a statement of the believer's likeness to Him. His manifestation of love in the sanctification process is in the person in such a way that true Christians are becoming like Him in thought and action; this is genuine Christianity. There is real transformation that has and is taking place. Again, John is not talking about perfection, but he is talking about a transformation that is radical from the old life to the new. This transformation takes place within. It produces such a change that *peace* with God is not merely positional, but experiential. Salvation in Christ is not something that will be seen only in eternity, but it is at work in the life of faith in the *immediate* sanctification process. That is what this entire epistle is about–the reality that exists in the present life when one is born again.

In verse 18, John adds clarity when he writes: **There is no fear in love; but perfect love casts out fear (4:18)**. The word used for **perfect** (*teleios*) means "fullness of age" or "maturity." As love is present and matures in the child of God, it **casts out** or removes **fear** (*phobos*, "fright or even terror"). The solace comes as the Christian progresses in his sanctified life of faith. John declares; **there is no fear in love**. In this context, love replaces fear before God. "The fear of the Lord is the beginning of wisdom" (Prov. 9:10). There is an appropriate fear of God that is associated with right reverence, which brings with it a right priority to spiritual matters (2 Cor. 7:1; Phil. 2:12). This kind of fear is not what is being referenced here. The fear in this context is terror, and has to do with God's just, eternal punishment. In Revelation 6:15–16, during the great tribulation, many will try to hide themselves from the wrath of God. This fear is the kind that John obviously has in mind, for he goes on to add, **because fear involves punishment, and the one who fears is not perfected in love.** The one who has this kind of fear is knowledgeable of, and has a sense of his hopeless guilt (Rom. 1:19), and that the punishment that is coming is deserved.

In contrast, the one who has his confidence in Christ and loves Him for what He has done, has love in the place of fear. He knows that "He who knew no sin became sin on our behalf that we might be made the righteousness of God in Him" (2 Cor. 5:21). God cannot and will not hold those in Christ accountable, because Christ has already paid their punishment in full. This sacrifice is why His children, guided by the Holy Spirit, love Him so much. John says, **and the one who fears is not perfected in love (4:18)**. This fear also becomes a source of testing true conversion. If there is the same manner of fear by the one claiming to be a Christian that exists with those who will be in fear when they see His coming in the clouds, then they have not this kind of true love that results in assurance. Both cannot be true. Paul speaks of those who do love His appearing (2 Tim. 4:8). In that context he uses "all" just as John does here to describe every true believer. John is not addressing a sense of anxiousness or discomfort at standing before the King of Kings. After all, such an event takes one's breath away. Rather, what he is addressing is the kind of fear of the unrighteous who know *they have no basis* to be kept from hell. They are devoid of love, and therefore, can only be filled with terror. The one who loves His appearing will stand in humility and trembling, but with love and assurance that he is *forgiven* in Christ. This assurance is the difference between a child of God, and one who really does not know God.

(2) Causes Us to Love as He Loves (4:19–21)

We love, because He first loved us. If someone says, "I love God," and hates his brother, he is a liar; for the one who does not love his brother whom he has seen, cannot love God whom he has not seen. And this commandment we have from Him, that the one who loves God should love his brother also.

First, its *source* (4:19): at this point one might think, "I am not sure I can generate this kind of love, or hold fast to this kind of love." John reminds his reader once again that what he is discussing is *supernatural*. It is from God and not from the person. The word for **love** here is again *agapaō*, the "God-kind of love," shown in sacrificial love and interconnected with relationship. He says, **we love, because he first loved us (4:19)**. In other words, no person would have this kind of love were it not for God doing something in the person *first* to give him this kind of love, or place him in this sphere of relational love. This love is not sourced from the person, or maintained by personal determination and energy. It is something that God has done *for and in* the person. That does not mean that it is mechanical. For he does say–**we love**. It is the Christian actually loving, but knowing that behind it all is the work of God. God is the source and receives the glory. This knowledge and attitude should permeate all of those who are recipients of true salvation. Whatever the loving person has received is by grace, and the focus of gratitude toward God should mark the life now, and into eternity.

Second, its *surety* (4:20): the "world" (meaning the unsaved of the world) naturally hates Christians, as the world naturally hates God. It will therefore also hate those associated with God, because as Christ said, "Men love darkness rather than light" (John 3:19), and Christians are the light of the world. Christ also said, "If the world hates you, you know that it has hated Me before it hated you" (15:18). Their hatred is not only directed toward Christians, but it is also directed toward one another (Titus 3:3).

Therefore, when John says, **If someone says, "I love God," and hates his brother, he is a liar (4:20),** he is reinforcing and clarifying the argument that *change must take place* in every true child of God (2 Cor. 5:17). God is different than natural, unsaved men, and those who have been changed by Him, and have His Spirit within them, are in His sanctification process and are different. Those changed cannot be full of love and hate at the same time. For this reason, John uses the strongest language regarding such inconsistency–**he is a liar**.

John continues his argument: **For the one who does not love his brother whom he has seen, cannot love God whom he has not seen (4:20b)**. To do so would be an unreasonable impossibility. God's children are going to love whom and what God loves. Here he uses the *lesser to greater argument* (in the sense of what is seen and not seen). If a person hates someone who God loves (who is a tangible being known by sight), how can he, at the same time love God, whom he has not tangibly seen? This contradiction is the same issue stated by Christ in John 8:42: "If God were your Father, you would love Me." There must be a consistency flowing from the heart. Just as light and darkness *do not mix,* neither do love and hatred. To talk about loving God is easy, for merely saying so is an intangible difficult to measure. However, the absence of love for a brother, who can be seen, *betrays* the absence of love for God. This love serves as another proof for the believer's assurance of relationship with God. Does he have a genuine love for the brethren? The only love that counts is a love that is shown in the actual circumstances of life. It is often a love that is tested in interactions with another, and it will remain if it is a true God kind of love. It is a love that matches the character of God's love. If it is absent, the life of God is also absent.

Third, its *statement* (4:21): the fact of the responsibility to love one another has been made clear (John 15:12). Also, Christ stated: "If you love me, you will keep my commandments" (John 14:15). This obedience is what John is referring to when he writes: **and this commandment we have from Him**. He goes on to add: **that the one who loves God should love his brother also (4:21)**. The word **should** is not present in the original Greek language. It was added by the translators. In the Greek the passage reads: "That the one who loves God loves his brother also." It is stated *as a fact,* and not an option. It goes hand-in-hand with loving God, which is a command. John is stating that no one can really claim to be a Christian and disobey God's command to love.

Pause and Reflect

This portion of John's test for the reality of true salvation is based on the abiding presence of God in the Christian. Because God the Holy Spirit abides in every Christian and God is love, then love must also abide in the Christian. This abiding presence of love is sourced from God, and will therefore produce God's kind of love. The love present in the Christian shows itself in the production of several characteristics. All of these are the supernatural work of God and are shown in His work of sanctification. As they are not perfected, sometimes they may be shown more than at other times, but they will be present. John addresses a type of peace that is not fearful of the judgment of God, but has overcome fear by the power of faith, and the presence of God's love. This kind of love replaces fear, and therefore provides assurance. Because this love is generated from God (1 John 4:19), it is supernatural and will manifest itself as John describes. The Spirit is also working to give a clear confession of the Person of Christ. Because of His work and His love, the Spirit also causes Christians to love as God loves. They love what He loves and whom He loves. These are all possessions within the process of sanctification that are present in true salvation. Rightly seen and correctly understood, these add clarity to whether one is born of God or not, because they are the marks present when God's sanctification work is taking place. The consistency of this fact is based on the reality of them being sourced from God. They are marks of true salvation, real and maturing according to John, in all of God's salvation recipients.

6

The Consequences of Fellowship

1 John 5:1–12

Outline context:

II. The Requirement of Fellowship with Christ (1:5—5:12)

    A. The Conditions for Fellowship (1:5—2:11)

    B. The Challenge for Fellowship (2:12–29)

    C. The Characteristics of Fellowship (3:1– 3:24)

    D. The Cautions for Fellowship (1 John 4:1–21)

    E. The Consequences of Fellowship (5:1–12)

        1. Victory over the World (5:1–4)

            a. Observable Earmarks of New Birth (5:1–3)

Whoever believes that Jesus is the Christ is born of God, and whoever loves the Father loves the *child* born of Him. By this we know that we love the children of God, when we love God and observe His commandments. For this is the love of God, that we keep His commandments; and His commandments are not burdensome.

    In the book of Ecclesiastes, Solomon recounts his experiments with life. He had a unique and providential opportunity given to him by God. God made him a great king during forty years of peace, and granted him wisdom. He had likely the most luxurious circumstances of any king in history. With his great mind, he asked a simple question: "What advantage does man have in all his work under the sun" (Eccl. 1:3)? The idea of the phrase "under the sun" means life in a fallen world without any consideration of God. This question was his way of asking: *how can anyone get the most out of life in this fallen world* (leaving God aside)? In answering that question, Solomon literally experimented with everything. He found that nothing fulfilled and nothing that he did, when he left God out, provided any sense of happiness. He concluded that all was "vanity of vanity." He likened it to chasing the wind.

Today many modern churches are following the same path, and are doing the same sort of thing that Solomon sought. They are on a path to have fulfillment in this life, a *fulfillment* that leaves out *the new birth* in Christ, but still promises happiness and success. This idea seeks to make the world system work toward something meaningful. In order to address this pop culture thinking, some so-called Christian leaders have taken words out of context from the Bible to serve as a *supposed* God-authored way to make the world system work to advantage. In reality, even a casual study of the Bible shows that it warns against agreeing or engaging with the world system. Instead, the "world system" (conceptually, a summary of the darkness of the fallen world, or all that is contrary to God), must be overcome by faith in Christ. God's truth, when honored in correct study, brings a completely different view. It is a real hope and one that is distinguishable because it acts *contrary to*, and *not in conformity with*, the world system of evil. John brings the reality of the Christian's true position as one being at odds with the world system, and when this at odds position is present, it serves as a mark of genuine Christianity.

John has already dealt with the earmarks (belief, love, & obedience) of true Christianity. He has shown that the true and only real confirmation of a relationship with God is based on a life changing faith in Christ alone, demonstrated by these characteristics: *love for God, love for God's people, love for the truth, and genuine obedience*. John has defined each of these and shown them to be essentials in the sanctification process. All of these earmarks must be present and real. If they are not present, no claim to genuine Christianity has merit. John now goes a step further to build on what has been addressed. He uses the phrase "**born of God**" twice, and "**born of Him**." By doing so, he demonstrates the interlocking nature of these earmarks, and their attachment to the work of God and with each other.

(1) Its Belief (5:1a)

Whoever believes that Jesus is the Christ is born of God,

The phrase "**is born of God**" is in the perfect tense and refers to an event in past time that has abiding results in the present. This question arises: Is faith the cause or result of the new birth? It is the result! The idea of **is born of God** means that God has acted supernaturally. Being born of God causes the person to be in a *different category*. Christ discusses this truth with Nicodemus in John 3. Christ stated: "You must be born again." The Spirit of God must move on the heart so that a supernatural work of God results, and produces faith (matching the context of John 3:16). Because men are "dead in sin," having no life or ability to believe (Eph. 2:1; 8–9), a saving belief must always begin with God. The work of God changes the nature and ability so that one receiving His work will believe. This belief is not a mere statement, but a belief that transforms the life. It is radical and is shown by evidence or works (as James states, Jms. 2:17). This has already been defined (1 John 4:2–3). The phrase **whoever believes that Jesus is the Christ is born of God** is also connected with other earmarks because the passage continues with "**and**." This is the unique addition to what John has already defined. These are not stand alone marks that describe the true child of God, but all of them *combined provide a picture* of God's work in salvation.

(2) Its Love (5:1b–2a)

and whoever loves the Father loves the *child* born of Him. By this we know that we love the children of God, when we love God

John further states: **and whoever loves the Father loves the child born of Him**. This kind of love has also been defined beginning in 1 John 2:7. This love is interlocked with a true belief that Christ is the incarnation. Belief of this nature cannot be separated from love. If the person has this kind of belief, he must possess love for other brethren. This reasoning is described by the love in 1 John 4:8: "God is love." If part of God's very essence is love, then how could someone **born of Him** not bear the same characteristic? Additionally, love is always measured in tangible ways. John does not allow men to get by with *mere love talk*. Just as faith must be real according to God's terms, so must love. John continues: **by this we know that we love the children of God, when we love God (5:2)**. As already seen, love for God cannot be separated from love for those born of God (4:20). These two very great commandments in Scripture (Mark 12:28–31) *interlace* with true belief. They must always go together. The phrase "**by this**" shows an interlocking relationship of necessity between belief and love. But John does not stop here.

(3) Its Obedience (5:2b–3)

and observe His commandments. For this is the love of God, that we keep His commandments; and His commandments are not burdensome.

When we love God, and keep His commandments underscores that love is shown, not in words, but in actions. John says that love must be interlaced with obedience to God. If obedience is not a reality (not perfect obedience, but effective actions), then love is not really present. Practically, how does one show his love for God? The answer–by obedience to what He commands (John 14:15). **Commandments** by their very nature are not options, but demands on the one claiming a relationship. Obedience then, is the real proof of love for God and the proof of true saving faith. The theology and interlacing nature of these three components—belief, love, and obedience—are *consistently* shown throughout the Scriptures. Christ asked, "Why do you call me, Lord, Lord, and do not do what I say" (Luke 6:46)? The act of calling Christ "Lord," shows a type of supposed belief and perhaps love, but is not confirmed by obedience. Therefore, it does not match what John says is true of the person **born of God**. Belief, love, and obedience are three marks connected with and *dependent upon one another,* and are true of every real Christian. These are not perfected in this life, but must be real because they are from God. Their interlaced presence becomes the means of distinguishing the genuine Christian. They are inseparable; never is one seen without the others.

John adds, **for this is the love of God, that we keep His commandments; and His commandments are not burdensome (5:3).** Once again John shows the circular nature of these interlacing realities. **For this is the love of God, that we keep His commandments** is another way of saying the same thing John has been emphasizing. He then adds, **and His commandments are not burdensome.** Why would John add that statement? At first glance, it does not seem to fit the context. The word **burdensome** (*barus*) means "weighty," "grievous," or "oppressive." The reasons that they are not troublesome, harsh, or difficult are three-fold, God Himself gives the ability, love for God and faith makes them desirable, and God Himself paved the way in Christ. Since the true believer has a new nature, his new nature is more in harmony to keep the commandments than not to keep them. For these same reasons, keeping God's commands are not for the unsaved. Indeed, for the unsaved they are impossible to keep. The unsaved find the commands of God more than burdensome; they find them unreasonable and unworkable. John has added this statement to clarify that the keeping of God's commands, or obedience to God, for the saved is not something unappealing. It is something challenging, but appropriate, reasonable, appropriate, and even desirous. They are, therefore, not burdensome to the new nature. This keeping of the commandments is part of the reality of the process of sanctification in the life of the true Christian.

b. Overcoming Nature of New Birth (5:4)

(1) Its Power (5:4a)

For whatever is born of God overcomes the world;

The phrase **whatever is born of God** is a peculiar phrase with a specific focus. **Whatever** is *pas*, meaning "all or every." It is as though John is saying **whatever** is touched by God is going to be radically different; it cannot help but be. **Born of God** is the strongest term for describing the mysterious supernatural work of God in salvation. The very idea is likened to a *physical birth*. There is nothing as mysterious and wonderful as birth; a new life that can be seen but not comprehended. John says that if God creates a new spiritual birth, it is a type of life that overcomes the fallen world of sin. This life is much more than something about religion, professions, or denominations. The heart of Christianity is found in *true conversion*; the work of God giving new life that is an overcoming life. There are no true Christians (**whatever**) who do not overcome the world. A Christian by definition must be an overcomer.

What does **overcome the world (5:4)** mean? The insurmountable impossibility for any person to overcome the world by their personal ability is understood by knowing man's woeful natural condition in sin. This condition began in the garden (Gen. 3:17), where mankind fell into the hopeless position of sinful suffering and death. Romans 3 states that "all are under sin." Paul states that "by the transgression of the one, [Adam] death reigned to all" (Rom. 5:17). This *curse of sin* is the world that everyone is born into. It is described by Christ as a place of darkness (sinfulness, deception, untruth), referring to the character of its despicable realm. John later writes: "the whole world lies in the power of the evil one" (5:19). Yet, John states that those born of God **overcome the world**. This overcoming ties back to the three marks of Christianity that are active and working in every true believer. These are contrary to the world system and used to defeat captivity to it. *Belief* is contrary because its opposite is living immersed in the world's ideas and philosophy. *Love* is contrary because its opposite is selfishness. *Obedience* is contrary because its opposite is living in sin and wicked behavior against the character of God. Therefore the overcoming can be defined by its two manners; *its power* and *its passion.*

The word **overcomes** (*nikaō*) means "to subdue," "prevail," or "conquer by overpowering and gaining the victory." To think of all the people that one has known and have passed away is sobering. Thinking of it helps to consider all the hurt, distress, and misery experienced in all of the people who have lived on the earth. All these difficulties are the result of this world system being under a curse. In contrast, John has incredible news! He says that the Christian overpowers these difficulties! The reason is because **whatever is born of God overcomes the world (5:4)**. Ultimately, the one born of God will prevail, and the reason he will is that God is with him, and his *prevailing is certain.* God has promised, and God has determined to work on his behalf. This overcoming is real. It shows God's glory; it is totally *effective* because His power is sustaining it, and nothing matters when compared to it. In Revelation 21:4 and 7 is its ultimate, future fulfillment. It is the complete reversal of the cursed condition from the Garden of Eden, and resulting in the most blessed state conceivable. The overcoming begins in the present as a result of the new birth. It is the component of salvation referred to in Scripture as "sanctification." The present tense of **overcomes the world** means that it is a reality now, and continues into eternity.

One of the most frequently used statements in Scripture concerning salvation being a work of grace is Ephesians 2:8–9. The apostle Paul explains that salvation is a work of God in its entirety, and is a gift of God. Most people stop there in their consideration. However, verse 10 goes on to state: "we are His workmanship created in Christ Jesus for good works, which God prepared beforehand so that we would walk in them." This latter part is the focus of John in this epistle, and cannot be separated from the gift of grace and faith, which may be thought of as the justification part. The latter part of "good works" encompasses the *new sanctified life* in Christ, and addresses the very power or ability to overcome the world. The beginnings may be in small increments, but they are nonetheless radical changes that characterize a new person. Those same changes are always in the three areas of faith, love, and obedience. The source is always Christ (John 16:33), for the one **born of God** is born into the new life by being found in Him (Rom. 6:3–4). Ultimately, the one spoken of will defeat sin, death, and hell by the power of God.

(2) Its Passion (5:4b)

and this is the victory that has overcome the world—our faith.

The passion, or drive and desire to succeed are seen in the recipient's faith, and this faith is being exercised and challenged every day. This faith is a fixation on all that encompasses the truth of God and His glorious promises. He calls it **the victory that has overcome**, meaning that it occurred in the past, beginning at its inception, is now occurring in the present, and will continue into the future. It is the true saving faith of God given as a gift resulting from the new birth. This faith includes all of the reality of Christ, His work, God's love, God's sovereignty, and God's ruling to see it through as He has promised. This faith will move the person through the sinful world as a sanctified overcomer, living *in* the world, but not *of* the world. This faith, because of the power of God, will make the person a foreigner to the world system. The true Christian will be marked by a passion to live for Christ.

Pause and Reflect

The life of obedience to Christ becomes a priority, but it is not something distasteful to the Christian. Because of the "new birth," it is a way of life not only far superior to the old life, but also it is desired by the Christian. There are three marks given by John that he has emphasized throughout this writing: faith, love, and obedience. Each of these has specific definitions. Not only must they be understood in God's terms, but they are inseparably interlocked so that each is contingent upon and builds upon the others. The source of each is God. God has initiated all three and provides the ability for all three. These earmarks are active at the point of the new birth (justification), continue throughout this life (sanctification), and will continue into all eternity (glorification). There might be periods of lesser activity of these marks, but they do exist in every true child of God. These earmarks serve to make the recipients of them overcomers in this life. To be an overcomer means that the person is able and will, not perfectly, but to an effective substantial degree, overcome the world system of sin and deception. He will further overcome his own selfishness through love, and live a life of obedience through faith. This overcoming is the trend of one's life in Christ.

2. Validity through Christ's Authentication (5:5–12)

a. The Centrality of Christ (5:5)

(1) Identification of the Recipient (5:5a)
Who is the one who overcomes the world,

Because of sin, the world is very treacherous. Even the theories that are considered in the present as scientific and generally unquestioned are often contradicted by additional or later knowledge. The Christian knows this treachery to be true in such matters as *evolution*, *global warming*, or even certain *health* instructions. Knowing what is real and what is not is often difficult. Concepts that a person might place his confidence in, and later find to be untrue can contribute to an attitude of skepticism. The attitude of many in society is that everything is relative, or it does not matter, or no one can know what is real.

In the world of religion, there are many ideas, fanatics, and philosophers that claim to have the exclusive right answer. For the observer to know what to believe is most difficult, if not impossible. The general attitude is that *all ideas are equal*. What a person believes or does not believe matters not. However, the person who knows God unashamedly points everyone to one Person–Jesus Christ. The true Christian is not tossed around "by every wind of doctrine" (Eph. 4:14). Instead, the true Christian points to one exclusive reality: Jesus Christ, "the Word" (John 1:1).

This section in John's letter begins with a question; a question that refers back to the previous paragraph and to verse 4: **whatever is born of God overcomes the world**. Now John brings the question specifically to a person. He has made clear that everyone **born of God** is an overcomer. He makes no exceptions, and goes further by asking in a different way: **Who is the one who overcomes the world?** He answers this question by dealing once again with one of the marks necessary for genuine Christianity: **but, he who believes that Jesus is the Son of God (5:5)?** The answer has already been given back in 5:1–2, so why does he restate it this way? Remember that John is providing clarity and assurance. For assurance to be sure, it must be built on a foundation that is so firm that there is no reasonable way to *misconstrue* what is being stated. Here the focus and foundation is Christ. Ultimately, John is building yet another connecting argument. He is *connecting* the recipient of faith with the exclusive and only glorious Savior. The overcomer is exclusively identified with those who believe **Jesus is the Son of God**. This emphasis has two major issues for clarity. *First,* it is specific in the richness of what one believes about Christ. **Jesus is the Son of God** encompasses all that the Bible says about Christ. He is the second Person of the Trinity (the One true and only God). The reader must be prepared to understand the seriousness of this statement in relation to describing the recipient's faith. This statement by itself denies all belief systems that do not embrace Christ as God. Such beliefs are not just wrong, but cursedly wrong.

Second, no other belief, no matter how sincere, close to true, popular, or humanly logical, can overcome the effects from the imputed sin in the garden; inherited sin, or personal sin. There is no overcoming except by the power of Christ, who is God (John 14:6; 10:1, 9). All other forms of religious activity that are built around ideas of a Jesus less than God, will never overcome the curse. The cults have many followers, who while may be sincere and nice people, are wrong according to John. They deny Christ, at this critical point of His deity, and John wants every reader to understand the connectivity essential to the recipient of grace with His Lord. Not only are faith, love, and obedience interlocked and inseparable, but John wants us to know that such faith is joined with a *right view* of Jesus as the **Son of God**.

(2) Identification of the Means (5:5b)

but he who believes that Jesus is the Son of God?

Within the scope of this great salvation, John also adds further clarity to the means: faith. As Paul told his readers, faith is "the gift of God" (Eph. 2:8–9; Rom. 12:3). He has made salvation this way so that no man can boast of any merit on his part, not even his unmerited faith. Neither does faith stand alone, as though faith is the object in itself. John makes clear the centrality, focus, and *object* that is inseparable from faith, is Jesus Christ, **the son of God**. The emphasis, in order to clear up any possible confusion, is that faith must be in the true and living God–Christ who became a man, and yet, was God who dwelt among men.

Pause and Reflect

This writing is a test, a personal test, so that one might be assured his salvation is genuine. John keeps drilling deeper and deeper into the necessities required in defining true salvation. Additionally, he continues to show the interlocking relationships that are the necessary ingredients.

> He has taken his reader full circle to show both the character of his faith, and the object of his faith. Faith cannot be resting in anything other than Jesus Christ. The Jesus Christ of which faith must rest is identified exclusively as the Son of God; deity. If either the object of faith or the person in whom one claims to believe is positioned in faulty thinking, then the reality of the persons salvation does not match that which is required.

b. The Certainty of His Credentials (5:6–11)

(1) Authentication by Unique Agreement (5:6–8)

This is the One who came by water and blood, Jesus Christ; not with the water only, but with the water and with the blood. It is the Spirit who testifies, because the Spirit is the truth. For there are three that testify: the Spirit and the water and the blood; and the three are in agreement.

John has taken the reader through the identity of the recipient in Christ, and the means that is used by God to bring about this great salvation. He now reminds us of the glorious *credentials* of the Savior. He provides a confident apologetic for salvation by Christ alone. The **One who came** is an obvious reference to Christ. Please note that **"One"** not only refers to Christ in a unique manner, but also to the exclusive nature of His Person. He alone is the Savior; there are not many saviors (John 14:6).

John, therefore, provides two of the three arguments for authentication of the credentials of Christ: **water and blood**. What does John mean by these two credentials? Keep in mind that this epistle is about reality, genuineness, and authenticity. John uses a similar reference to water in John 3:5, where Christ is speaking to Nicodemus. In John 3, some think that Christ is referring to water baptism, but the context is the new covenant, promised long before by the prophets (Jer. 31:31; Ezek. 36:25–27; 1 Cor. 11:25), of which the church, having been grafted into the life of God (Rom. 11:17), is a part. This "new covenant" is essential if anyone is to be saved. Jesus was speaking to a Jewish leader, someone familiar with the Scriptures. By expressing **water and blood (5:6)**, He was depicting with the water the *necessity of cleansing* (seen in Ezek. 36:25) used in temple rituals to picture cleansing from sin (Ex. 30:20). Nicodemus would have been familiar with this essential ritual. He was using something physical as a metaphor for that which God must do spiritually. There is a need for purity, and water depicts and is used for cleansing, always with a view to the necessity of spiritual cleansing from sin. Christ was pure (John 8:46), but became sin on behalf (2 Cor. 5:21) of the elect that they might be cleansed or purged from sin and made pure like Him. Water, therefore, is a picture of cleansing and signifies God's work of purity and holiness. It testifies to who He is; that is why He is here called the **One**. This picture is also one reason baptism is used as the *ordinance of initiation* into Christ; it is a physical picture of an act of spiritual cleansing. Christ was baptized, not for personal sin, but in order to be identified with those who are baptized to be identified in Him. He was sinless, and yet, baptized to be identified with sinners. He testified by water. When the Christian is in Him, he is born of that same water; he is baptized into His death, and cleansed because He became sin for him (2 Cor. 5:21). Therefore, he must be born of water (figuratively water), to declare the essential work of Christ in cleansing and the Spirit in making us new.

John does not stop there. He says **not with the water only**, but he adds **and blood**. The means whereby the perfect Lamb of God could be the believer's sacrifice was not only by living a holy life, but also, by *actually dying* in his place, and by shedding His precious blood. Peter expresses this idea best: "Knowing that you were not redeemed with perishable things like silver or gold from your futile way of life inherited from your forefathers, but with precious blood unblemished and spotless, the blood of Christ" (1 Pet. 1:18–19). John does not stop with the uniqueness of the pictures, types, and acts prophesied from Old Testament writings. He goes on to state: **it is the Spirit who testifies because the Spirit is the truth** (5:6b). This is now the third witness, as John will go on to state that **there are three that testify (5:7)**. At the time of Christ's baptism, there was a visible testimony of the Spirit descending as a dove (Matt. 3:16). God the Father spoke from heaven in confirmation of His Son (Matt. 3:17). Additionally, His works testified (John 14:10); Christ stated: "The Father abiding in Me does His works." All that He did while on earth testified to the Spirit of God working, giving absolute identity as the Messiah promised from the beginning. The **Spirit** is the primary supernatural testimony for Christ, actively showing Christ's authenticity. As this is something seen in identifying Christ, it continues to be seen in His people who have the same Spirit. John calls Him **the Spirit is the truth** because He cannot tell a lie. Such would be impossible since God the Spirit is truth in His essence. In the Old Testament, before judgment was passed on a person convicted of a serious crime, there had to be at least *two witnesses*, and three were preferred (Deut. 17:6). John demonstrates that Christ met all the standards perfectly and that His *three witnesses* are aligned in perfect agreement. These three witnesses (**three that testify**) are irrefutable proof of identifying the glorious Savior. Implied in this context is the Spirit working in every Christian in a similar manner, identifying the Christian through the three witnesses of faith, love, and obedience.

> ## Pause and Reflect
>
> Since the Savior is authentic and genuine and His authenticity is shown by His work and testimony, does the believer not know that the salvation that He brings to His people will also be authentic, and its testimony shown by the works or testimony in the lives of those saved? The use of the metaphor water is emphasis upon the necessity of the Spirit working in the purification of life, and the use of blood is a reference to the actual work of Christ on the cross. The overcoming influence of the Spirit is at work in the life to transform the nature of the saved. By the Spirit of God, these witnesses identify Christ as the true Savior. In similar manner, the Spirit works to identify the Christian by three witnesses: faith, love, and obedience. The evidence of these three witnesses God provides as those testifying to the new life in Christ.

(2) Authentication by the Father's Testimony (5:9)

If we receive the testimony of men, the testimony of God is greater; for the testimony of God is this, that He has testified concerning His Son.

If we receive the testimony of men, the believer is constantly acting on reasonable beliefs that what others tell him is true. He could not get by a single day if he did not react to information from others. He does this unless he has reason to suspect the information is false. He must trust people to get along in business and with family and friends. However, people are often untruthful, deceived, or just wrong. God is *never* wrong. He can always be trusted. His testimony is what ultimately counts. He has given the believer the testimony of His validated Holy Word. He has even worked His testimony in the *providential* events and circumstances of history. There is not one thing in His Word or in the history of the world to invalidate the message God has given. Quite the contrary; prophecy given and fulfilled exemplifies His truthfulness. John simply means that **the testimony of God is greater**. Why then do men want to foolishly believe all kinds of unreasonable and unsubstantiated theories such as evolution, false religion, humanism, and atheism that emanate from unsaved men rather than

God? The central message from God Himself is **for the testimony of God is this, that He has testified concerning His Son**. God the Father gave believers His testimony in Matthew 3:16, and His testimony concerning Christ in many other places in His Word (Is. 42:1; Ps. 2:7). Christ Himself gave His children the works that only the Father could do (John 10:37–38). Indeed, the *entirety* of Scripture is a testimony of Christ (John 5:39). The *bottom line* is an issue of believing God, or of denying Him against reason, and believing theories and ideas of lost mankind. The person studying this book (1 John), written under inspiration, will either receive what is stated or will reject it. The reader should consider carefully, because to reject this writing in any manner, is to reject God's testimony.

(3) Authentication by Changed Lives (5:10–11)

The one who believes in the Son of God has the testimony in himself; the one who does not believe God has made Him a liar, because he has not believed in the testimony that God has given concerning His Son. And the testimony is this, that God has given us eternal life, and this life is in His Son.

John's statement, **the one who believes in the Son of God has the testimony in himself**, is precisely what he has been referring to in this epistle. The **testimony in himself** is a *radical* transformation of life. The Scripture describes it as being "a new creation" (2 Cor. 5:17), which is precisely what John has been addressing in the three key areas that must be affected: faith, love, and obedience. These three elements of life cannot be successfully *imitated* or generated by man through personal rehabilitation or self-induced reform. No true Christian is a *self-made man*. Transformation is the work of God, and therefore, the saved person **has the testimony in himself**. Paul states in Romans 8:16: "The Spirit Himself testifies with our spirit that we are the children of God."

And the testimony is this, that God has given us eternal life, and this life is in His Son. God has shown this statement to be true by the transformation of individuals. To have **eternal life** never merely refers to existing forever, but it has the idea of the life of God; to exist eternally with Him. Even the wicked are spoken of as in eternal destruction or some form of existence in hell, but here, the idea of **life** is the rebirth in Christ. God has made this life available and testified of it in the manner described. Those who reject God reject His precious gift and do not have **eternal life**.

> **Pause and Reflect**
>
> There can be no neutrality concerning the Christian's approach, or lack thereof, to God. If a person does not believe the testimony of God, he is defying all evidence and reason. In his rejection, the person is challenging God and calling Him a liar. This lack of neutrality is because God has obviously spoken and is continuing to speak (Rom. 1:18; Heb. 1:1–3). Even the plan of God cannot possibly be explained in any human theory. God sent His Son to die. The person who rejects His message and testimony has rejected God. Nothing could be more offensive, absurd, or wicked. The person rejecting God's testimony cannot plead ignorance, neutrality, or wish away the fact that God has testified before the world. God has made a testimony that is clear and complete. In a similar and lesser sense, the Christian makes a testimony of the work of God that serves as the prominent evidence, and of the reality of personal salvation. He does so first and foremost by trusting God through His Son.

(4) Authentication of His Ownership (5:12)

He who has the Son has the life; he who does not have the Son of God does not have the life.

The simplest summary of the Christian is this very statement: **He who has the Son has the life; he who does not have the Son of God does not have the life**. Notice the black and white nature of this statement. The reader, any person, either has the Son, and with Him **the life**—the true and exclusive salvation of which John has been writing—or he does not have the Son, and therefore does not have **the life**. John has already gone into some detail about the meaning of to have **the life**. Ultimately, having **the life** is all about whether or not one *belongs* to Christ (John 10:27–28). Clearly, from this basic statement that reality must be present. John does not say, "he that accepts Jesus or is religious and sincere," but he says who **has the Son of God** by *true possession*. John is all about reality in providing this personal examination concerning assurance.

7

The Confidence from Fellowship

1 John 5:13–15

Outline context:

I. The Reality of the Person of Christ

II. The Requirement of Fellowship with Christ (1:5—5:12)

III. The Reassurance of Eternal Fellowship with Christ (5:13–21)

A. The Confidence from Fellowship (5:13–15)

1. Assurance from the Writing (5:13)

In coming to the close of this letter, John specifically identifies his purpose in writing: so that **you may know that you have eternal life**. The person will know if he has eternal life by how he matches the examination given by John. He says that by reading and studying this writing, a person can receive assurance of his salvation, assurance that his salvation is real. Here is a review and summation of the precise truths stated as evident in real Christianity:

- (1 John 1:6) True Christians do not walk in darkness; they do not follow the thinking and ways of non-Christians.

- (1 John 1:8) True Christians have a recognition, humility, and repentant attitude about their sin.

- (1 John 2:4) True Christians are in tune with God; they are concerned about pleasing Him and doing His will.

- (1 John 2:9) True Christians cannot hate their brother in Christ.

- (1 John 2:19) True Christians persevere in their belief.
- (1 John 3:9–10) True Christians are not addicted to, or ruled by the practice of sin. While they still sin, that is not the general character of their lives. Instead, the manner of their lives is love.
- (1 John 4:6) True Christians listen to the words of Scripture.
- (1 John 5:2) True Christians have three obvious realities present in their lives: faith in God, love for God and for God's children, and obedience to God's Word. These truths interplay and overlap.
- (1 John 5:4) True Christians "overcome the world" (the world system of thinking, sinning, and opposing God).

a. Evident Purpose (5:13)

These things I have written to you who believe in the name of the Son of God, so that you may know that you have eternal life.

Once before in this letter, John used this phrase **these things I have written** (2:26). This identifying purpose was in the section concerning false teachers, and it served as a warning. This thought was obviously a subset. **These things I have written** in the present context, is obviously referring to the letter as a whole. In today's culture the purpose of the writing would normally be included at the beginning of a letter, but such a practice was not necessarily true in John's day. As with his Gospel writing (John 20:31), he tells the reader the purpose of the writing near the end of the letter. He says **so that you may know you have eternal life** is a purpose statement to remove all confusion, speculation, or guessing. God had John write this letter and to include it in the *canon of Scripture* for the purpose of personal examination, and with it, assurance for those who meet the qualifications. The assurance of salvation must be anchored in the Scripture itself from which the reader derives the message of salvation. No other validation from a church, preacher, religion, or any other source will do. This Word is the exclusive means God has given to clear away all speculation so that **we may know we have eternal life**. This understanding brings supreme comfort to those in harmony with the truth of this epistle, and at the same time, great discomfort to anyone who is playing religion or *professing* without *possessing* (James 1:23–24). This epistle is the *measuring stick* as it were. Does the reader "measure up" to the descriptions in this epistle? If not, he is encouraged to turn from his mere religion, to Christ alone. He must confess his sin and recognize Christ as his only hope. He should call on Him that he might be saved, and thereby comply by living out the description of the work of God found in this epistle.

b. Exclusive Recipients (5:13a)

These things I have written to you who believe in the name of the Son of God.

The target audience of the epistle is **to you who believe**. Interestingly, John writes to those with faith, and yet, by the writing, tests whether the faith of the readers is of the type that is saving faith. Of special note is that John is really only writing to those **who believe in the name of the Son of God**. The concept of **the name of the Son** is a statement of belief that encompasses all that Christ is as the God/Man/Savior and Lord. It is bringing together the infinite summation of the Christ of the Bible by stating **the name of the Son of God**, all that He is as shown in the Scriptures. The kind of faith that John speaks of is the kind of faith that *believes all that the Scripture says* of Christ, and is thereby, manifested in the life as clarified in this epistle. Indeed, there is a type of faith in the Scriptures that is insufficient for salvation. Christ spoke in John 8:31 to: "those Jews that had believed Him," and yet, this kind of belief was inadequate, for He later condemns them in the harshest terms. Peter speaks of a faith in writing his second epistle: "to those who have received a faith of the same kind as ours" (2 Pet. 1:1), implied is the fact that there is a faith that is not adequate for salvation. This same idea is seen in James 2:19, where James says the demons "believe in God and tremble," but there is no salvation for them; their kind of faith will not save. Therefore, the examination of this epistle is to be overlaid on the reader's life to see if the reader's faith is of the *same kind* that John says is necessary. In other words, a physician has to periodically take examinations to show he is up-to-date (qualified) with the latest information to practice medicine. The examination gives assurance to the physician and to the patients that the one practicing medicine is qualified. In Christianity, the stakes are much higher. Each person needs to know he belongs to Christ before he passes from this life.

c. Eternal Life (5:13c)

that you may know that you have eternal life.

As previously stated, **eternal life** is not merely referring to the everlasting length of existence, but also, to the quality of that existence. It is the *antithesis* of eternal damnation in hell. The best way to describe this **eternal life** is to read Revelation 21:3–7. This description is so glorious that it cannot be comprehended, while the antithesis in hell is so terrible that it cannot be imagined either. **To know you have eternal life** makes all the difference, and that difference begins in this life. If a person knows who he is in Christ and where he is going, all of the issues with which he is temporarily dealing *seem small* (2 Cor. 4:17). Nothing is more encouraging and life-changing than to know Christ and to be secure in that knowledge. So, verse 13 is the summation and purpose of this epistle: to bring assurance of salvation and confidence by seeing the work of God in a believer's life, and by having confidence that the promises of God are absolutely true (Titus 1:2). Passing God's examination through John is **to know you have eternal life**.

2. Assurance from Confident Prayer (5:14–15)

a. Expectation He hears (5:14)

This is the confidence which we have before Him, that, if we ask anything according to His will, He hears us.

Knowing the God of the universe through His Son, Jesus Christ, is the most blessed state conceivable. Because the believer's relationship with God has been restored through Christ (Rom. 5:1), he has immediate and real communion with Him. He can come before the "throne of grace" (Heb. 4:16) and speak to Him. In itself, this concept is significant and unthinkable, but the Christian is none-the-less commanded to "pray without ceasing" (1 Thess. 5:17).

John uses the term **confidence (5:14)**, which is related to the believer's faith in Christ. Christians see the world differently. They recognize that God is in control and is doing all things according to His divine plan. Nothing then, is more encouraging and carries more **confidence** than to be able to come into His presence in prayer, and to commune with Him. This statement should give the Christian boldness and confidence as he prays. Now, John makes reference to all that has been discussed. He is not merely addressing prayer in some general manner, but in reference to living the Christian life. After all, *living the Christian life* is what this letter is about; it is about living and *demonstrating* that he has a relationship with the God of glory. It is to know that he is somewhere along the path of God's sanctification. How does he do that? He must have God's strength and His power to enable him.

Paul writes in Philippians 2:12–13: "So then my beloved, just as you have always obeyed, not as in my presence only, but now much more in my absence, work out your salvation with fear and trembling; for it is God who is at work in you, both to will and to work for His good pleasure." This passage sums up the very truth being addressed by John. The Christian *struggles* in his efforts to live out his faith, but at the same time, his faith is lived out because God *is on his side* (Rom. 8:31), and is ultimately behind the believer's effort to give him the ability for overcoming power. Knowing by clear command that the Christian has a responsibility to pray, he knows he is to ask of God and seek Him constantly. John says that if the believer should **ask anything according to His will, He hears us**. There are two very important concepts to note about this phrase. First, whatever he asks for must be **according to His will**. Much could be said of this concept, but John is putting this praying into a context of being successful in living the Christian life. He is not referring to *frivolous prayer*, but for strength, providence, and guidance in sanctification. Second, the phrase **He hears us** means that He hears not merely because He, as God, is aware of everything, but also that He takes what is asked into account. God's plan and good pleasure is for true Christians to *successfully* overcome the world, and live their Christian lives as described in this letter (Rom. 6:22; 1 Thess. 4:3). The amazing thing is that God has not only determined the end result of the Christian's life (Phil. 1:6), but He has also determined the means to accomplish it. One of the chief means is through prayer. Through prayer, the believer actually becomes the *instrument* of God's will. Prayer is fellowship, relationship, trust, and obedience all in one. It is essential in the life of the Christian. Prayer shows dependence on God to do for His children what they cannot do for themselves.

b. Expectation He answers (5:15)

And if we know that He hears us *in* whatever we ask, we know that we have the requests which we have asked from Him.

John writes: **and if we know that He hears us in whatever we ask**. Three times in these three verses John writes **"we know."** John reiterates this phrase as a source of great comfort and blessing. There is no speculation that the believer's prayers only reach the ceiling. No, they reach the very ear of God. God promises through John that He will acknowledge the prayers of His people. John goes on to state: **we know that we have the requests which we have asked from Him**. There is great comfort in knowing this. He is saying that the believer, as God's child, can have the absolute confidence of God's interest and concern for his prayers. He is with him. There are times when heaven might seem as if it is made of brass. God might not seem to pay attention to the believer's prayers, but John *assures* us that God does listen. The true comfort comes from understanding that whether he receives an immediate answer, or whether he does not receive the answer he expected, God does hear His child and He has his *best interest* in mind (Rom. 8:28). God knows all things actual and possible. He knows better how to answer prayers than the believer knows how to pray. There is great comfort in knowing that God is working for His child and actively so. Consider the prayer of Paul in 2 Corinthians 12:7–10. Paul had a profound reason to ask God to remove something seriously troubling him. He could rationalize that he is trying with all his effort to serve God, and that this "thorn in the flesh" (whatever it was), was something that did or could inhibit his ability to serve. However, the context says that God *had a reason* for giving it to Paul, and God was not going to remove it. When Paul received God's answer, he was completely comforted and truthfully stated "most gladly . . . I am well content . . . for when I am weak then I am strong." If the Christian really turns his concerns over to God, he can *shift* all to Him, and be content, and rest in the reality that He hears and is doing what is best and right for His children. This assurance is the meaning behind the phrase **we know that we have the requests which we have asked from Him**. The believer can stop fretting over whatever the burden is, and know that God has everything under control and is doing, and will do, what is best.

Pause and Reflect

God has promised to hear the prayers of His people. The emphasis is on the prayers for overcoming the world and living the Christian life. The Christian is far from being alone in his overcoming in the world. He has the God of all glory with Him, and is able to commune with Him at any time. The idea of "hearing" carries with it the fact of God consciously, and specifically, acting upon the prayers of His children. In this, the believer can have absolute confidence. Therefore, since God promises to act upon those prayers, the believer can find great solace in turning everything over to Him, and then resting in whatever decision or direction God reveals.

> How can the believer so rest? Scripture says that God knows all things and always acts with the best interest of His glory and His people in view. Even if God's answer to a prayer is ultimately a "no," the believer can find contentment in trusting Him and knowing that He made the best decision. This contentment is a matter of faith, and it brings great comfort.

8
The Conclusion from the Writing
5:16–21

Outline context:

I. **The Reality of the Person of Christ**

II. **The Requirement of Fellowship with Christ (1:5—5:12)**

III. **The Reassurance of Eternal Fellowship with Christ (5:13–21)**

  A. The Confidence from Fellowship (5:13–15)

  ## B. The Conclusions from the Writing (5:16–21)

    ### 1. Prayer Guidance (5:16–17)

One of the better things about our otherwise morally decaying society, is that there has been an increase in volunteerism. Much of this is done for the wrong motives, but there are some useful endeavors being done to help others. Many volunteers are working in hospitals, serving in food banks, and building homes. These acts are good things, but they do not compare with the spiritual. What if a person possessed the greatest and most important ability to help others? That person might even hold the key to the greatest success and joy for another person. Christians have that key. It is the *key* of prayer. John has given an exhaustive explanation of the difference between a true Christian, and one that is merely a Christian by profession. True Christians are born again and have characteristics of love, faith, and obedience. In verses 14 and 15, John addressed the Christian's *relationship* to prayer. As true children of God, Christians have access to God, and as true children of God, He is interested in their prayers. Now John, in keeping with the context, provides very practical guidance concerning the prayer requests of Christians on behalf of those he has been discussing. This passage is considered extremely difficult by many theologians.

a. Possible Interpretations (5:16a)

If anyone sees his brother committing a sin not *leading* to death, he shall ask and God will for him give life to those who commit sin not leading to death.

Some say this passage has a reference to the classifications of sin based on Old Testament passages. These are sins called *mortal sins* and *venal sins*, sins that were punishable by death and those that could, on the other hand, be forgiven. However, this interpretation does in no manner fit the context. There is not any evidence to conclude the connection.

Others believe this passage could be referring to the unpardonable sin of Matthew 12:32, which was blasphemy against the Holy Spirit. Blasphemy is the idea of speaking evil directly about God (the 3rd Person) Himself. It is a total rejection of God and His work. The passage before us is the context of a lifestyle or behavior in sin (as we shall see), and not a direct attitude of rejecting the very Person and work of God. There is no indication from the context that the person engaged in the sin is directly accusing God of injustice, or denying His work, or even confronting God's authority. Rather it appears as someone actively engaged in sinful activities contrary to God, His Word, and or His commands

Other theologians believe that John is addressing physical death as a result of sinning. References here are made to Numbers 18:22 and Isaiah 22:14. This reference is also seen with Moses' death before entering the "Promised Land," because of his sin (Deut. 32:50–51). In the New Testament, there are also references to death resulting from sin (1 Cor. 5:5; 11:29–30; 1 Tim. 1:20; James 5:15; and Heb. 12). Some of these references can be argued to be saved individuals, dying prematurely (as Moses), while others might be in reference to non-Christians dying as a result of sin. Another account is that of Ananias and Sapphira (Acts 5), who lied against the Holy Spirit and died on the spot. The idea then, under this interpretation with regard to the passage, is that sin is such an affront to a Holy God, and the patience or endurance of God is at its end, thus causing the person to be prematurely taken by Him in physical death. This interpretation is usually applied to Christians who are engaged in sin, and God determines that He will not allow them to continue. This illustrates the severest form of discipline; removal from the earth. So in verses 16–17, the thought is that these passages have a reference to praying for Christians who commit sin. However, there is the recognition that praying for those who commit more serious sins, **sin leading to death**, might well be too late. Then it is God's will to take them in early physical death.

There is one final interpretation of this passage. The theory is that John is referring to "spiritual death." This view takes the context into account, within the antithetical (either/or) framework of one being a true Christian or merely a *professor* and not a *possessor*. John is therefore addressing eternal life and eternal death in providing guidance for prayer. True believers possess eternal life (John 5:24), and unbelievers remain in spiritual death (3:19–20; 1 John 3:14). Thus the **sin leading to death (5:16)** is not sin committed by true believers necessarily, but by unbelievers, referring to those who by their practice of sin show that they are not truly saved. Keep in mind the repeated context in 1 John is that unbelievers are identified by their slavery to sin, and this slavery is the reason for their practice of sin. This sin would be viewed by John as **sin leading to death**. This view is in keeping with the context of those held captive by the practice of sin, being the same ones that, by their actions, are involved in **sin leading to death** (eternal separation from God). They are seen by their manner of life in sin as those who have not been reborn, and are engaged as all non-saved are in continued sinful practices. Therefore, the Christian is instructed to pray for professing Christians who are engaged in sin in the same manner as expressed in the first chapter of 1 John (where John states that Christians do sin). However, they are not to expect prayer to be answered for those who are showing by their continual sinful activities and non-repentance, the strong possibility of their actual lost condition (3:8–10). Those shown in this lifestyle are presenting evidence of not really being saved, and bringing into question the effectiveness of any prayer for restoration of fellowship, as that fellowship does not exist.

Pause and Reflect

The correct understanding of this passage must be found as one of the last two interpretations. It is referring either to preventing sin, and possibly the early death of a Christian by his sin, or to differentiating between the saved and the lost regarding prayer guidance, accountability, and expectation. Ironically, the outcome in either of these situations is similar. In either case, recognizing that sin is a very serious offense against God and that it must be overcome, the Christian is praying for another professing Christian. Christians also must have prayer to face their remaining battles

> against personal sin. Christians alone can pray for one another, and are commanded to do so.

In order to understand this passage, some academic work associated with the context is essential. First, who are these persons potentially being addressed? They are those **"committing a sin"**. This phrase is a little misleading from the original language. The word for **sin** is *harmatia,* the typical word for sin. However, the words **"committing"** and **"a"** do not commonly align together. The word **committing** is the same base word for **sin** (*harmatanō),* except that it is plural. The literal translation is "sinning sin," or the idea is the plurality of sin or the practice of sin. The translators have added **leading**, so if the initial phrase is taken literally, it reads: "if anyone sees his brother sinning, sin not to death." Some interpret the phrase as "sin that is going towards death." That the context is referring to one big sin is very unlikely. In fact, if it was one big sin, it would likely be specifically named, so the faithful could avoid it, and pray concerning it. Instead, John, using sin in a plural manner, is addressing the on-going captivation to sin or practice of sin leading to death. **Death** is *thanotos,* the typical word for "separation," used both physically and spiritually. However, the only other time it is used in 1 John is in 3:14, where it is definitely addressing spiritual death, not physical death. Also, the context of 3:14 is discussing the practice of sin (3:4, 7–8), and the resulting comments about spiritual death reflect on the fact that those who are engaged in practicing sin have not passed from death (spiritual death) to life (the spiritual work of God in the heart). This author suggests that this context is a continuation of the general theme. The **sin[s] to death** refers to a lifestyle demonstrating that the person considered is not truly born from above, for he is immersed in the practice of sin. He is practicing sin in a manner reflecting the unsaved, engaged in **sin to death**. If, as the passage states, he has committed offenses **not sin[s] to death** (5:16b), then there is hope for him to be truly saved. His sins are not so extreme by practice, so there is yet hope that he is a Christian.

This explanation is consistent with the text already spoken of in 1:8–10 and 3:4–10. **Sin[s] to death** refers then to a lifestyle demonstrating that the persons considered are *not truly* born from above. Their practice of sin is *incompatible* with being a child of God. This context has reference to the deliberate and persistent preference of darkness to light, falsehood to truth, or sin to righteousness. One writer explains the phrase along these lines: it is the difference between the person who sins, but hates his acts, compared to the person who has *a love affair* with sin, and thereby practices it as the characteristic of his life.

Some make their determination of position on this text based on the term **brother**, *adelphos* meaning "the womb, showing connectivity." They believe when this word is used it must be a true **brother** in Christ. This interpretation is used in the argument for the premature physical death of a Christian. The argument is that since the **brother** term is used, John must be addressing true Christian brothers. This interpretation, however, is not emphatic in all other contexts where the term can merely be addressing those claiming or professing to be Christians (Heb. 3:12–13; James 5:19–20). In both of these cases, the failure was spiritual death. Also, and most importantly, the same thing is seen in the greater context of 1 John: 2:9, 11; 3:10, 15; 4:20. All of these passages use **brother** entwined with those who are only bearing a profession, but not the reality of the new birth. These being spoken of as brothers in these contexts are spiritually dead. Whether then, saved or unsaved, what can be concluded of the person who is the object of prayer, is that he is behaving indistinguishably from an unbeliever.

The last bridge to cross with this passage, under the interpretation referring to spiritual rather than physical death, is the phrase **give life**. To what is this phrase referring? Is it referring to physical life or spiritual life? If it is referring to physical life, the one praying is seeking that God would spare the **brother** a form of discipline leading to premature death. However, if it is spiritual life, to what is it referring? In the latter "spiritual life" interpretation, it would simply be the *opposite* direction from what sin holds. The idea would be that the sinning true brother would get back on track, and live the Christian life in a manner showing that he is moving toward life (spiritual life), instead of toward death (spiritual death). One must keep in mind that the word **life** is found in ten verses in 1 John. In all of these verses, the reference is not to physical life, but to spiritual life, which is being contrasted with spiritual death. Two clear examples of this obvious use of spiritual life are in verses 1:2 and 3:14; the point being that John is discussing spiritual life throughout this letter. Why then would he suddenly change only to physical life in contrast to physical death, and how would that fit the entire context? The word **give** is *didōmi*, meaning "bestow," "bring forth," "or commit." It also is used in other places in 1 John. In verse 5:11, it is referring to eternal life, and so it is in 3:1, as love "bestowed" on us by the Father. The word bestow in these passages is also related to spiritual life, not to physical life. Again, spiritual life is the theme of the entire epistle. Therefore, the author believes it may well be that both of these interpretations are relevant, in the sense that the person praying needs only to recognize the determination of the effectiveness of his prayer is in God's sovereign, wise assessment, and purpose. The object (person) of the prayer may be a Christian or perhaps, not a Christian. If the person (object of prayer) is truly a Christian, he will be restored because all true Christians will persevere in the faith (Phil 1:6). If he is not a Christian, he cannot be restored, as he was really never saved (1 John 2:19), and only had a profession.

Going a little deeper, the structure of the statement **he shall ask and God will for him give life to those who commit sin not leading to death (5:16)** seems awkward. However, we must think contextually. John is writing from the viewpoint of a person, *showing by his life*, whether he has spiritual life or whether he is spiritually dead. The evidence of spiritual life throughout this epistle is the issue and whether or not God has actually "bestowed," or "given" life in Christ. If the person is involved in sin, the person comes under question as to whether there is true life. Here, the observer must gauge whether the involvement in sin is so dynamic that there is yet a possibility that he could be a Christian. The situation is addressing whether there is evidence with the manner of life so that the one praying can determine if he is praying for a saved person, or for a lost person. If one is praying for a saved person, there is appropriate expectation of the person's turning from the sin. If the sin is not **sin . . . to death,** but rather, demonstrates that the person is likely unsaved, and advanced in the practice of sin (as in Rom. 1:24–32), then the Christian can pray that God may **give life**. Whether the person is saved or unsaved, the Christian can pray that God will establish them on the righteous path where spiritual life is real and demonstrated. However, if the person is so immersed and given over to sin, John says: **I do not say that he should make request for this**. The statement back in 1 John 3:22 promised *a positive answer* to prayer for those living out their relationship with God. This by definition would be praying according to God's will. Here, the person praying cannot assume the one living in sin is a Christian, and therefore have the expectation that prayer for correction will be effective. This person's case before God may already be judged by God, and if so, there is no guarantee of the person turning. The reader must keep in mind that this evaluation comes after all that John has already written about understanding the truthfulness of one's profession. John is simply giving guidance as to how one should pray for others who might have a profession of Christianity, but are living sinful lives, and what the expectation from prayer should be.

The question might arise: why was this written and included here? There are several possible reasons, and again these all point in the direction of John referring to spiritual life or death, and not just physical life or death.

- The entire epistle is about differentiating mere Christian professions from true Christianity. That John, as he comes to a close, provides some guidance regarding how a person should pray for those being observed along the way, is not a surprise. For those who are judged to be Christian, but momentarily are off the path, there is hope; and there should be prayer with expectation. For those who are judged to be hopeless, John does not say not to pray for them, but he says that prayer must be made with the recognition that there is no guarantee for God to be seen in their lives. They have had a profession only, and therefore cannot persevere in the faith.

- The theme of the epistle is needful because of the apostasy taking place within the church. John is writing, not only to identify those outside of Christ, but also to understand how one must think and deal with their situation.

- The epistle has much to say about love for one another. There is no greater display of love than to pray for one another. Praying is a true test of love, and John gives guidance about praying in love, and also, guidance as to what can be expected.

- The epistle is about fellowship with Christ, and the greatest degree of fellowship is always associated with communication. The communication that the Christian has with God in prayer is not only an essential (for it shows his trust and interest), but it also demonstrates his love for Christ and his love for others.

- The epistle is also about the Christian having discernment in regard to self, and in regard to others within the professing church. As John reaches the end of his letter, and moves into the practical side of living surrounded by a variety of professions, he provides discernment in praying.

To summarize the best interpretations, we consider two.

First, there is the possibility that this passage is referring exclusively to Christian discipline, and is discussing it from the standpoint of responsibility for prayer on behalf of others. Under this interpretation, a true believer who continues in sin can continue to such a degree that God will remove him by physical death as a disciplinary measure, and for the betterment of the church. The question is can "sinning-sins to death" in this context, be what John is referring to? This interpretation is possible. However, the words and context also lean toward providing a delineation of what to expect when a Christian prays for someone else, and taking into account the relationship that the person is shown to have with God by the degree of their practice of sin. This interpretation does not rule out that God deals with His own in a disciplinary manner (example of Moses), but along with the context of the epistle, it also deals with whether or not the person who is the object of the prayer is a Christian at all. Here are some considerations for interpreting the passage when assuming it is not exclusively referring to Christian discipline:

- The context has consistently shown that practicing sin is an identifying factor of the unsaved, and according to John, it is one of the principle means of determining true salvation.
- Death is always shown in the epistle context as spiritual death. If this passage is referring to physical death, it stands alone, by itself, and therefore, is not consistent with the rest of the context.
- Likewise, life in the writing is always referred to as spiritual life.
- The use of brother has been shown in this context, not to be an absolute endorsement that everyone he refers to as "brother" is saved, but rather, a term used for all who profess salvation, thereby allowing the instruction by John to dictate whether the profession is real or not.

Second, is the interpretation of what we might simply call *apostasy*. This interpretation is looking at one who persists in sin to such a hardened degree that he shows himself more likely to be unsaved than saved, and is therefore on the road to eternal death. Not only is this view consistent with the context as described, but it is also consistent with other passages and truths of doctrine presented in the Word of God. For example, Paul says sin shall "not be master over you" (Rom. 6:7, 11, 14, 23). In the context of John, this one is obviously being referred to as being mastered by sin. In Hebrews 10:26–27, within a setting where truth has been taught and rejected, the same thing is seen: "If we go on sinning willfully after receiving the knowledge of the truth, there no longer remains a sacrifice for sins." This verse fits perfectly with the context of **I do not say that he should make request for this**. All of these verses serve as serious warnings. John states that the praying believer has no guarantee of success in prayer, for these, who by their life practice, appear to be lost. The phrase **I do not say** does not tell us not to pray, but instead, to reason the circumstances with the understanding that our prayer of restoration or **life,** may not be in the will of God. God hears our prayers, and desires His children to pray in faith, but He is never under obligation to respond positively concerning someone who has rejected the truth, and willfully sins (Heb.10:26).

b. Position of Responsibility (5:16b)

he shall ask and *God* will for him give life to those who commit sin not *leading* to death. There is a sin *leading* to death; I do not say that he should make request for this.

On the other hand, for those who are truly battling against sin, there is an appropriate prayer and a promise from God. The prayer is guaranteed an answer: **will for him give life**. This interpretation complements other promises within the Scripture, such as John 10:27: "My sheep hear My voice and I know them and they follow Me, and they will never perish, and no one will snatch them out of My hand." It also is consistent with John 6:39; 1 Corinthians 1:8; Philippians 2:12; Luke 15:5, and many other passages. There is a struggle with purity going on in every true believer in the world, and the persons are shown in these passages as Christians, not mastered by sin, but as those struggling against sin. God has included as part of the battle against the believer's sin that Christians pray for one another. This praying for one another is woven into the dynamic process of sanctification and God's eternal security (or perseverance). Christians, then, are continually praying for each other as they engage in the battles of the sanctification process. The prayer of intercession is taught throughout the New Testament epistles, and shown by example in the Old Testament (think of Moses). There are many passages requesting prayer from brethren (1 Thess. 5:25; 2 Thess. 3:1; Heb. 13:18–19; 2 Cor. 13:9; Eph. 6:18–19; and James 5:16). God has included prayer as a priority. Salvation is never to be taken for granted, but worked out through God's strength. This process requires prayer. It is also a privilege (Gal 6:1–2). Christians must, therefore, value the power and importance of prayer.

The phrase **will for him give life** appears by the translation to be moving from a state of being unsaved, to being saved (if applied spiritually). The word **give** is *didōmi*, a verb used in a variety of applications and is here used in the future, active, indicative mood. It is pointing forward to the ultimate outcome, with something going on now, that is real. It is elsewhere translated *offer, commit, deliver*, and *minister* among others. Neither the word translated **give,** nor the tense of the word, requires it to be translated as an initiation of life (either spiritual or physical). If the phrase **give life** means the granting of life from the dead, then the phrase fits neither of the strongest positions. In either case, it means the continuance of life (either physical or spiritual), with an emphasis upon restoration. Taking into account both interpretations, if the person engaged in the sin is not to the degree of the unsaved (to death), then those praying are praying for a Christian, and are used of God to intervene in his well being. If then praying for a Christian who has sinned, the prayer may be used of God in both the continuance of physical life, and living as God would have the person live spiritually. In either of the best interpretations, prayer is a means that God uses for blessing and or restoration.

c. Personal Discernment (5:17)

All unrighteousness is sin, and there is a sin not *leading* to death.

John does not leave the topic without bringing an admonition and warning against a careless mindset over the fact of sin. So there will not be confusion in the reader's mind, John is not excusing Christians from sinning by discussing the fact that Christians do sin. All manner of sin is sin, and God's children can *never feel comfortable* about sin. **All unrighteousness is sin**, John emphasizes that all sin is against God and contrary to Him. The true child of God is never in the mindset of purchasing "indulgences" (as those in false religion prior to the reformation), before or after he has sinned. Neither is he in the habit of establishing some kind of boundary, within being sinful, over which he will not cross. No, he says **all unrighteousness is sin**. Sin is hideous, destructive, grievous, and abominable to God. John goes on to state: **and there is a sin not leading to death (5:17)**. Again, the word **leading** has been supplied by the translators. A better rendering of this statement (which is exactly the same as in the previous verse) is "and there is sinning-sin not to death." The reader must interpret between this verse and the next (5:18), where John states **no one who is born of God sins**. He must recognize that John is drawing a discerning differentiation between the sins of God's saved, who have sin struggles, and those who have a lifestyle given over to sin. This differentiation is the issue in recognizing the Christian struggling with sin, as separate from the sinner enslaved to sin in the *fullest* measure. The latter drinks sin like water, without reservation.

This discernment in praying appears throughout Scripture. Think of Christ Himself as He focused His personal prayer for His own (John 17:9). He did not pray for those "sinning-sin to death." As Christ prayed for His own, does He not show that God's will is for His children to pray in the same manner? Prayer to honor God must always be consistent with His nature and His purpose. His purpose is known by being in His Word, and becoming discerning of His nature and will. Even the prayer for all men (leaders) in 1 Timothy 2:1, is a prayer ultimately beneficial in the providential care for God's true children so that they may "lead quiet and peaceable lives in godliness and dignity."

> ## Pause and Reflect
>
> Christians are commanded to perform the greatest act of good and display of love by praying for one another. God also promises to act on the prayers for His own. He has woven answered prayers into His providential plan and purpose. On the other hand, God has made no promise of hope for those who willfully continue to reject Him, and who show their rejection by their disobedient practice and consumption in sin. Christians must be discerning in their praying, and mature in appropriate prayer by being in God's Word, discerning God's will, and thereby praying accordingly.

2. Proper Perspective (5:18–20)

a. Protection (5:18)

We know that no one who is born of God sins; but He who was born of God keeps him, and the evil one does not touch him.

John summarizes what he has elaborated throughout this letter. He does so by repeating in snapshots those truths explained. He has made it abundantly clear that there are three main aspects to being a true Christian. These are obedience (2:4), love (3:15), and faith (5:13). These are shown to be interlocked (5:1–4), and are the basis for the testimony of overcoming the world. In summarizing, he focuses on the protection that is absolute, because it is God who is doing the keeping. Once again, John uses the word **know**, addressing the believer's surety, and the very reason this book is one of assurance.

What does he remind believers that they **know**? **We know that no one who is born of God sins (5:18)**. This statement refers back to 1 John 3:6 and 9. The practice of sin is incompatible with the new birth in Christ. The word **sins** is *harmartanō* and is in the present (continuous action) tense, meaning that it is not referring to occasional actions, but to a continuous series of actions or a course of sin. The idea is (as discussed in chapter 3) that the continual practice of sin shows that an individual has no spiritual life, but as all natural (unsaved) men, is enslaved to sin. A child of God still sins (1:8), but is not immersed or controlled by sin. The Christian does not *practice* sin as a manner of life as the non-Christian does. Christians do not engage in sustained, willful rejection of God and His will. They are instead *characterized* by their new nature and the presence of the Holy Spirit, so that their lives are characterized by holiness, and not by sin.

The fixed logic for the **we know** means that it is a settled conviction and is something clearly seen and understood. It is similar to that found in Matthew 7:16–17: "You will know them by their fruits. Grapes are not gathered from thorn bushes nor figs from thistles, are they? So every good tree bears good fruit, but the bad tree bears bad fruit." There is nothing hidden or unreasonable in this concept; therefore–**we know**. The basis for the certainty on one side, and the clear lines of distinction, is the change made by God. The change made by God does not stop with the distinction, but is reinforced, as John states: **He who was born of God keeps him**. This phrase has been correctly rendered by the New American Standard Bible translators with the emphasis on the One who keeps the child of God by the capitalization of **He,** being a reference to Christ. The Lord, not only creates a new birth in a true child of God, but He also sustains him. These words are precisely what Christ means in John 10:27–28: "No one will snatch them out of My hands." The idea of "keeping" is in reference to falling away from the new reality of relationship to God, which would be evidenced by a falling back into the practice of sin.

John goes on to add: **and the evil one does not touch him**. Satan has no authority or hold on those re-birthed in Jesus Christ. This case is far different than what John states next in verse 19 concerning all those outside of a relationship to Christ. Here is a glorious reality–Satan cannot get the best of the child born of God. The reason is not the person's own strength, but because God, by His *omnipotent* power, will not allow it. The basis for the certainty of the **we know** is the very power and authority of God. This interpretation harmonizes with the doxology found in Jude 24–25: "Now to Him (God) who is able to keep you from stumbling, and present you faultless before the throne of His glory." God's power keeps the true child of God. Therefore, there is absolute certainty concerning all the evidence that John has provided in this epistle. The evidence of the life that has been freed from the bondage of captivity to sin provides assurance.

b. Position (5:19)

We know that we are of God, and that the whole world lies in *the power of* **the evil one.**

John brings a distinguishable contrast of summation between the true children of God and those who are of Satan. The difference is not merely in name only, but in attachment, character, likeness, and therefore–action. Once again John uses the phrase **we know**, *oida,* with the meaning of consistent and absolute perceived assurance. He says **we know that we are of God**, and the evidence has been made clear. Those who have *passed* the examination are in full assurance with settled conviction. God has made them alive to Him, and the character of their lives is now consistent with what John has written. By contrast, he says that **the whole world lies in the power of the evil one**. John means that he knows that only those born of God are not under Satan's control, but instead, are under God's control. The latter part of the verse in the Greek is actually **in the evil one**. The phrase **the power of** has been added by the translators. John means that there are only *two possibilities* for any person. There is no neutral ground, and there are two distinct realms in which people dwell; therefore, any person not found **of God** is found **in the evil one**, that is, in Satan. This understanding is taught throughout the Scriptures (2 Tim 2:26, held captive; 2 Cor. 4:3–4, keeps blinded; Eph. 2:2, living according to his dictates). All of these passages address Satan's hold on all mankind outside of Christ. At the same time, the Scriptures teach the cross of Christ as the means of overcoming Satan. In Revelation 5:9–10, Christ is described as the One who purchased for God "men from every tribe, tongue, people, and nation." These men are those identified as belonging exclusively to the **of God** category which is the only exception category from **the whole world that lies in the power of the evil one**. John makes clear in this entire epistle that the people **of God** can be, and are, identified with God. They have been called out of the *realm of Satan* into the new realm **of God,** and are known because of their new nature, a nature that he has described in this epistle as one engaged in the active process of sanctification.

c. Partnership (5:20)

And we know that the Son of God has come, and has given us understanding so that we may know Him who is true; and we are in Him who is true, in His Son Jesus Christ. This is the true God and eternal life.

This is John's final **we know,** and the concluding summation of all John has written. The **we know** (*oida*), perceive or understand, again emphasizes the certainty of understanding. With this certainty of Christ's first coming is the certainty of His granting to believers understanding so that they do **know Him who is true**. This second **know**, *ginōskō*, is an experiential knowledge, a knowledge that is consistent with relationship. This is the union that God's true people have with God through Jesus Christ. The phrase **Him who is true** speaks specifically of Christ (John 14:6). As Christ is God and one with the Father (John 10:30, having the same exact nature; Hebrews 1:3), John is again pointing to the certainty and reality of those He saves. He forms this thought by stating **and we are in Him who is true**, that is, instead of being under the realm, power, and authority of Satan, we are in the *absolute* security and blessing of being **in Him** (here a reference to the Father because of the Son). He adds **in His Son Jesus Christ**. Being in God and **in His Son Jesus Christ** are the same. There is the one realm of blessedness of which John appropriately closes out by stating: **this is the true God and eternal life**. This epistle has provided insight into the unity of God's own with Him. Those who belong to Him are being transformed through a process of sanctification, and are thereby, showing their kinship. This growth process will culminate in glorification (Rom. 8:30). With this process, there is *unity* with the Father in the same manner that there is unity in the Godhead (John 17:22–23). Those to whom he is referring belong to this realm. Within this realm is a blessed state because of the union between God the Father, God the Son, and those who are **in Him**.

3. Practical Command (5:21)

Little children, guard yourselves from idols.

With all that John has written concerning the reality of the relationship with God by those described as having faith, obedience, and love, he provides one simple closing command. The phrase **little children** has been used throughout the letter as a term for great affection and endearment. This title is perfect for John's last counsel. The word **idols** is the standard word for anything other than God that receives worship, or takes the place of the true and living God. Serving idols was what the Thessalonians were doing when Paul encountered them (1 Thess. 1:9), and what all people outside of Christ do; they do not serve God, and therefore, are idolaters.

John's last command, then, is to be aware of worldly allurements. Getting the believer's attention fixed on something other than God is always a danger. All of the **"we knows"** have reminded the reader of the true value of Christ, and of the infinite separation that exists between idols and the true God. Knowing who God is, and who they are in Him, and acting by God's power, believers are to be on **guard** from idols. **Guard** is *phulassō*," to guard," or "to keep watch." The idea is to look at everything with precision. Be aware of what is going on all around. Satan has many traps. This last command supports the entire context. Everything that does not conform to the Word of God is evil or wrong. Believers are to examine everything and cling to that which is good (Rom. 12:9). Ultimately, all sin is idolatry and is unfitting for the child of God; therefore, John writes **be on guard** as his last command to those who "know Him" (Christ), as they wait for His coming.

Pause and Reflect

Because this has been a book of sobering reality, and of identifying that which is genuine from that which is false, closing out this last section with a whole series of interconnecting "we knows" is fitting. The true Christian is not some unknown entity, but is known by his new birth identity. This identity becomes best explained by a summary of the "we knows." We know that no one born of God will continue in a lifestyle dominated by sin. Those dominated by sin are identified with the realm of Satan. We know that Satan cannot ultimately destroy the one who is born of God, because God keeps him. We also know that those born of God are different from unsaved humanity, because all who are outside of Christ are controlled and held captive by Satan. This difference and the many "we knows" make the distinction not only evident, but glorious. True salvation in Christ is not an "I hope so" (in the modern usage of the term hope as wishful thinking), but a solid reality identified in the person and supernatural work of God. Christians know that they have an inseparable union to Christ and to the Father. The clarity of this writing and the evidence of true relationship is the *biggest deal* (most important matter) that there is! The Christian can know that he has eternal life and can experience wonderful assurance. For those who read this epistle and cannot honestly identify themselves as those belonging to the definitions of the saved, there is the admonition to seek the Lord of grace for His mercy. There is nothing in this letter that presents salvation as being a work of man. Salvation is, in its entirety, a work of the Lord within the man. It is a work of grace. And, as it is not a work of merit, and because God is a God of mercy and grace, the unsaved reader should not rest until he has found his hope exclusively at the foot of the cross of Christ. He should seek God for His mercy, which He abundantly supplies to all who ask (Matt. 11:28). God is able to transform a person into a new creation (2 Cor. 5:17), who will then have assurance when examining this epistle.

Closing Thoughts

I determined to write this commentary because of being convinced there are many professing Christians, even those sitting in Bible teaching churches, who are not truly "born again." The easy-minded theology of the day has swept into the minds of many, and they have not been confronted, as only the Word of God can, and my comments have simply followed what John has clearly written. There is also a theology in conservative evangelical churches that attempts to explain John's writing in altogether different terms. According to their analysis, this writing is not an examination but an exhortation. They say–it is not really for personal assurance, as it is not defining essential salvation at all, but is intended to correct and exhort the reader to be a better person. If the reader is under this kind of ministry, he will hear and see many twists of the clear text. An honest evaluation of the comments made in this commentary will show that no such liberties with the Word have been made in this writing. Comments have been made sensibly and simply as John has revealed, and clearly stated. John obviously believed (under inspiration) that many professing Christians are deceived about their salvation. Personally, I went for years attending church in my youth and was blessed with the witness of real Christians, but there were also many around me who were *mere professors*. I was deceived about my own relationship to Christ, and was for years unconcerned. Are you, reader, concerned? I have personally never met anyone soberly concerned about his salvation who has not then found true peace with God. God's invitation for salvation is throughout the Word. There are many though, who are complacent about their salvation, accepting the modern theology of a faith that does not reflect any change of life. For anyone to come to Christ, he must come on Christ's terms. Only then will transformation take place. As a pastor, I have met many who take comfort in a shallow religious life while assuming that all is well with their souls. The importance of preaching, teaching, and providing exposure to biblical truth is of the utmost importance. This generation needs to be powerfully shaken from its blind condition of complacency, face the problem of separation from God, and come to grips with true transforming salvation. I believe that this is the necessity of honestly matching ourselves with John's writing.

As stated at the beginning of this commentary, salvation is not only justification (God declaring someone not guilty), but it is also sanctification (God making someone into a new person). God does not justify people and then let them continue in their life as they were–living in their sin. That does not mean that the person is perfect, but the person is changed and in the process of moving toward Christ-likeness. Everyone whom God justifies, He also sanctifies (Rom 8:29–30, "conforms to the image of His Son"). This epistle focuses on the matter of sanctification, and defines from the process of sanctification, whether true salvation has or has not become a reality.

There are three big components seen throughout this epistle that must be very prominent in the sanctification process of every Christian. These serve as the evidence, or marks of salvation as John defines them. These three distinctions John reiterated over and over from every angle. They are defined biblical understandings of faith, love, and obedience. These three components are so integrated that no one of them can exist without the others. Each one must be understood from the Bible. This understanding requires significant effort, yet, on the other hand, the concepts are remarkably simple.

What would I do if I were personally struggling with the issue of my salvation? This struggle is something that I have faced in the past. *The first thing to do* is to be honest in your approach to Scripture. Do not read it for what you want it to tell you, but read it for what it will tell you. The effort of this commentary has been to precisely follow the thinking of John, and his God inspired, and needful evaluation of who is truly saved. *Second,* honestly seek God privately. No one needs to tell you how to seek Him. Talk to God and ask Him for help to know Him. There are many assurances in the Word of God that those who truly seek Him will find Him. *Third*, do not be satisfied until you have confidence that God has heard you, and has done His work in you. Study the approach of the Canaanite woman (Matt. 15:22–28). You will know you are His as His work in you progresses. There is nothing that comes close to being as important as your salvation, and when you have arrived at the point of knowing that God has dealt with you in His grace–you will know! You will have assurance as you study His Word because faith, love, and a desire to be obedient will all come together. His hand of assurance will be on you at the same time His work is in you. Nothing is more wonderful than living a life of love to God now, and having the assurance of being with Him throughout eternity.

God bless you on your journey!

About the Author

Jim Bryant has been a serious student of the Bible for more than forty-five years. He has served in leadership capacities in three separate Bible Churches since 1975, and on both a Christian school board and a mission board. For more than thirty years he has served as a teaching elder. For the last fifteen years he has ministered as chairman of the elder board, and Pastor of Grace Bible Chapel in San Antonio, Texas. Jim holds a BS from West Texas A & M University, and an MBS (Master of Biblical Studies), from Tyndale Theological Seminary. He and his wife Jan, have been married for forty-five years and have five children and twelve grandchildren.

For more information:
Grace Bible Chapel
www.gbcsa.org

Made in the USA
San Bernardino, CA
26 October 2017